Language in History

In *Language in History*, Tony Crowley provides the analytical tools for answering such questions as: What are the relations between language and class? How has language been used to construct nationality? Using a radical re-reading of Saussure and Bakhtin, he demonstrates, in four case studies, the ways in which language has been used to construct social and cultural identity in Britain and Ireland. Examples include the ways in which language was employed to construct a bourgeois public sphere in eighteenth-century England, and the manner in which language is still being used in contemporary Ireland to articulate national and political aspirations.

By bringing together linguistic and critical theory with historical and political consciousness, Tony Crowley provides a new agenda for the study of language in history. In particular he draws attention to the fact that this field has always been firmly rooted in a deeply political context. And he demonstrates how that context has directed the study of language in history.

Language in History represents a major contribution to the field and is an essential text for anyone interested in critical and cultural theory; it also provides an important contextualisation of many debates which have influenced literary studies.

Tony Crowley is Professor of English at the University of Manchester. His publications include *Proper English*, also published by Routledge, and *The Politics of Discourse*.

THE POLITICS OF LANGUAGE

Series editors: Tony Crowley,
University of Manchester,

Talbot J. Taylor,
College of William and Mary,
Williamsburg, Virginia

'In the lives of individuals and societies, language is a factor of greater importance than any other. For the study of language to remain solely the business of a handful of specialists would be a quite unacceptable state of affairs.'

Saussure

The Politics of Language Series covers the field of language and cultural theory and will publish radical and innovative texts in this area. In recent years the developments and advances in the study of language and cultural criticism have brought to the fore a new set of questions. The shift from purely formal, analytical approaches has created an interest in the role of language in the social, political, and ideological realms and the series will seek to address these problems with a clear and informed approach. The intention is to gain recognition for the central role of language in individual and public life.

Language in History

Theories and Texts

Tony Crowley

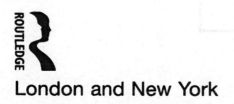

London and New York

First published 1996
by Routledge
11 New Fetter Lane, London EC4P 4EE

Transferred to Digital Printing 2004

Simultaneously published in the USA and Canada
by Routledge
29 West 35th Street, New York, NY 10001

© 1996 Tony Crowley

Typeset in Baskerville by J&L Composition Ltd, Filey, North Yorkshire

British Library Cataloguing in Publication Data
A catalogue record for this book is available from the British Library

Library of Congress Cataloguing in Publication Data
A catalogue record for this book has been requested

ISBN 0–415–07244–1 (hbk)
     0–415–07245–x (pbk)

For
Ursula Armstrong
Tam Hood
and
Edmund Papst

Contents

Acknowledgements

There are as usual so many people to thank that it is difficult to know where to start. The institutional debts are the easiest. I acknowledge gratefully the support of the University of Southampton, the British Academy and the Leverhulme Awards Committee. All three have been generous and have enabled me to undertake research which would otherwise have been impossible. In a general way I would like to thank the students with whom I worked at the University of Southampton between 1984 and 1994. I would particularly like to thank my colleagues at Southampton during those years. They made it a difficult and challenging place to work by their sheer energy, enthusiasm and intellectual commitment. I am grateful that they were so supportive yet critical, uncompromising and yet humane and humorous. Their students were lucky, and so was I.

Specific debts are more difficult and so have to be paid more carefully. I would like to thank Julia Hall, my editor, for her encouragement and help, and Tolly Taylor, my series co-editor, for his interest in, and commitment to, this project. For her careful reading of the original book proposal I want to say thanks to Debbie Cameron. For his critical reading of chapters I would like to acknowledge my debt to Ken Hirschkop; he made me think again about important issues. To Viv Jones I owe thanks for pointing me in the right direction in eighteenth-century debates. And my Ph.D. students are and have been a constant source of stimulation; I thank them too.

So to personal debts, the hardest of all to acknowledge. To Ursula Armstrong, again thanks for the support and love. To Alan Girvin and Lucy Burke, thanks for the same. To Kath Burlinson, Edmund Papst and John Peacock: well, how to say how much I've gained and learned from that unlikely trio. To Tam Hood, a special thanks for being a good mate and companion; this book is dedicated in part to his memory. Finally, thanks to Anita Rupprecht, for the love and all else; she knows how much it means.

Introduction
Language in history

'Language in history: that full field.'

(Williams 1984: 189)

The aim of this book is to examine the significance of language in history, and to do so from two distinct but related points of view. First, we will consider this question from the theoretical perspective. That is, we will look at how two of the major thinkers on language in the present century have discussed the question of the relations between language and history. The major theorists we will consider under this heading are Saussure and Bakhtin, who both, in different ways, reflect dominant trends in the study of language. Second, we will attempt to show how language is of fundamental importance to our understanding of history by means of a number of case studies. These, it will be argued, show us the various ways in which language has been used in order to help to construct historical formations such as nations, classes, genders and races. The examples studied focus upon Britain and Ireland from the eighteenth century to the present.

We can take these two points of view in turn in order to demonstrate the purpose of each. One of the most noteworthy things which strikes the student of language in history is bound to be simply how poorly the area is theorised. There is of course the work of French thinkers such as Balibar and Laporte, Achard, Calvet, Faye and Bourdieu; and the Italian work of Rossi-Landi. In Britain there is a gap, although the work of Raymond Williams is the outstanding exception. His theoretical work in *Marxism and Literature*, inspired by the pioneering work of Vološinov, offered a clear break and opened up a new way to a relatively new field. It was a break which developed out of his work in *Keywords*, which in turn was sparked by the concentration upon the significance of the particular vocabulary of culture and society in his central work of that title. *Keywords* itself emerged from Williams's reading of the incompletely theorised work of thinkers such as Empson and Trier. Williams's work apart, however, the field was inadequate theoretically, though there has been important work in Britain in recent times gathered by Corn-field, Burke and Porter. Of course from one perspective the study of language was always historical, or at least social. For since the 1960s there has emerged the field of sociolinguistics, which could be considered as nothing less than the study of language in history. This work too, however, has tended to be extremely empirical in its bias and, again, relatively unsophisticated in terms of social theory. This is not of course to deny that such work has either interest or significance; but that it studies language in history from a fully theorised perspective can hardly be sustained.

Why has this lack of theory occurred, and what are its roots? One account would point the finger at Saussure, usually described as the founding father of modern linguistic study, and it would argue that his crucial methodological distinctions are such that any reference to history in the study of language is prohibited in advance. And thus there would be no need for any theoretical account of the relations between language and history. A marxist such as Jameson, and it has been marxists in particular who have levelled this accusation, has argued that Saussure makes precisely this move (Jameson 1972: 7). And thus, the critique follows, structuralism, engendered by Saussure's work, cannot cope with the historical perspective and so can only be either simply formalist or reductive. Whether that is an account of structuralism which does it justice is a question which we can set on one side here. Whether this is an accurate account of Saussure's attitude to the study of language and history is one which will be explored in the first chapter. It will be argued that although it is correct to point out that Saussure did rule out any study of linguistic change through time in the science of language which he was delimiting, it is not the case that he ruled out the study of language in history *tout court*. In fact it will be argued that Saussure eliminated both the study of language change through time, and the study of language in history, from the science of language. That, how-ever, does not mean that he ruled them out of play on the grounds that they were insignificant; unscientific perhaps, but not insignificant. Indeed it will be demonstrated that Saussure specifically argues for the study of language in history, that he does so in the *Course in General Linguistics*, and that he does that in ways which show how important he considered it. It will be argued too not only that Saussure points to this new field, but that he outlines some of its major concerns and areas of interest. We will be arguing then both for and against Saussure.

One of the major thinkers on language in history in the twentieth century, usually classified somewhat awkwardly as a literary theorist, is of course Bakhtin. He, it might be argued, is a student of language and its relation to history who offers new and radical concepts and ways of understanding. That opinion will be put to the test in Chapter 2 in order to see if it can be validated. It will be argued that although it is clearly the case that Bakhtin does give us new ways of comprehending in this area, it is also the case that when they are tested they are sometimes found wanting. This will be the value of the case studies which follow the first two theoretical chapters. It will be argued that Bakhtin's central concepts in relation to this field are precisely unhistoricised. We have the theoretical input with Bakhtin, then, but not the history. And this stems from the rigidity of his model, and a combination of undue optimism and undue pessimism. It will be proposed, therefore, that Bakhtin's concepts are of central importance to the study of language in history only when the concepts themselves are understood historically and politically. The work of Gramsci in this field will be of importance here. If the central concepts of monoglossia, polyglossia and heteroglossia, along with monologism and dialogism, are not understood politically, then they run two dangers: first, that of being simply empty, that is, never quite specific enough; and, second, that of being as reductively formalist as many of the central concepts of Saussure's work which were taken into structuralism. We will then also be arguing both for and against Bakhtin.

Having established our theoretical starting-points, therefore, we can then move on to our four case studies. In doing so we will see how useful, or not, the modified ideas of Saussure and Bakhtin are to our understanding of the field. We will take as our starting-point an observation made by a character in Friel's play *Translations*: 'it is not the literal past, the *facts* of history, that shape us, but images of the past embodied in language' (Friel 1981: 66). We will consider this in relation to four case studies: (1) the roles of language in eighteenth-century Britain; (2) language and cultural nationalism in nineteenth-century Ireland; (3) language, class and nation in nineteenth- and early twentieth-century Britain; (4) language in history in contemporary Ireland. We can take these areas in turn. First, we will examine how language played a central role in the various social formations which appeared in eighteenth-century Britain. By using the concepts, or better the clues, given to us by Saussure and Bakhtin, we can see how language played a number of roles which had previously been unrecognised. Central to these is the importance of language to the construction of the bourgeois public sphere, whose rise has been classically described by Habermas (1989). We will attempt to show, however, how language was used in other ways which foreshadow, importantly, questions which were to become of great significance later: questions such as the relationship between language and nationality; the identification of language as the key site of history, both past and present; the way in which language has been used for the purposes of exclusion along the borders of class and gender. In all of these ways, it will be the aim of the chapter to show how eighteenth-century Britain used language to create and validate its various social formations. It will also be the purpose of the chapter to show precisely where many of the later debates originated.

In our second case study, that of language and cultural nationalism in nineteenth-century Ireland, we will build upon and extend arguments made in the first three chapters. Of central importance here will be the philosophical account of the relations between language and nationality rendered by Kant and the post-Kantians, primarily Fichte and Humboldt. It will be argued that at three distinct points in Irish history, over a century or more, language became the focal point of the process of nation-building. It will also be important, however, to remember that Ireland, as Britain's first colony, offered a blueprint for the consequent models of language and colonialism practised throughout the world. We will examine, then, in relation to this question, the ways in which the model was set in place and enacted at different times. This story is a complex and often contradictory one. We will also examine how the same model, only placed in reverse, became the focus of attempts to resist the colonial power. We will see too how the language is figured in all sorts of curious and strange ways in order to construct a pure, 'proper', Irish identity. And we will find again how the language was used to exclude, as well as to include, on the grounds of race, religion and nationhood. Finally, we will consider the role accorded to women in the 'language war', as it was called.

Our third case study also builds on the work in the previous chapters. Here we will look at how the English language is figured in relation to nation and class. One question which will be demonstrated here is how continuous the debates are between the eighteenth and nineteenth centuries. Against this, there is a view which holds that in the nineteenth century the study of language became scientific, principally by means of dropping its prejudices and adopting instead the scientific methodology of positivism. It will be part of the aim of this chapter to show that such a view is wrong; and this will be accomplished precisely by identifying the various biases which dominated the study of language in this period. These, it will be shown, vary between different points of historical conflict. At times they are related again to questions of national identity; for nineteenth-century Britain was at least as obsessed with establishing its identity as in the preceding century. At other moments, and more pressingly, the relationship between language and class, already clearly formulated in the eighteenth century, was of the utmost significance. In such debates language was taken to be at once the index of social division, and the only possible source of its healing. It was the one sure means, in an uncertain and rapidly changing society, by which social identity could be reliably estimated. And nineteenth-century Britain was obsessed with it, as both linguists and social observers freely admitted. Of great importance in such debates was the question of what was to be known, after its coinage in 1858, as 'standard English'. We will examine in this chapter, then, the origins and consequent fortunes of that phrase, which was to gain enormous power in the debates which followed. This is of interest not least in the fact that it is a phrase which continues to be significant in contemporary debates; it is of further interest since it is usually used in confused and misleading ways.

The fourth and final case study returns to Ireland and attempts to show the importance of language in history today. With the advance of linguistic study in all its various modes, it might be thought that the 'language question', as it has been known at least since Dante, could be dealt with objectively or neutrally. However, as this chapter shows, the significance of language in history transcends any scientific approach to language. The examples demonstrate that language is still being used in a particular context of historical crisis as the key to social and political identity. It has been argued widely and recently that nationalism is dead, and that cultural nationalism is a relic from the past in a world of global capitalism and cosmopolitanism. Our final analysis demonstrates such a view to be at least a gross underestimation of historical reality. What our example shows us is old models of cultural nationalism, posited on the link between language and nation, struggling with new models of language and nation. What we can clearly find too is that the old models are residual, that they have not lost their force and that they are underestimated too easily. This, of course, is not true simply of Ireland, for we see the wider significance of that particular context when we look to the breakdown of the Soviet Union. There too nations are reappearing; there too nationalists are once more fighting with rifles in one hand and dictionaries in the other.

As was pointed out above, the book has two aims: first, to clarify certain theoretical concepts and ways of understanding in relation to language and history; and, second, to use these concepts, and thus test them, in order to produce readings of language in history. What we will find are some extraordinary claims about language and languages; bizarre and almost unbelievable assertions backed up by the most unusual evidence. But their oddity should not lead us to underestimate their power and significance. For language in history is not only a full field, it is also an important one.

Chapter 1

For and against Saussure

'Il faut d'abord distinguer *la langue dans l'histoire et l'histoire de la langue.*'

(Saussure 1957: 38)

THE SCIENCES OF LANGUAGE

The explicit aim of Saussure's *Course in General Linguistics* is to establish the science of language. Such an intention does not at first sight seem remarkable, since the nineteenth and early twentieth centuries saw the establishment of a number of new sciences. The extraordinary nature of this goal, however, is revealed when it is placed in its intellectual and historical context. For it is one of the peculiarities of the study of language in the post-Enlightenment period that not one but two sciences of language have appeared. Or, to be more accurate, there have been two methodological approaches to the study of language which have laid claim to the status of science. Again this would not in particular be of major interest, given that the status of scientificity for any new discipline is one to be devoutly sought in the cultural order of modernity. Yet it is significant for our purposes since Saussure, at different times in his life, belonged to both of the sciences of language. Or, again to be more precise, in his later work he denounced the claims of the first science of language, in which he had produced his only non-posthumously published text, and articulated the methods by which the second, and for his purposes the *only*, science of language could be brought to light. Any comprehension of the aims of the *Course*, then, and indeed of the vehemency with which they are stated, has to begin with a brief account of the first discipline which claimed for itself the mantle of the science of language.

It is a characteristic of language debates in the eighteenth century that they concentrated upon two main areas of interest. The first was the origin of language, signalled by texts such as Rousseau's *Essay on the Origin of Languages* (1781), Monboddo's *Of the Origin and Progress of Language* (1773–92), and Adam Smith's essay 'Concerning the First Formation of Language', which was added to the second edition of the *Theory of Moral Sentiments* (1761). The culmination of this work was Herder's prize essay *Über den Ursprung der Sprache* (1772). The second area of interest, stemming from a Cartesian influence, was that which took as its object the search for universal grammar. The central text here was the *Grammaire générale et raisonée* (1660), in which the Port Royal grammarians outlined their goal as the formulation of a universal account of grammar which would demonstrate that the operations of language acted according to the principles of reason. This intention served in the eighteenth century generally as the model for the 'philosophical grammars', of which Harris's *Hermes, or a Philosophical Inquiry concerning Universal Grammar* (1751) was a leading example, and acted as an inspiration for the rationalism of the encyclopaedists.

The concern with language in general, then, was characteristic of the eighteenth century. Yet it was also the case that the period saw a growing interest in particular languages. This double focus had in fact been presaged in the preface to the *Grammaire générale et raisonée*, in which Lancelot comments on his search for 'the reasons for several things which are either common to all languages or particular to only some of them' (Arnauld and Lancelot 1975: 39); though it was, of course, the interest in language in general that the work of the Port Royal grammarians primarily inspired. The concern for particular languages also took two different forms. It arose on the one hand from the interest in the propriety and antiquity of the vernacular languages, exemplified in the preceding century in the burgeoning production of vernacular dictionaries such as the *Vocabolario degli Accademia della Crusca* (1612) and in the founding of the Académie Française in 1635, and in the eighteenth century itself by Swift's *Proposal* and Johnson's *Dictionary*. It also took the form of antiquarian inquiries such as those related to the English language by Somner, Skinner, Junius and Hickes in the seventeenth and early eighteenth centuries. On the other hand, the interest in particular languages was evinced in the attention paid later in the century to those languages which were brought to European notice as a result of colonial conquest and consequent cultural confrontation.

The most famous of the discoveries which resulted from colonial rule was that made in the late eighteenth century by Sir William Jones in his work on Sanskrit. Jones's most important observation on Sanskrit was articulated in his 'Discourse on the Hindus' (1786):

The *Sanscrit* language, whatever be its antiquity, is of a wonderful structure; more perfect than the *Greek*, more copious than the *Latin*, and more exquisitely refined than either, yet bearing to either of them a stronger affinity, both in the roots of verbs and in the forms of grammar, than could possibly have been produced by accident; so strong indeed, that no philologer could examine them all three, without believing them to have sprung from some common source, which, perhaps, no longer exists: there is a similar reason, though not quite so forcible, for supposing that both the *Gothick* and the *Celtick*, though blended with a very different idiom, had the same origin with the *Sanscrit*; and the old *Persian* might be added to the same family, if this were the place for discussing any question concerning the antiquities of *Persia*.

(Jones 1807: III, 15)

In practical terms, Jones's scepticism towards etymology, which was often linked to the concern with the origin of language in the eighteenth century, and which Jones describes as 'a medium of proof so very fallacious', and his attention to grammar, the 'groundwork' of a language, were important steps on the road to the science of language. And his prescience in positing a vanished ancestor to Sanskrit, Latin and Greek, along with his challenge to the cultural superiority of the latter two, were to have important repercussions in academic fields such as language study, history and theology. Yet it is the simple fact that he drew attention to the importance of Sanskrit that ensures his historical place. For in that act he directed attention on to Indian language and culture more generally and further encouraged the turn to the East.

One figure who followed this interest was Friedrich von Schlegel in his essay '*On the Language and Wisdom of the Indians*' (1808). And it is in this text that we find the first use of the term which was to be the key to the nineteenth-century study of language:

> There is, however, one single point, the investigation of which ought to decide every doubt, and elucidate every difficulty; the structure or comparative grammar of the language furnishes us with as certain a key to their general analogy, as the study of comparative anatomy has done to the loftiest branch of natural science.
>
> (Schlegel 1849: 439)

Schlegel's announcement of 'the great importance of the comparative study of language' was prophetic; the comparative method, though still undeveloped and inaccurate in the works of Jones and, particularly, Schlegel, was in various forms to sweep all before it in the nineteenth century. It marks the beginnings of the first science of language.

By definition the method of comparativism was to compare languages in order to trace their historical relations; that is, to establish a chronology by which we can see how languages have developed and affected each other. The basic fact upon which this method is grounded is that languages change as they develop through time, that is, diachronically. Given this, it is possible to compare different languages, trace the changes and then construct historical relationships between them. In the first stirrings of such work the aim had been to trace a path through the alterations in order to discover the oldest, and therefore source, language. Such an aim is clearly a leftover from the eighteenth century's concern with the establishment of the origin of language. In later research, however, this became a quest to establish a chronological hierarchy of languages, usually in the form of a family tree, which would outline their ascendancy and descendancy. At a later point still, taking us almost to the dawn of the second science of language, the aim of linguistic research was understood as the search for the binding laws which governed the diachronic changes which had taken place in any particular language or between languages.

An illustration of the early comparative method can be taken from Rask's *Investigation Concerning the Source of the Old Northern or Icelandic Language* (1818). In this example Rask compares Latin and Greek with a Teutonic language, here Icelandic. Ranging words against each other, Rask discovers a number of regular patterns between the languages. His examples are:

p to *f,* e.g.: *platus* (broad) *flatur* (flat), *patēr fadir*
t to *þ,* e.g.: *treis* (read *trís*) *þrir* . . .
k to *h,* e.g.: *kreas* (meat) *hræ* (dead body) *cornu horn* . . .
b most often remains: *blazanō* (germinate) *blad, bruō* (spring forth)
d to *t*: *damaō* (tame) *tamr* (tame) *dignus tíginn* (elevated, noble) . . .

(Lehmann 1967: 34)

By noting the 'most frequent of these transitions from Greek and Latin to Icelandic' what Rask does here is to give an unrefined model of how comparativism was to work. That is, by comparing the different languages he notes regularities in the changes which take place beween them (in this example, Greek and Latin *p* becomes *f* in the Teutonic language, *t* becomes *þ*, and so on). It is by this method that the linguist can trace the regularity of diachronic change. That offers the possibility, as Rask puts it, of understanding the diachronic changes in languages through 'comparison of all of them' (Lehmann 1967: 35). This most basic form of comparativism can be summed up in Rask's formulation:

A language, however mixed it may be, belongs to the same class of languages as another, when it has the most essential, concrete and indispensable words, the foundation of language, in common with it . . . when in such words one finds agreement between two languages, and that to such an extent that one can draw up rules for the transition of letters from one to the other, then there is an original relationship between these languages.

(ibid.: 32)

The early comparativists, however, did not rely solely upon correspondences between the vocabularies of different languages. And thus in the work of Bopp and Grimm a distinct methodology, which marks the beginning of comparative philology proper, was developed. Reliance upon lexical correspondence ran the risk of being misled by word-borrowings in the attempt to sketch the historical relations of a particular language. A more solid body of evidence was required and that, as Schlegel had pointed out, was that furnished by grammatical structure. The reasoning behind this is that although words may be borrowed between languages which have no linkage other than such borrowing, it is highly unlikely that grammatical features could be borrowed in this way. Therefore a link in, for example, the way in which tenses are formed or the plural is created was taken to be the most firm evidence of an historical relationship between languages.

Comparisons of vocabulary and grammatical structure, then, were the principal methods used by the early comparativists, largely to the neglect of sound changes between languages. And the method of comparativism was most clearly vindicated in the case of Sanskrit, since it had been formerly conceived of as being wholly unrelated to languages such as Greek, Latin or the Teutonic or Celtic languages. However, once it became clear that Sanskrit did have a grammatical structure and vocabulary which was related to those other languages, it then also became evident that a whole group (or family, as it was later described) of languages was linked in ways not previously considered possible. This group became known as the Indo-European family of languages, of which it was at first though that Sanskrit was the source. By the time of the publication of Schleicher's work *Die Darwinische Theorie und die Sprachwissenschaft* (1863), translated into English in 1869, it had become clear that Sanskrit was not only not the source language, but that Sanskrit itself was derived from a language which had now disappeared. This led to the important step of attemtping to reconstruct this lost language, known as proto-Indo-European; it took the form of an hypothetical language created by way of calculated estimates based on the rules of diachronic change worked out by the comparativists. It was an attempt to read back into the history of a group of languages in order to arrive at its origin.

To this point the nineteenth-century science of language had viewed itself as scientific by dint of its use of the comparative method. And it is difficult to overestimate the extent to which comparativism had become the paradigm of scientific methodology. At this conjuncture, however, the presentation of Darwin's theory of evolution affected deeply the nineteenth century's view of science. And it is not surprising that the science of language also took an organic turn, principally in the work of Schleicher. Schleicher, influenced by Hegel as much as by Darwin, takes as given 'the struggle for existence in the field of human speech' (Schleicher 1869: 64). He continues to specify that Darwin's methodology is appropriate for the study of language: 'the rules now, which Darwin lays down with regard to the species of animals and plants, are equally applicable to the organisms of languages' (ibid.: 30). The science of language, which had been constructed on the basis of recording the connections between languages in time, was now given a new basis and indeed a new name, 'glossology' (which was presumably intended to echo biology). The new science of language was to proceed by the methods set out by Darwin:

> We may learn from the experience of the naturalist, that nothing is of any importance to science but such *facts* as have been established by close objective observation, and the proper conclusions derived from them; nor would such a lesson be lost upon several of my colleagues. All those trifling, futile interpretations, those fanciful etymologies, that vague groping and guessing – in a word, all that which tends to strip the study of language of its scientific garb, and to cast ridicule upon the science in the eyes of thinking people – all this becomes perfectly intolerable to the student who has learned to take his stand on the ground of sober observation. Nothing but the close watching of the different organisms and of the laws that regulate their life, nothing but our unabated study of the scientific object, that, and that alone, should form the basis also of *our* training. All speculations, however ingenious, when not placed on this firm foundation are devoid of scientific value.
>
> (ibid.: 19–20)

It follows, therefore, that the science of language should take its place alongside the other Darwinian sciences:

> Languages are organisms of nature; they have never been directed by the will of man; they rose, and developed themselves according to definite laws; they grew old, and died out. They, too, are subject to that series of phenomena which we embrace under the name of 'life'. The science of language is consequently a science of nature; its method is generally altogether the same as that of any other natural science.
>
> (ibid.: 20–1)

Schleicher's swipe at his more historically orientated colleagues is based on what he construes to be their lack of scientificity, since what they ought to be undertaking is the 'close objective observation' of 'facts' and 'the laws that regulate their life'. Rather than the idle speculation of the early comparativists, what is demanded here is the rigour of science. This was not the last time that this complaint was to be heard in the study of language.

If Schleicher's biological naturalism did not carry the day in the struggle for dominance in the study of language, then his conception of positivist scientific method as the establishment of facts and the laws which govern them did. For, not long after Schleicher's theoretical pronouncement appeared, there also came to the fore a group of linguists who rejected his naturalism but accepted his positivist methodology of science. This group by-passed Schleicher, recovered the principle of the historicity of language but now made it scientific by holding that language change takes place by means of determinate, all-encompassing laws. Fanciful historical speculation gave way to biological scientificity only for it in turn to be superseded by a form of historicism which claimed the status of science.

The appearance of the *Junggrammatiker* or neogrammarians (*Junggrammatiker* is coined by analogy with the 'young Hegelians' or 'young Irelanders', and any such coinage was usually dismissive in its first intent), in the 1870s and 1880s was an event of considerable historical moment in the study of language. For not only did Schleicher's work come under attack; that of the early comparativists was criticised too. The principal advances made by the neogrammarians were founded upon three factors: the focus upon modern languages, the use of phonetics, and the belief in the necessity for rigorous and formal explanation of linguistic change. The attention to modern languages had the effect of lessening the importance of Sanskrit (a point which they took from Schleicher's stress on the proto-language from which Sanskrit derived), and gave them empirical evidence with which to work. The result was the most detailed tracing of linguistic facts and the laws which governed them that had as yet been achieved; though later critics, including Saussure, were to argue in effect that in following the detail of diachronic facts they lost sight of the object of linguistic study itself – language. The use of phonetics was likewise a major advance. In the first edition of Grimm's *Deutsche Grammatik* there is little analysis of sound; there is little else in the work of the neogrammarians. The significance of this step is that the early comparativists often worked to a large extent with the relationships between written forms in different languages. With the development of phonetics, however, it became clear that there were often correspondences which were hidden by their written form and which became clear only when the forms were understood as sound-forms. The vagaries of the English spelling-system suffice to demonstrate the importance of this breakthrough. The final advance over the early comparativists, stemming from the second, was the ability to explain apparent exceptions to the rules of linguistic change. In the study of the pioneers such as Rask, Bopp and Grimm there were often anomalies in the regularities which they noted in the processes of diachronic change; these were usually regarded as peculiar irregularities. The major step taken by the neogrammarians, however, was to use the field of phonetics, in conjunction with the methods of comparativism, to produce sound-laws which were completely rigorous and all-inclusive. In fact the laws which govern linguistic change were thought to be so all-encompassing that Verner claimed, in a manner which demonstrates the enormous confidence of the new science, that apparent irregularities were simply regularities whose governing laws had not yet been discovered:

> Comparative linguistics cannot, to be sure, completely deny the element of chance; but chance occurrence . . . where the instances of irregular shifting are nearly as frequent as those of regular shifting, it cannot and may not admit. That is to say, in such a case there must be a rule for the irregularity, it only remains to discover this.
>
> (Lehmann 1967: 138)

In the preface to the *Morphologische Untersuchungen* (1878), Osthoff and Brugmann put it more succinctly: 'every sound change, inasmuch as it occurs mechanically, takes place according to laws that admit no exception' (ibid.: 204). Schleicher's doctrine of immutable laws which govern the development of facts had been transferred to the realm of history from that of nature.

The account of linguistics as an historical rather than a natural science, albeit history governed by rigid laws, was effectively assured of its triumph by dint of the successes of the neogrammarians in their explanation of exceptions to the rules formulated by the earlier students of language. And ultimately it was this version of the scientific, historical viewpoint that dominated the latter part of the century, particularly in Britain, where the publication of Paul's *Principles of the History of Language* (1890) set the seal on the victory. Paul's defence of the title of his book gives an indication of the confidence and status of the historicists:

> I have briefly to justify my choice of the title 'Principles of the *history* of Language.' It has been objected that there is another view of language possible besides the historical. I must contradict this. What is explained as an unhistorical and still scientific observation of language is at bottom nothing but one incompletely historical, through defects partly of the observer, partly of the material to be observed. As soon as ever we pass beyond the mere statements of single facts and attempt to grasp the connexion as a whole, and to comprehend the phenomena, we come upon historical ground at once, though it may be we are not aware of the fact.
>
> (Paul 1890: xlvi–xlvii)

From the logic of this argument there is of course no escape; if we think we are being scientific while not deploying the methods of historicism, we are simply mistaken. There is no other methodology which fulfils the criteria of scientificity.

Yet even at the height of their dominance the scientific historicists were faced with other opponents, the 'independents', such as Schuchardt, and the linguistic geographers, of whom the best representative was Gilliéron. These were linguists who, while not on the side of the naturalists, were deeply sceptical of the claims of the neogrammarians, on the grounds of the excessive rigidity of the neogrammarian account of linguistic laws. For these two influential linguists in particular the main concern was with what can be described as the more individual and subjective aspects of language rather than with objective laws. The attention paid to the geographical aspects of linguistic change and innovation, for example, directly contrasted with the neogrammarians' insistence on the purity of linguistic relations. And Schuchardt's view that language is individually created, and thus that linguistic innovation is a question of individual psychology rather than mechanistic laws, represented a radical challenge to the neogrammarians. This split was eventually to lead to two utterly opposed camps in which abstract formalists were faced by aesthetic idealists such as Croce and Vossler, for whom language was more like poetry than geometry, shifting in every moment of its existence rather than operating by means of a closed set of laws. The ideas of linguists such as Gilliéron and Schuchardt also helped to inspire the group of Italian scholars known as the neolinguists, of whom Bartoli was the leading proponent. The influence of this school on the work of Gramsci will be considered in Chapter 2.

This, then, was the critical state of the study of language in the late nineteenth century. The neogrammarians, having defeated the biological naturalism of Schleicher, and having overhauled the methods of their comparativist forerunners, were predominant. Yet the work of their opponents had the effect of bringing to the fore a set of significant questions in relation to the study of language which will be recognisable to anyone familiar with Saussure's *Course*. They signal the key areas of methodological differences between the competing schools of linguistics and thus the important issues which were up for debate. Examples of these questions are: Is the study of language to be undertaken from an objective or a subjective viewpoint? Is it to be concerned with the individual or the social aspects of language? Is language law-governed or random? Is it abstract and formal in its operations, or constantly creative in the manner of poetry? Is it subject to human agency, or blind in the anti-humanist workings of its rules? Is the study of the development of a language to take precedence over the study of language in the present? These, then, are some of the questions which were being contested towards the end of the century. And what was at stake of course was the most important prize of all: the scientificity of the study of language. In the light of this methodologically confusing and contradictory context it comes as less of a surprise to find Saussure complaining of 'the utter ineptness of current terminology, the need for reform', and therefore asserting the imperative 'to show what kind of an object language is in general' (Saussure 1964: 93). It is also unsurprising that Saussure should take the terms which were up for debate and use them for his own clarificatory purposes. It was by any standards an impressive aim, and one which he seems to have undertaken unwillingly, as he set out to prove that the first science of language had not been scientific at all. To do so he needed to delineate from the prevailing confusion both the science of language and its object.

GAINING SCIENTIFICITY, LOSING PRAXIS

If, as Saussure claims at the beginning of the *Course*, 'it is the viewpoint adopted which creates the object', then his task was to find the viewpoint which would render the object of the science of language. He does this by a series of rhetorical moves which have the cumulative effect of defining what is to count as the object of linguistics. The method is outlined aphoristically: 'ni des axiomes, ni des principes, ni des thèses, mais *des délimitations*, des limites entre lesquelles se retrouve constamment la vérité, d'où que l'on parte' (Saussure 1957: 51). Delimitation then was Saussure's procedure in the *Course*, and it took the form of a constant questioning of ways of looking at language in order to find the key methodology which would render that obscure, pure, scientific, delimited object: language 'in itself and for its own sake'.

The aims of linguistics in the *Course* are threefold:

1 to describe all known languages and record their history. This involves tracing the history of language families and, as far as possible, reconstructing the parent languages of each family;
2 to determine the forces operating permanently and universally in all languages, and to formulate general laws which account for all particular linguistic phenomena historically attested;
3 to delimit and define linguistics itself.

(Saussure 1983: 6)

It is evident from these aims that Saussure felt that the object of linguistic science, to say nothing of linguistics itself, had not yet been clarified. This conclusion is also made clear in his brief account of the history of linguistics. Given then that linguistics had not yet found its object, what could Saussure's attitude be towards the work of the historical linguists who had declared themselves to be the first practitioners of a 'science of language'? Saussure's attitude on this point was unequivocal and was made clear in a letter to Meillet:

> The utter ineptness of current terminology, the need for reform, and to show what kind of an object language is in general – these things over and over again spoil whatever pleasure I can take in historical studies, even though I have no greater wish than not to have to bother myself with these general linguistic considerations.

He adds: 'there is not a single term used in linguistics today which has any meaning for me whatsoever' (Saussure 1964: 93). Reluctant revolutionary he might have been, but such a total rejection of the terminology and methodology of the historical linguists could leave him with no other option.

The drive towards science then derives from Saussure's impatience with what he conceived of as the pre-scientific complacency in the study of language in which he had served his apprenticeship. To work in that tradition, he complained to Meillet, was inevitably to face 'the general difficulty of writing any ten lines of a common sense nature in connection with linguistic facts' (ibid.). Against the background of confusion and intellectual quarrels between the different schools of the 'science of language', Saussure's first step was to assert that his study was to be related to the other, 'proper' sciences, in taking as its object a part of reality. In fact it is no small paradox, in view of the importance accorded by Saussure to the science which studies signs, that he begins the classification of his object with a negative claim about language. After beginning to articulate 'the place of language in the facts of speech', thereby disarticulating *langue* from *parole*, he continues by making an ontological claim about language:

> It should be noted that we have defined things, not words. Consequently the distinctions established are not affected by the fact that certain ambiguous terms have no exact equivalents in other languages. Thus in German the word *Sprache* covers individual languages as well as language in general, while *Rede* answers more or less to 'speech', but also has the sense of 'discourse'. In Latin the word *sermo* covers language in general and also speech, while *lingua* is the word for 'a language'; and so on. No one corresponds precisely to any one of the notions we have tried to specify above. That is why all definitions based on words are in vain. It is an error of method to proceed from words in order to give definitions of things.
>
> (Saussure 1983: 14)

In many ways this is a remarkable claim since it appears to place Saussure firmly in the camp of those who betray a distrust towards language, a fear of the potential confusion brought about by words, and a preference for the reliable solidity of things. This wariness towards language is typical rather of the seventeenth-century philosophers than of the founder of the modern science of language, and in fact Saussure's claim here echoes Descartes:

> because we attach all our conceptions to words for the expression of them by speech, and as we commit to memory our thought in connection with these words; and as we more easily call to memory words than things, we can scarcely conceive of anything so distinctly as to be able to separate completely that which we conceive from the words chosen to express the same. In this way most men apply their attention to words rather than things, and this is the cause of their frequently giving their assent to terms which they do not understand, either because they believe that they formerly understood them, or because they think that those who informed them correctly understood their signification.
>
> (Descartes 1968: 252)

If it really is the case, as Saussure claims, that 'all definitions based on words are in vain', then why continue with the writing of the *Course*, since its principal aim has been declared as a set of clarificatory delimitations concerning language and its study? And if it is 'an error of method to proceed from words in order to give definitions of things', then what can be done except to point to the thing itself, in the manner of the early Wittgenstein, and leave it at that?

Rather than Cartesian scepticism, however, the preference for things rather than words here sounds like a maxim of seventeenth-century empiricism, and it is therefore all the more unusual that Saussure should appear to endorse it. His complaint echoes that of Bacon when he notes that 'words plainly force and overrule the understanding, and throw all into confusion' (Bacon 1857: 164); and his aim recalls Bacon's intention to expose 'the false appearances that are imposed upon us by words' (Bacon 1861: 134). The desire to avoid words and rely upon things also replicates Locke's sceptical caution with respect to the imperfections of language, 'where the signification of the word and the real essence of the thing are not the same' (Locke 1975: 477), and the consequent problems for those who 'set their Thoughts more on Words than things' and thus 'speak several words, no otherwise than Parrots do, only because they have learned them, and have been accustomed to those sounds' (ibid.: 408).

However, although Saussure's claim is at first sight rather odd, it is in fact perfectly compatible with the scientific project of the *Course*. Another of his assertions serves to show why this is so. He insists that the idea that language is a nomenclature, 'a list of terms corresponding to a list of things', is incorrect. For Saussure language is a systematic structure of sound-patterns and concepts, and rather than being the means by which we name the world, it is in fact a system of representation which does not necessarily, if at all, involve the world. This of course is a highly contentious point which has provided the focus for a great deal of discussion amongst philosophers and linguists on the question of reference. However, for scientific purposes the crucial epistemological significance of the distinction, and its centrality to understanding Saussure's project, lies in the rejection of the commonly postulated duality of language and world. As already noted, Saussure rejected those accounts of language which took it to be the medium by which consciousness named the pre-linguistic objects of the world. But his radical break went even further than a simple rejection of the language–world duality. For his claim here is that world and language do not belong to distinct orders of being, but in fact belong to the same ontological order. The break amounts to this: that Saussure conceived of language as a thing to be found in the world of other things; not of course as a material thing, and this is where Saussure entirely parts company with the empiricists, since that would be to mistake language for one of its material modes – either sound or writing (which are to be studied by phonetics and philology rather than scientific linguistics), but a thing nonetheless. As such of course, and like other things, language became open to the methods of objective scientific study. Once liberated from its status as but a pale shadow of the world of things into its proper place standing alongside those things, then language could join those other items of reality in the privileged status of scientific object. Hence the perfect sense of the claim to have 'defined things not words'. Once we are clear that we are no longer dealing with mere words, with which it is impossible to give definitions of things since words are not necessarily related to the world of things, then we can be certain that we have focussed our attention away from misleading forms and on to one of those more reliable things: that is, as the last sentence of the *Course* puts it, 'language, considered in itself and for its own sake'. We are then in a position to know that we have passed into the realm of science rather than that of mere words, words, words.

The transformation of language from its position as a poor (or even perfect, it does not matter) speculum of the world has important consequences. Not the least is the denial of the centrality of human activity in the study of language. As language becomes reified it loses its roots in praxis, in practical human labour; the realm of practice is relegated to the position of mere shadow of the thing itself. Abstracted from the realm of history, language becomes a thing which science can investigate with all its full rigour. As Lukács, following Marx, pointed out, the basis of any such reification is that a relation between people takes on the character of a thing and thus acquires a 'phantom objectivity', an autonomy that seems so strictly rational and all-embracing as to conceal any trace of its real nature: the relation between people.

(Lukács 1971: 83)

Once language has become a thing, its role as the practical constitutive factor of human social being is banished in favour of objectivity, autonomy and rationality. It becomes what Vološinov summarises as an 'abstract-objective' entity, the governing characteristics of which are that it is immutable, self-enclosed, and determinedly rule-governed (Vološinov 1973: 57) What this amounts to is the delineation of the real object of the science of language at the expense of the loss of history. And once Saussure had delineated language as a thing 'in itself and for its own sake', then the crucial distinction between *langue* and *parole*, the thing itself and the uses to which it is put, follows logically. Furthermore the hierarchical ordering of *langue* over *parole* is the next logical step, in that for the type of scientist that Saussure had in mind, the study of things demanded the necessary condition that they should be stable and static rather than constantly in flux, in order that they could be reliably identified and theorised. Only *langue* could fulfil these necessary conditions.

THE REJECTION OF HISTORY?

Saussure's delimitation of *langue*, then, dictates that history, in the sense of the practice of human labour, is lost from his account of the study of language. Yet is this tantamount to arguing that the historical perspective is entirely rejected in his work? It is certainly a commonplace of the accounts of twentieth-century linguistics that Saussure was the founder of a discipline which turned away from the achievements of the historical linguists of the nineteenth century in order to achieve a new, and as it happens second, 'science of language'. And this is an accurate assessment, although in fact Saussure's only published work was the *Mémoire sur le système primitif des voyelles dans les langues indo-européennes* (1878), a major contribution to the field of historical linguistics. But does this amount to a full rejection of history? It is evidently the case that his reputation has been consolidated as 'le créateur d'une linguistique anti-historique' and a proponent of a view of language which considers it 'hors de la vie sociale et de la durée historique' (De Mauro 1972: 448). However, reputations can be unmerited and this view of Saussure's work, as being anti-historical, and agnostic (at best) towards the political aspects of language, is a version which needs to be examined. It will be argued here that this account is indeed accurate in some respects, but reductive in others; fair, perhaps, in terms of his theoretical stance, once that is properly understood, but unjust in its blindness both to his overall aim and to his particular understanding of the question of language in history.

That Saussure was opposed to a particular use of the historical perspective in the study of language can be, and often is, evinced by the quotation of selected extracts of the *Course*. In the discussion of 'Static linguistics and evolutionary linguistics', for example, we find:

> The first thing which strikes one on studying linguistic facts is that the language user is unaware of their succession in time: he is dealing with a state. Hence the linguist who wishes to understand this state must rule out of consideration everything which brought that state about, and pay no attention to diachrony. Only by suppressing the past can he enter the state of mind of the language user. The intervention of history can only distort his judgment.
>
> (Saussure 1983: 81)

The rejection of history here appears emphatic: the fact that linguistic facts succeed each other in time (diachronically) is of no relevance. Indeed not only are such considerations unimportant, they are positively harmful to proper judgment, and therefore both history and any consideration of the past have to be banished.

And yet if history is to be suppressed in this stark manner, why is it that the alleged founder of anti-historical linguistics cites the following 'important matters' which 'demand attention when one approaches the study of language'. First, he claims:

> there are all the respects in which linguistics links up with ethnology. There are all the relations which may exist between the history of a race or a civilisation. The two histories intermingle and are related to one another. . . . A nation's way of life has an effect upon its language. At the same time it is in great part the language which makes the nation.
>
> (ibid.: 21)

Another important set of questions is cited:

> mention must be made of the relations between languages and political history. Major historical events such as the Roman Conquest are of incalculable linguistic importance in all kinds of ways. Colonisation, which is simply one form of conquest, transports a language into new environments and this brings changes in the language. A great variety of examples could be cited in this connection. Norway, for instance, adopted Danish on becoming politically united to Denmark, although today Norwegians are trying to shake off this linguistic

influence. The internal politics of a country is of no less importance for the life of a language.

(ibid.)

And finally:

> A language has connections with institutions of every sort: church, school, etc. These institutions in turn are intimately bound up with the literary development of a language. This is a phenomenon of general importance, since it is inseparable from political history. A literary language is by no means confined to the limits apparently imposed upon it by literature. One only has to think of the influence of salons, of the court, and of academies. In connection with the literary language, there arises the important question of conflict with local dialects.

(ibid.: 21–2)

The 'important matters' which Saussure notes then are: language and race, language and the nation, the relations between language and political history (conquest, colonisation, internal politics), language and institutions, and the relationship between the literary language and the dialects. Can this be the same author against whom the charge is laid of being anti-historical? Perhaps this apparent dichotomy between the two Saussures would be explained if these comments were tucked away in the manuscript sources, those enigmatic and unsystematic students' notes from which the *Course* was derived. Perhaps; but these citations of important questions are all contained in chapter 5 of the Introduction to the *Course*. How then are we to reconcile these apparently contradictory statements: on the one hand the proposition that the past, history, distorts and must be suppressed; and on the other the claim that historical questions are important and have to be addressed? The answer to this problem can only lie with a detailed reading of the other theoretical delimitations by which Saussure brought the new science of language to light.

THE DELIMITATION OF SYNCHRONY AND DIACHRONY

The same demand for scientificity which produces the *langue–parole* division is that which is responsible for the privileging of the synchronic study of language over its diachronic relation. For again only the synchronic *état de langue* can offer the stability and staticity demanded by the gaze of science. Yet just as the *langue–parole* distinction and its precondition, the reification of language, were based upon the formal repression of human activity, likewise this other central distinction has its basis in the process of rigid delimitation which Saussure had announced as his method. The dimension which is excluded here is what Saussure calls 'history', but what would be better understood as the fact of change through time; and this is excluded on the grounds that it represents a distorting and problematic force which prevents the stability required for the operation of science. Synchronic study, by contrast, lends itself to scientific method by dint of its being by definition static, since 'although each language constitutes a closed system all presuppose certain constant principles' (ibid.: 98).

However, although change through time is excluded here, it lies at the heart of the definition of the synchronic state of language. Saussure claims that the synchronic system 'occupies not a point in time, but a period of time of varying length, during which the sum total of changes is minimal. It may be ten years, a generation, a century or even longer' (ibid.: 99). This is not so much an exclusion of the temporal perspective, or 'history' to use Saussure's term, as its relegation to the realm of irrelevance. Since it does not matter whether a linguistic state lasts a day or a century, time can have no relevance in the matter of the demarcation of the linguistic state. This refusal of the significance of time is stressed further when Saussure adds a rider to his definition of the synchronic state:

> An absolute state is defined by lack of change. But since languages are always changing, however minimally, studying a linguistic state amounts in practice to ignoring unimportant changes. Mathematicians do likewise when they ignore very small fractions for certain purposes, such as logarithmic calculations.
>
> (ibid.: 100)

Linguistic change through time then, although acknowledged as central in Saussure's definition of the language state (since it has to occupy a period of time, and 'languages are always changing'), must be understood from the particular viewpoint of his 'scientific' approach. For in fact what is being argued here is that not all change is significant, and that some changes have to be ignored in order to gain the mathematical precision of 'science'. To engage in this process of deliberate exclusion, however, is to make the linguist not an observer of linguistic facts, but a judge of which facts are important and which are not. That is, it is to have the linguist engage in presciptivism rather than the description of linguistic states. It is also to admit that the all-encompassing scientific study of language proposed by Saussure is based on a myth: 'the notion of a linguistic state can only be an approximation. In static linguistics, as in most sciences, no demonstration is possible without a conventional simplification of the data' (ibid.: 100). The fact of linguistic change even at the synchronic level is not denied by Saussure, but either ignored or relegated to a secondary position in the interests of science. This has the effect of reversing the usual function of time: rather than time being the measure of the duration of a linguistic state, it is the language that becomes the means by which time is to be calibrated. The flow of time is discarded in favour of a series of static systems whose alteration alone can allow the temporal perspective to be momentarily important. Yet this hierarchy, as with that of *langue–parole*, can only be bought at the price of exclusion and simplification in the interest of science. In the case of *langue–parole* it is history as human practice that is left out; in that of synchrony and diachrony, it is time itself.

Of course readers conversant with the *Course* will know that Saussure mentions the 'important matters' of language and race, nation and political history, precisely in order to relegate them to the realm of 'external linguistics' rather than to include them within the scientific gaze of his theoretical study ('internal linguistics'). It is just this sort of distinction that has led to the claim that Saussure rejected history, and it is to this claim that we shall return shortly. However, it is worth noting for the moment that the founder of General Linguistics viewed the topics outlined above as not only significant for linguists but important in a more general sense. For Saussure this is the case because, he asserts, 'in practice the study of language is in some degree or other the concern of everyone'. He also makes the forceful contention:

> In the lives of individuals and societies, language is a factor of greater importance than any other. For the study of language to remain solely the business of a handful of specialists would be a quite unacceptable state of affairs.
>
> (ibid.: 7)

Arguing against the prevailing trend in linguistic thought in the twentieth century, and indeed the trend which his own work at least in part engendered, Saussure argues that the study of language should not be a sealed and impenetrable field for specialists alone but a discipline whose significance is general precisely because its object is of singular importance in social life. Already in such declarations we can find a clear recognition that Saussure is aware of the importance of language in history; that is, he recognises the relevance of thinking about language not only in relation to 'political history' but also with regard to the importance of the study of language for its users in the historical present.

The commonplace claim that Saussure regarded history as at best an irrelevance in the study of language, and that it could only function by 'suppressing the past' is an important one, and it is necessary to be clear about the assertion which Saussure makes in this regard since it is central. What he argues here is the cardinal point that General Linguistics concerns itself only with the system of language which exists at a particular abstract moment (the duration of which is determined not by time but by the requirement that any changes within the system be judged minimal and not significant). That is, it attempts to describe the state of a language from the language-user's point of view, in the form of a system in the present, the nature of which is, by definition, static. Despite this, it is clear from the *Course* that Saussure is not arguing against work on the relations between language and history *per se*. Rather, he is arguing against the confusion of the synchronic and diachronic viewpoints. That which is constantly affirmed is the need to keep these viewpoints separate and, in the interests of scientificity, to render a hierarchical ordering in which the synchronic takes precedence over the diachronic. The question to be addressed is why Saussure deems this necessary to his project and, more importantly, why this is taken to be a rejection of history.

Before embarking upon an attempt to answer this question it is necessary to clarify one point. That is that Saussure did not evince a lack of interest in diachronic linguistics. Not only was his training and only self-penned publication in this field, he also devoted by far the longest section of the *Course* to the problems of diachronic study.[1] However, be that as it may, it is certainly clear that in the theoretical model, synchrony is privileged over diachrony. The reason for this hierarchy is quite simply that diachronic facts are not systematic, and therefore stable, in the same way as synchronic facts appear to be. 'Diachronic linguistics', Saussure claims, 'can accumulate detail after detail, without ever being forced to conform to the constraints of a system.' Thus the diachronic evolution of language offers not a closed, logical order of relations but a series of 'facts' which can be interpreted in a number of different ways. The synchronic system of 'facts', on the other hand, 'admits no order other than its own' (ibid.: 23). Briefly put, the problem with diachronic linguistics is that it deals with units which 'replace one another without themselves constituting a system' (ibid.: 98).

The privileging of the synchronic view, then, stems from the requirement for systematicity in language study, and this in turn derives from the drive towards scientificity. In contradistinction to the sequences of diachronic units which need to have an order and regularity imposed upon them, the relations of synchronic units already exist, and merely await discovery by the scientist of language. Yet even given this distinction (and its validity in the context of the more self-reflexive developments in the modern sciences is open to question), it is still not the case that Saussure can be said to have rejected history. And this is the point at which Saussure's use of the term 'history' itself, and indeed its extension in the phrase 'historical linguistics', needs to be clarified further. When Saussure uses 'history' in claiming that for a linguist 'the intervention of history can only distort his judgment', what he means is simply the fact that signs change through time; just as the phrase 'historical linguistics' really means the tracing of linguistic change through time. For the scientific linguist the fact that a sign had a different value in the past is of no consequence, since the object of study is the language in the present. For the historical linguist, on the other hand, the fact that languages may have mingled because of political conquest, or that language may give some indication of how national identities are formed, is of no consequence either; since for the historical linguist the aim is to trace the history of a language, and of language in general, in the sense of recording the changes which have taken place through time. This is the significance of Saussure's choice of the term 'diachronic' instead of 'historical linguistics' or 'evolutionary linguistics'. 'Evolutionary linguistics', though preferable to Saussure to 'historical linguistics', might have had unfortunate echoes of Schleicher's biological naturalism. And 'historical linguistics' dismissed by Saussure as 'too vague' might be misleading in the sense that it appears to suggest that the field is concerned with the study of the relations between language and history (itself to be given the new title of 'external linguistics'). The term 'diachronic', however, has the advantage of signalling, ironically by way of its etymology, the tracing of linguistic change through time (*dia chronos*). What has been argued then is the rejection of the privileging of the diachronic over the synchronic, on the basis that systematicity demands synchronicity. This cannot in any meaningful sense be described as a rejection of history, since the diachronic perspective for Saussure means simply the 'evolution' or succession of units through time. And it is a reductive and poor view of history (and a view, more-over, which cannot be ascribed to Saussure) that sees it simply in terms of events succeeding each other in what Benjamin called 'homogeneous, empty time' (Benjamin 1970: 266). To summarise, then, Saussure argues against the privileging of the diachronic point of view in language study; he does not rule out the importance of the relations between language and history, nor does he dismiss the significance of the study of such links; though it can be argued reasonably that the *Course* permits this confusion to take place by dint of its lack of distinction between time and history.

It is important to establish this point in that it returns us to Saussure's assertions in relation to language in history. For what is evident in those extracts is that Saussure does not conflate external linguistics with diachronic linguistics, or internal linguistics with synchronic study. And this is crucial. The set of distinctions, external–internal – diachronic–synchronic, are not to be seen as two sets of terms in correspondence (in which external and diachronic are paired as inadmissable, and internal and synchronic paired as the allowed terms), but as a series of terms in which each has its own significance. For although in the overall model it is the synchronic and internal perspectives that are privileged, it does not therefore follow that the diachronic and external are relegated in the same way, for the same reasons, and with the same stress. To put it simply, in order for the science of General Linguistics to get off the ground in the first place both the stress on the internal system and the synchronic viewpoint have to be given precedence. But it is not a necessary consequence of this methodological step that we are to consider external linguistics and diachronic study to deal with the same material, to be united in perspective, or indeed in any important way to be related.

   In fact Saussure makes it clear that the areas of external linguistics and the diachronic study of language deal with very distinct material and that they must not be confused. We have seen above how he specified the 'important matters' with which external linguistics concerns itself. We can now remind ourselves of the definition of diachronic study: 'Diachronic linguistics studies the relations which hold not between the coexisting terms of a linguistic state, but between successive terms substituted one for another over a period of time' (Saussure 1983: 139). The object of study for these two approaches is very different. In external linguistics it is the relation between language and political history construed in its broadest sense; in the diachronic study of language it is the relation between units which come to replace each other in time. Moreover, not only are these two fields to be distinguished; Saussure argues that they cannot lend each other support. For in the last few pages of the *Course*, in which he considers 'linguistic evidence in Anthropology and Prehistory', including such topics as 'languages and races', 'ethnicity', 'linguistic palaeontology' and 'linguistic types and group mentality', Saussure explicitly warns against using the diachronic method in order to give accounts of the relations between language and political history. For example, he discusses the reconstruction of former languages which have long disappeared, this being a central concern in diachronic study. Of this he asks:

> Can these reconstructions tell us anything about the peoples themselves, their race, their social structure, their customs, their institutions, etc? In other words, can the language throw light on questions of anthropology, ethnography and prehistory? It is generally held that it can. But in our view that is largely illusory.
>
> (ibid.: 221)

Again, later, when discussing 'linguistic types and group mentality', he reconsiders the nature of diachronic evidence:

> It is always interesting to determine the grammatical typology of languages (whether they are historically attested or reconstructed) and to classify them according to the procedures they adopt for the

expression of thought. But from these analyses and classifications no conclusions can be drawn with any certainty outside the linguistic domain proper.

(ibid.: 226)

The point is that diachronic studies never leave 'the linguistic domain proper', by which Saussure means that they never quite manage to escape the task of detailing the successive units with which they are concerned. The significance of external linguistics, on the other hand, is left untouched by these objections to diachronic study since the two fields are distinct and take different objects for analysis.

The argument then is that the rejection or, better, the relegation of the diachronic viewpoint is not a rejection of history. Rather, what appears obliquely in Saussure's account, though it is hardly developed, is the field of external linguistics which takes as its object of study the role of language in history. There is no absolute rejection of history then, but a new positioning of the historical viewpoint in the field of linguistic study. There is even evidence that it is a viewpoint which Saussure might have favoured once the arduous task of clearing the ground for the science of language had been completed. For in the letter to Meillet in which he had complained of the confused state of language study, he also commented:

in the last analysis, only the picturesque side of a language still holds my interest, what makes it different from all others insofar as it belongs to a particular people with a particular origin, the almost ethnographic side of language.

(Saussure 1964: 93)

The account then of Saussure as the creator of an anti-historical linguistics is, as stated earlier, both accurate and reductive: accurate if we take Saussure's 'anti-historical' stance to mean a study of language which relegates the importance of linguistic change through time, but reductive if it is taken to mean a study of language which rejects altogether the significance of language in history. It is fair in terms of his theoretical stance, since the delimitations he makes are in his view those required for the purposes of science. But the account is unjust in taking these methodological manoeuvres as indicating a negative stance on Saussure's part towards the types of relations between language and history which he outlines under the title of 'external linguistics'.

The importance of this re-reading of Saussure's attitude to the study of language in history is that it suggests a possible new departure in linguistic study. For if the argument that he did not reject the historical viewpoint but relocated it is accurate, then we can begin work in a field which, though hinted at in an abstract way, has not yet been worked upon to any great extent. And if we are to take seriously Saussure's claim about the importance of the study of language to everyone, then this will have repercussions for our ways of thinking about linguistic study: about its objects, its methods and its aims.

We can begin by saying that the study of language in history must pose a threat to the formal, abstract forms of linguistic study which have dominated the twentieth century. Whether these be in the post-Saussurean or Chomskyan schools (the dominant branches in the last seventy-five years), it is clear that the decontextualised, ahistorical approach to language must be called into question by a method which does not seek for an abstract structure but looks instead for the uses, and their significance, to which language is put at the micro- and macro-social levels. And this is not just a question of turning away from *langue* to *parole*, or from competence to performance, since that would be to accept the misleading alternatives on offer in the established models. The new approach would seek and analyse precisely neither abstract linguistic structure nor individual use but the institutional, political and ideological relationships between language and history. It would take as its object, for example, the ways in which language has been used to divide some groups, to unify others, to convince some of their superiority, to make others feel outsiders. It would look to the role of language in the making and unmaking of nations, of forms of social identity, of ways and patterns of ideological and cultural beliefs. In short, it would consider the modes in which language becomes important for its users not as a faculty which they all share at an abstract level, but as a practice in which they all participate in very different ways, to very different effects, under very different pressures, in their everyday lives. It would seek neither the abstract linguistic structure fixed in a static present nor the evolutionary unfolding of linguistic elements in empty time. It would take as its focus the complex, changing, often contradictory and difficult relations between forms of language in history. And it would attempt to have as its basis the belief that 'in the lives of individuals and societies, language is a factor of greater importance than any other'. It might even change the unacceptable state of affairs in which the study of language is 'solely the business of a handful of specialists'.

CONCLUSION

The first pretender to the status of the science of language was Historical Linguistics. But by this use of the term 'historical' is meant nothing more than the story, or account, of changes which have taken place in the past in respect to a language or languages. It is the story of a language as it has altered through time; it is 'l'histoire de la langue'. It is not, however, the study of a language, or a number of languages, in relation to the political context in which they are produced, of which they form a part, and in which they have a significant role. *That* study is a question of language in history, 'la langue dans l'histoire'. The record of that set of complex relations is certainly external to any particular 'état de langue', and it is most likely to be rather unsystematic in its nature. It is, however, a field to which Saussure pointed in an important way. He noted it but could not, by dint of his aims in the *Course*, pursue his interest in that area in that text.

But if language is to become more than the object of concern of a small number of scientists, and if we are to recognise its central importance in social and individual life, then it will be necessary not only to reject the view of language as an abstract formal entity, sealed off from praxis and time, but also to distinguish carefully between the history of language, and language in history.

Chapter 2

For and against Bakhtin

'historical linguistics is still far from historical . . .'
(Gramsci 1985: 170)

THEORY IN THE STUDY OF LANGUAGE IN HISTORY

One of the most salient facts about research conducted in the area of language in history until relatively recently is its resistance to theoretical work. This is surprising given the centrality of questions concerned with the relationship between language and history in modern critical theory. It is also peculiar in the light of the enormous theoretical and speculative connections of the discipline of historical linguistics in the nineteenth century – ranging from anthropology to geology. Yet it is nonetheless true that the field of language in history has been relatively untouched by the sorts of questions, and answers, which have had such a transformative effect upon literary studies in the past twenty years. One pertinent, if historically odd, reason for such an omission is that the field has been characterised by a rigorous adherence to the Saussurean division (examined in the last chapter) between what is properly internal and what is external to the study of language. As we have seen, internal linguistics was to concentrate upon the formal relations between units in a system; external linguistics on the relationship between language and ethnography, language and political history, language and institutions, and so on. This rigorous delimitation, by which the science of language was brought about, has had the effect of causing the study of language in history to be regarded either as a categorical mistake or as a sort of sideline which serious linguists might follow in their spare time.

If there has been a single figure whose work has stood out against this prevailing trend, although the tardy transmission of his texts delayed their effect greatly, that figure would be Mikhail Bakhtin. In a sense his work is a part of a series of shifts which have taken place in modern theory and which have produced a new situation. The theoretical drift away from the more arid types of formalism to what can be described as more discursive and, both implicitly and explicitly, political forms of critique has had deep effects. Across the fields of language study, literary theory, philosophy and historiography, there has been a significant understanding of the social constitution of both their objects and the political implications of their modes of treatment of such objects.

In this change the texts of Bakhtin have had a pivotal role, and his influence appears to grow apace. Yet if his influence in these domains of research has been significant, not least in the production of an historical self-consciousness, it is ironic that his works have had little or no effect in the very field in which their importance seems obvious. For, like the work of many other major theorists, Bakhtin has been overlooked in the study of language in history, despite the fact that his texts offer a number of crucial insights which open up new directions in research. His theoretical and historical treatment of forms of discourse appears to provide the foundation for bridging the gap between the internal and external approaches outlined by Saussure – or, if not bridging the gap, then exposing the division as theoretically untenable and disabling. The importance of this development is that if the chasm were to be bridged, or the division to be exposed as false, the field of language in history would be radically altered in terms both of its methodology and of its aims. The aim of this chapter therefore will be to explore this possibility by considering the relevance of Bakhtin's work for the study of that field.

THE KEY CONCEPTS

It is possible, and indeed his translators frequently do it, to draw up a glossary of the key terms which Bakhtin uses in his writings. If such a glossary were to be compiled with particular reference to this work on language in history, it would necessarily include the coupling of dialogism and monologism along with monoglossia (*odnoyazychie*), polyglossia (*mnogoyazychie*), and heteroglossia (*raznorechie*). Although this technical vocabulary is most frequently used by Bakhtin in his discussions of literary texts, they are in fact terms which are specific to language. Therefore in considering the usefulness of these terms for the field of language in history, it will be necessary first to ascertain the ways in which Bakhtin uses them in his own analyses. It will be argued that, like Saussure, Bakhtin opens up a significant field of research in the area of language in history but fails to exploit it in any sustained way.

The two terms dialogism and monologism are evidently central to Bakhtin's work, and yet, as Hirschkop has noted, they are words whose function and significance alter across his texts (Hirschkop 1986: 93–5). The change can be characterised as the politicisation or historicising of philosophical concepts and takes place between the earlier and later works. In their early use these terms refer to what Bakhtin calls 'worldviews'. In the schema he sketches out, one of these 'worldviews' (monologism) is superseded by the other (dialogism) in what can best be described as an ethical and teleological progression. This idealist account, however, is replaced in the later works in which the terms are employed in at least three distinct ways. First, the pair of terms is used to refer to the historical forces which are in constant conflict in discourse: monological versus dialogical forces. Second, they are used to indicate the effects brought about by the conflict: monological and dialogical forms of discourse. And in their third use they specify the nature of the conflict itself: given that the forces are always in conflict, the form which is dominant at any particular time has to engage in active dialogical renegotiation and struggle with the other in order to retain its position of superiority.

The development in Bakhtin's thought from a static view of either simple opposition or a progression from the inferior 'worldview' of monologism to the superior one of dialogism, to the perception of active historical conflict in discourse, is crucial. For the stress on dialogical struggle as the basis of all forms of discourse allows for the relation between particular dialogical and monological forms to be theorised from an historical perspective. They can thus be viewed as the results of specific social struggles in which their status and position are always at stake. This in turn means that, rather than reflecting an ethical and teleological viewpoint, these terms embody a political mode of analysis which can help to facilitate the understanding of past formations of language in history. The contrast with Saussure's view of a static synchronic state fixed in an apparent 'eternal contemporaneity' (Williams 1986: 23) as the proper object of linguistic analysis could not be more stark. Rather than history being considered as external to language, Bakhtin's account takes history to be the internal force which produces states of language in particular contexts as a result of a conflict between opposing forces.

In fact the general principle to be abstracted from this theoretical politicisation is that all forms of language – from the smallest units to the national language and beyond – are scored through with social and historical conflict. For the study of language in history this is a revolutionary principle, since it threatens to deconstruct the rigid polarisation of interests which had been its central tenet since Saussure had theorised it. Rather than privileging internal over external concerns, Bakhtin's theoretical premiss means that the Saussurean hierarchy would have to be overturned. More significantly perhaps, it would mean that those forces which had been excluded as not belonging to the study of language proper would now be viewed as constituting it. For the Saussurean model the complex relations between languages and political history are characterised by a total split: language state on one side, language and political history on the other, each to be treated differently. For Bakhtin, however, such relations are taken to embody the conflict of social forces which will produce particular linguistic forms, effects and representations. In the field of language in history, if Bakhtin's views were accepted, it would mean that the static conception of language, in which any particular language moves from one state to another, owing nothing to the past and having no concern for the future, would have to be replaced by the Bakhtinian view that the very concept of *a* language is already the product of historical conflict. The field would then have not only to be more concerned with questions of history and struggle but would also engage in a self-conscious reflection upon the role of the field in such struggles. That is, how particular representations of language have their own effects in the historical arena: the hailing of a linguistic golden age in comparison with our currently debased usage, and the vision of some languages as superior to others, are two such representations with resonant historical effects. It is this self-consciousness that has been so markedly absent from the study of language in history as yet, despite the fact that it is this that is necessary for the field to give an adequate account of its object.

If monologism and dialogism are keywords in Bakhtin's work in general, then monoglossia, polyglossia and heteroglossia have particular importance for the study of language in history. Yet these terms also shift their signification, and it is important to distinguish their differing uses too. In the early use of these terms, mirroring the static conception of opposed forces set out in the monologic–dialogic pairing, they refer to actual stages in the history of a language. Monoglossia therefore was the primary historical stage of a language, and its 'purity' and closedness to derivation from other languages reflected directly the self-enclosed monologic 'worldview' of its speakers. Homeric Greek could be cited as such a monoglossic form, signalling as it did its blindness to difference and its desire for purity in its division of the world into Hellenes and *barbaroi* (Greek-speakers and then the other inarticulate babblers). Such a form is represented as self-sufficient and self-originating and is often accorded a theological status, typified for classical Greek when Socrates refers in *Cratylus* to the language 'in which the Gods must clearly be supposed to call things by their right and natural names' (Plato 1970: 138). The same type of assertions of purity and superiority were made for Irish in the eighteenth and nineteenth centuries, including one assertion that Irish was the language of Eden, as we shall see. Another example of the representation of the monoglossic language might be Anglo-Saxon, since it too was often portrayed as the purest form of a particular language. In this account Anglo-Saxon represented the 'true

English' before it was bastardised, and 'feminised', by its miscegenation with Norman French.

According to the teleological order adopted by Bakhtin in his early work, monoglossia is superseded by polyglossia when the self-enclosed language becomes aware for the first time of linguistic otherness. In *Cratylus* such alterity is already present in the references of Socrates to geographic, historical, social and gender-related variation which needs to be suppressed, by way of a return to the *etumos logos* (the 'real' meaning of a word), in order to recover the divine language of truth. However, once the perception of difference has entered, then the self-enclosed Ptolemaic language becomes irreversibly transformed into the open Galilean set of languages in a variety of relations with each other. In this historical account, Latin would play the role of polyglossia to the Greek monoglossia, since Latin, and indeed Roman civilisation, came into existence as precisely not self-sufficient but derived at least in part from its Greek forebear. In such a shift the absolute confidence of self-origination and self-standing is relativised and undermined by the acute awareness of historical roots and therefore dependence. Polyglossia can thus be characterised as a stage which induces linguistic and cultural anxiety for a previously monoglot community.

The final stage in Bakhtin's schema occurs when polyglossia is sup-planted by heteroglossia, a process which results in the bringing to light of internal and external linguistic difference. In this stage a language drops both the absolute and the relative unity characteristic of its former stages and thus reveals the fully dialogic and heteroglot reality of its pluralistic character. Thus Bakhtin writes of

> the internal stratification of any single language into social dialects, characteristic group behaviour, professional jargons, generic lan-guages, languages of generations and age groups, tendentious lan-guages, languages of the authorities, of various circles and passing fashions, languages that serve the specific sociopolitical purposes of the day, even of the hour.
>
> (Bakhtin 1981: 262–3)

For Saussure of course the task of accounting for this 'internal strati-fication' is relatively simple. Either the fact of such variation is relegated to the realm of parole, and therefore does not count in linguistics proper; or, if such usage can be shown to be derived from a systematic synchronic state which facilitates it, then the linguist's job is to describe that state of language (to draw up the units, and the rules which govern them, of, for example, the social dialects, generic languages, and so on). For Bakhtin, any such positing of an underlying unity is a transparent fiction by which the complex interrelational differences of all these languages are sup-pressed. It is the construction of a language out of the fact of language.

The teleological and ethical tone which accompanies Bakhtin's account, as a language moves historically from worse to better stages, is one that he never quite manages to lose. It is almost the counterpart of Saussure's underlying vision; where Saussure sees the need for unity and systematicity, Bakhtin celebrates difference and plurality. The two are in a sense as absolutist as each other; and they are caught on the opposite horns of a dilemma as a result of failing to comprehend fully the role of language in history.

It is always and everywhere the case for Bakhtin that dialogism is preferable to monologism, and heteroglossia to either polyglossia or monoglossia; polyglossia of course is also superior to monoglossia. The validity of this view, and its lack of historical specificity, will be challenged later, but it is necessary first to demonstrate the limitations of such a view and the attempts made by Bakhtin to overcome them. For Bakhtin it is clearly the case that polyglossia and heteroglossia are ethically superior to monoglossia since, in the transformation from the earlier to the later stages,

> language is transformed from the absolute dogma it had been within the narrow framework of a sealed-off and impermeable monoglossia into a working hypothesis for comprehending and expressing reality . . . .. Only polyglossia fully frees consciousness from the tyranny of its own language and its own myth of language.
>
> (ibid.: 61)

In this transformation the forces of liberation and pluralism are victorious in their linguistic conflict with those of narrow dogmatism, and the result is a new, polyglot stage of language. Yet if such a view is taken to its (teleo-)logical conclusion, then it must follow that we live today in a world in which the forces of linguistic liberation have triumphed. It is an argument made by Bakhtin when he claims that we live in a world which is beyond monoglossia:

> We live, write and speak today in a world of free and democratized language, the complex and multi-leveled hierarchy of discourses, forms, images, styles, and linguistic consciousness was swept away by the linguistic revolutions of the Renaissance. European *literary* languages – French, German, English – came into being while this hierarchy was in the process of being destroyed . . . . For this reason these new languages provided only very modest space for parody: these languages hardly knew, and now do not know at all, sacred words.
>
> (ibid.: 71)

This is Bakhtin at his most idealist, and in terms of a blindness to history such a stance can only be compared to Saussure's declaration of what Bourdieu describes as 'linguistic communism': 'at any time a language belongs to all its users. It is a facility unreservedly available throughout a whole community' (Saussure 1983: 73–4). For both writers their theoretical stance obviates the historical realities. Saussure's declaration, though theoretically necessary, is historically naive. A language simply does not, except in an idealist, abstract sense belong to all its users, since linguistic capital, and the uses to which it may be put, are distributed very clearly along the lines of power. This historical blindness stems from Saussure's subscription to the model of the nation, articulated by the nineteenth-century cultural nationalists, in which the nation is a mono-lingual community. We will consider the development of this theoretical model later in our analysis of the role of language in cultural nationalism at various points in Irish and British history. Saussure's own equation of the nation with a monolingual group, however, is further evinced in his treatment of the geographical diversity of languages. Its 'ideal form', he claims, occurs where 'different areas correspond to different languages' (ibid.: 192).

In contrast to Saussure's historical naivety, Bakhtin's misleading optimism is brought about by rigid adherence to a teleological schema whose historical accuracy is disproved by even a quick glance at the conditions which prevail in our world. To argue that languages such as French, German and English know no 'sacred words' is to fly in the face of the history by which each of them became the language of an empire which elevated its own language and determined to stamp out the languages and cultures of the colonised. To claim that we live 'in a world of free and democratised language' is to be blind to the fetters and restrictions placed on actual language use. Like Saussure's claim about the availability of language to all in the community, Bakhtin's assertion of linguistic democracy is similar to the proposition that all are equal before the law. This is clearly true in a formal sense, but in lived experience it is quite as clearly not; to pretend otherwise is to render a disservice to the dispossessed and to be ignorant of historical reality.

THE POLITICISATION OF THE CONCEPTS

If Bakhtin had kept to this unbending historical model he would have remained at the level of a theorist who acknowledged the importance of language in history but was unable to account for it in any specific sense. In fact there is much in this charge, as will be demonstrated later. But it is at this point that we have to recognise that the shift which takes place in his work in the use of monologism and dialogism as theoretical terms has further relevance. For under the influence of the politicised conception of these terms the relations between monoglossia, polyglossia and hetero-glossia appear very differently. Rather than conceiving of these terms as referring to chronological stages of linguistic being which occur in an irreversible teleological process, the politicised standpoint takes them as forms and representations of language engendered by social and historical conflict. This means that rather than their evolution being guaranteed, with progress from the least good (monoglossia) to the best (heteroglossia), their appearance depends upon the contingencies of history and the balance of forces at a particular point. Thus monoglossia, from the politicised viewpoint, is one of the forms of language, or a set of representations of language, which are the product of the dialogical struggle between opposing tendencies. Moreover, although it achieves a certain stability, its status can never be as absolute as it pretends:

> it must not be forgotten that monoglossia is always in essence relative. After all, one's own language is never a single language: in it there are always survivals of the past and a potential for other-languagedness.
>
> (Bakhtin 1981: 66)

This is the principle of the historicity of language cast in a new light, for even in a language represented as monoglot there will be historical traces. Monoglossia is now seen to be a result of historical circumstances which can be altered rather than as a primary, pure stage of language. The introduction of the historical principle here also allows us to account for Bakhtin's hailing of French, German and English as revolutionary, democratising languages. For if understood historically it can be seen how the vernacular languages (from the Latin *verna* meaning home-born slave) were in thrall to the authoritative, imperial and sacred language of Latin; and how during the Renaissance they threw off that yoke and flourished in their own right. But if we maintain the historical principle it means that we cannot halt our analysis there, which is the weakness of Bakhtin's account. For what were once revolutionary languages, whose rise to independence signalled so many other political and cultural changes, were later to become the languages in which other forms of slavery were to be practised. Once admitted, the historical principle has to be pursued to its fullest limits.

Once Bakhtin had made this crucial theoretical shift, the rejection of the conception of monoglossia, and in consequence polyglossia and heteroglossia, as fixed stages of linguistic being led to the axiomatic statement on the processes of historical becoming in language:

> At any given moment of its historical existence, language is heteroglot from top to bottom: it represents the co-existence of socio-ideological contradictions between the present and the past, between differing socio-ideological groups in the present, between tendencies, schools, circles and so forth.
>
> (ibid.: 291)

In the same sense in which dialogism can refer both to a form of language and to the founding principle of all such forms, heteroglossia is one of the historical representations of a language as well as it grounding characteristic. To make these distinctions clearer we can give two examples. A monological form of language, say an order from a commander to soldiers in a unit, appears to be self-authorising, absolute and unquestionable. But in Bakhtin's account this is not the case. For in his analysis what in fact is happening is that a monological form is in conflict with and, by dint of the balance of forces in the struggle, triumphant over dialogical forms. What could happen of course is that the soldiers ask why such an order has been given; or they might refuse the order, question the authority of the commander, and so on. So the monological form is only dominant if it suppresses the possibilities which oppose it; but, far from being self-standing and self-assured, it keeps a wary eye on the possibilities of dialogical response. This conflict in which the dominant form gains victory is not then one which comes already decided; it is in its nature dialogical and thus open to change. Likewise with heteroglossia. For Bakhtin all language is in fact heteroglot, just as all forms are dialogic. But a particular language might only appear heteroglot under particular circumstances: say, for example, when someone wanted to undermine the argument that the English people are a 'pure' group who have never been influenced by 'foreign' cultures. In this context it would be very easy to point to the bastardised nature of the English language – the fact that it is formed primarily out of Teutonic and Romance stocks, which occurred as a result of invasions and conquests – as evidence to the contrary. However, that very same language, despite being of its nature heteroglot, might be *represented* as monoglot in order to achieve exactly the opposite effect to that achieved by its representation as heteroglot. An example of this can be seen in the work of a Victorian linguist writing of the education of the English schoolboy of his day:

> Perhaps the next important step, is that his eyes should be opened to the Unity of English, that in English literature there is an unbroken succession of authors from the reign of Alfred to that of Victoria, and that the language which we speak *now* is absolutely *one* in its essence, with the language that was spoken in the days when the English first invaded the island and defeated and overwhelmed its British inhabitants.

> (Skeat 1873: 221)

Here the representation of *the* English language as monoglot, unified, '*one* in its essence', with that of King Alfred, is acting to serve specific historical and political purposes (in this particular case a form of English nationalism). But in this it has everything in common with the representation of the same language as heteroglot; both are intended to achieve positions of dominance for the values they embody. By way of the theoretical distinctions which these examples illustrate, Bakhtin demonstrates the historical and conflictual nature of language; and this of course is of the utmost significance for the study of language in history.

The conflict of opposing tendencies in language is characterised by Bakhtin as the perpetual dialogic struggle between centripetal forces whose aim is to centralise and unify, and centrifugal forces whose purpose is to decentralise and rupture. The crucial point is that in this struggle the relations between such forces will differ in their forms and effects at distinct historical periods. At one time, and under specific historical conditions, centripetal forces will organise a certain form of language as the centralised, unified, authoritative form of language, and thus monoglossia and monologism will be effected. An example of this process would be that whereby a particular class accent becomes the dominant and usual form used in broadcasting; the accent demanded by the state broadcasting organisation in Britain in the 1920s and 1930s is typical here. At another historical moment the centrifugal forces will be victorious and attempts at unity will prove futile. An example of this would be the resistance to particular dominant accents in popular culture and youth sub-cultures; in these examples identification with accents which are marginalised acts as a force which prevents the dominance of the 'standard' form. What happens in these processes is that all forms of language, and representations of language, become dialogised as effects whose forms are created by the specific historical arrangements of the opposed forces at any one time.

Another example of the type of representation of language to which Bakhtin is referring here is the 'unitary language'. The unitary language is not, as the misleading title of the sub-discipline 'the history of *the* language' suggests, an historical fact waiting to be discovered, but a linguistic form which has to be fought for and gained. As Bakhtin puts it:

> Unitary language constitutes the theoretical expression of the histor-
> ical processes of linguistic unification and centralization, an expression
> of the centripetal forces of language. A unitary language is not
> something which is given (*dan*) but is always in essence posited (*zadan*).
> (Bakhtin 1981: 270)

Both the formal unity which the language has, and the cultural unity whose purpose it serves, are the effects of the massive centralising forces overcoming heteroglot differences. The sites of such struggles, ranging in Bakhtin's account from Aristotelian poetics to Indo-European philology, are the fields in which such significant effects are achieved. The disci-pline carved out by Saussure of course is a perfect example of an

approach to language which concentrates on the centralising and unifying aspects of language.

POLITICAL CONFLICTS

The brief account of Bakhtin's work outlined above has concentrated
upon the important transformation of Bakhtin's idealist concepts; in this
outline the significance of the politicised versions of these concepts for
students of language in history has been noted. The shift was crucial
since it focusses attention on the various institutionalised sites of struggle
in which the competing forces meet. This is important since it allows us
to trace the battle-lines of the conflict, and the complex relations by
which forms of language and power are tied together. There are,
however, problems with Bakhtin's account which specifically involve
the level of abstraction at which his concepts are deployed, the lack of
historical specificity, and a consequent failure to lose entirely the ethical
and teleological tone attached to the early use of the concepts. These
problems in turn mean that the specific questions concerning the relations of language and power are not fully answered. Therefore we have
now to turn to particular examples of historical struggle between centripetal and centrifugal forces in order to see both the limitations and the
possibilities of Bakhtin's politicised concepts and to tackle the problem of
historical specificity. The specific example which affords the clearest
results is that of the 'unitary language'.

Bakhtin's argument in relation to the 'unitary language' claimed that
linguistics, stylistics and the philosophy of language had been major
centralising forces in the history of cultural formations whose principal
method had consisted of seeking for unity in the face of diversity. Such
methodology focussed upon both formal unity, by means of the identification and stabilisation of common linguistic features and their uses,
and cultural unity, by means of an ordering of particular cultural
functions of language (representing the historical status of the nation,
for example). The attempt to forge unity took many forms:

> The victory of one reigning language (dialect) over the others, the
> supplanting of languages, their enslavement, the process of illuminat-
> ing them with the True Word, the incorporation of barbarians and
> lower social strata into a unitary language of culture and truth.
>
> (ibid.: 271)

The double-edged nature of unifying processes is significant in the task of
achieving hegemonic rule in that it not only seeks the centralisation and
solidification of grammatical or cultural forms but also insists at the same
time that the cultural significance of such forms be solidified and

centralised. Without the successful fulfilment of both tasks, the aim of centripetalising forces (hegemonic rule) cannot be achieved.

A good historical example of the ways in which centripetalising forces operate on both the linguistic and the cultural level to create a 'unitary language of culture and truth' was the formation of 'standard English' in the work of nineteenth-century linguists in Britain. This will be discussed in detail in Chapter 5. Suffice it to say here that this example fits perfectly into Bakhtin's account of the construction of a monoglossic and monologic form of language: a language which was thought of as pure, central to English national life, superior to other languages, and carrying with it the mark of both rectitude and cultural status. It appears to be the model of a language which is elevated to the position of the medium of truth, selected from a variety of weaker forms, and banishing those forms to an inferior existence. In all it represents everything which is bad in Bakhtin's schema.

And yet there are difficulties with Bakhtin's argument. For if the conflict which takes place in language (and indeed for Bakhtin in culture generally) is resolved in one way, then monoglossic and monologic forms dominate, the word of the father is the last word, and authoritative discourse appears to be the only form permitted. If the conflict is resolved in another way, however . . . then what? At this point there is a genuine problem in Bakhtin's work which centres upon the difficulty of what it is which is to oppose monoglossia and monologism. For surely in social life certain forms of unity and organisation (the main features of centripetalisation), are necessary. Without them it is impossible to see how social life could be conducted, to say nothing about how change could be brought about. But if this is so, then it must follow that there would need to be a suspension of absolute heteroglossia (the form so lauded by Bakhtin) in favour of unifying tendencies. In Bakhtin's work such a suspension does not seem conceivable, and instead an authoritarian form of monoglossia faces an ineffectively pluralist heteroglossia in a sterile binary opposition. This opposition clearly needs to be avoided since it is a return to the idealist position taken in the early use of Bakhtin's concepts. The means of getting around this lies in taking the later political concepts which he articulated to their logical conclusions by stressing the importance of the historical context in which particular forms of language emerge.

Bakhtin's stress on the differing relations between the concepts set out in the politicised version of his account of language in history is evidently correct. Yet it is also clear that his preference for heteroglossia and dialogism, always and everywhere, typified in his extravagant claims for novelistic discourse, needs to be challenged. This challenge has to read his work against itself by arguing that if the forms and representations of language, and the roles they play, *are* dependent upon their historical and political contexts, then it is possible that in certain contexts a preference for dialogism and heteroglossia would be politically regressive. If monoglossia and monologism are not essentially absolute static forms, then it is possible that they could play a role in the struggle against particular authoritarian forces rather than serving to reinforce them. The question is this: if the dominant forces can adapt monoglossic, polyglossic and heteroglossic forms and representations to their own purposes (and it will be shown later in the textual studies that they can), then why cannot the forces which oppose them do likewise?

In order to answer this question both theoretically and with regard to empirical evidence, it is necessary to turn to another historical philologist, a contemporary of Bakhtin, whose work was also, in part, concerned with the connections between language and power. Gramsci commented in one of his *Prison Notebooks*:

> Every time the question of language surfaces, in one way or another, it means that a series of other problems are coming to the fore: the formation and enlargement of the governing class, the need to establish more intimate and secure relationships between the governing groups and the national-popular mass, in other words to re-organise the cultural hegemony.
>
> (Gramsci 1985: 183–4)

Gramsci's stress on the importance of language in the formation of cultural hegemony is essentially a political theorisation of Bakhtin's more elliptical assertions. For Gramsci, however, the importance of language lay not merely in this area but in the fact that at a more abstract level it functioned as a paradigm of the operations of social change and the achievement of hegemony. Thus it was at one and the same time engaged in political practice, and a blueprint for it. As Franco Lo Piparo has argued in *Lingua intellettuali egemonia in Gramsci* (Lo Piparo 1979), the concept of hegemony was derived at least in part from the work of the 'spatial linguists' at Turin, and in particular from the work of Gramsci's thesis supervisor in historical linguistics, Bartoli.[1] Essentially the argument of the spatial linguists was that linguistic change is brought about by the effect of the prestigious speech community's language in its contact with the languages of the non-dominant neighbouring speech groups. Rather than by means of direct imposition, the spatial linguists saw change as being effected by the operation of prestige on the one hand and active consent on the other. Thus the spread of any particular linguistic feature, as it passed from the dominant community through to its subordinates, would be brought about by consent rather than coercion and would eventually become universal. The diffusion of the English language in Ireland in the eighteenth and nineteenth centuries is a good example of this process. English came to be seen as the language of prestige, of commerce, of progress; Irish on the other hand came to be considered with shame as the language of backwardness and poverty.

If this argument as to the formation of Gramsci's concept of hegemony is correct, then the importance of language to his work is central. For not only does it operate as the marker of social conflict; it also functions as the model for the means by which such conflict is to be broached and resolved. Given the central role ascribed to language, it is no surprise to find that Gramsci asserts explicitly the necessity of a language programme for any group which aspires to cultural hegemony. However (and it is at this point that his work takes a theoretical and practical position that is distinct from that of Bakhtin), Gramsci's contention is that in the historical and political conjuncture in which he was located, rather than arguing for heteroglossia, what was required was precisely the organising force of a form of monoglossia. In particular what Gramsci argued for was the teaching of prescriptive grammar to the children of the working class and peasantry in order to empower them with literacy as a part of a larger radical project. Bakhtin, faced with the increasing centralisation and brutal forms of unity engendered by Stalin (including the imposition of Russian as the 'national' language of the Soviet Union), argued for the importance of diversity and pluralism. Gramsci on the other hand, faced with a divided and multi-factional national-popular mass, stressed the need for unity.

It would be incorrect, however, to explain Bakhtin's favouring of the heteroglot and diverse aspects of language entirely in terms of the political situation in which he was located. For his preference also stems from a critical, but at times close, engagement with the views of a group of linguists which we have already touched upon in the previous chapter. Reacting against the development of positivism in the study of language which we noted earlier, Bakhtin positions himself in opposition to both the neogrammarians and Saussure. Indeed he rejects Saussure's diagrammatic account of communication, which occurs in the *Course*, as a 'scientific fiction' (Bakhtin 1986: 68). Rather than the Saussurean model then, Bakhtin turns to a viewpoint which is, he comments, 'as unpopular as de Saussure's is popular and influential' in Russia (Bakhtin 1983: 37). This Bakhtin called 'idealistic neophilology' but was known more generally as 'aesthetic idealism'. Deriving in part at least from the work of those linguists such as Gilliéron and Schuchardt who had opposed the rigorous positivism of the neogrammarians, the aesthetic idealism of Croce and Vossler stressed the creative, diverse and ever-changing nature of language. In fact, as Bakhtin properly points out, aesthetic idealism had its earliest and in many ways most significant articulation in the work of Humboldt. Be that as it may, however, the principal proponents of the school with whose work Bakhtin engaged were Croce and Vossler.

Croce's work is of particular interest here since it was explicitly attacked by Gramsci, and the central tenet of his approach can be summed up in his own formulation: 'language is perpetual creation' (Croce 1953: 150).[2] It is this doctrine that is developed in his *Aesthetic as Science of Expression and General Linguistic* (1907). Equating language with poetic creation, the expression of spirit, Croce is led to equate the science of language itself with aesthetics:

> Aesthetic and Linguistic, conceived as true sciences, are not two distinct things, but one thing only. Not that there is a special Linguistic; but the much-sought-for science of language, general Linguistic, *in so far as what it contains is reducible to philosophy,* is nothing but Aesthetic. Whoever studies general Linguistic, that is to say philosophical Linguistic, studies aesthetic problems, and *vice versa. Philosophy of language and philosophy of art are the same thing.*
>
> (Croce 1953: 142)

In contrast to the positivist aim of the science of language, which attempted to trace the general laws which govern particular facts, Croce's study concentrates upon the non-iterable aspects of language:

> Linguistic also discovered the irreducible individuality of the aesthetic fact, when it affirmed that the word is what is really spoken, and that two truly identical words do not exist. Thus were synonyms and homonyms destroyed, and thus was shown the impossibility of really translating one word into another, from so-called dialect into so-called language, or from the so-called mother-tongue into the so-called foreign tongue.
>
> (ibid.: 146)

Asserting later that 'language is always poetry', he quotes Humboldt in order to reject the positivists:

> Languages must be considered not as dead products but as an act of production . . .. Language in its reality is something continually changing and passing away. Even its preservation in writing is incomplete, a kind of mummification: it is always necessary to render the living speech sensible. Language is not a work, *ergon*, but an activity, *energeia* . . .. It is an eternally repeated effort of the spirit in order to make articulated tones capable of expressing thought . . .. True and proper language consists in the very act of producing it by means of connected utterance; that is the only thing that must be thought of as the starting point or the truth in any enquiry which aims at penetrat-

ing into the living essence of language. Division into words and rules is a lifeless artifice of scientific analysis.

(ibid.: 327)

It is this stress upon the protean, diverse, non-static and non-unified aspects of language to which Bakhtin is sympathetic and which he echoes in much of his work. It is also this emphasis, however, that leads to the idealist tendencies in his analyses of specific forms of language.

By contrast to the concentration on heterogeneity and diversity, Gramsci's argument in favour of a unitary language was based on the difficulties of organising an illiterate mass in a society in which literacy was largely the prerogative of the governing class. In this context too it is significant that Croce asserts 'the impossibility of normative grammar' (ibid.: 147), a position which Gramsci damns as '"liberalism" of the most bizarre and eccentric stripe' (Gramsci 1985: 186).[3] Gramsci's argument is a useful reminder of the need to historicise theoretical debates:

> If one starts from the assumption of centralising what already exists in a diffused, scattered but inorganic state, it seems obvious that an opposition on principle is not rational. On the contrary, it is rational to collaborate practically and willingly to welcome everything that may serve to create a common national language, the non-existence of which causes friction particularly in the popular masses among whom local particularisms and phenomena of a narrow and provincial mentality are more tenacious than is believed. In other words, it is a question of stepping up the struggle against illiteracy.
>
> (ibid.: 182)

Bakhtin's tendency to prefer heteroglossia to any other form is the type of 'principle' to which Gramsci is referring here, since in this historical situation a preference for heteroglossia over monoglossia would be a reactionary stance. This is the case in Gramsci's view, since such a preference would serve only to heighten the linguistic differences which might prevent other forms of social or political unity. In a situation in which a linguistic hierarchy exists, a refusal to work for common and unifying forms may be tantamount to support for an unjust distribution of power. If that refusal to intervene institutionally is based on an abstract rather than an historical evaluation of monoglossia and hetero-glossia, then what in effect is brought about is a denial of access to the forms by which organisation can take place and thus 'in practice the national-popular mass is excluded from learning the educated language' (ibid.: 187). It is possible of course to differ from Gramsci in the specifics of his case (he argues, for example, that the working class and peasantry should learn the spoken standard language of the ruling class), but in the general drift of his argument he is surely right to put the case for empowerment through literacy. Even literacy in a unified, common and stable form of monoglossia.

Another example of the way in which Bakhtin can be read as taking a position closer to Croce than Gramsci is that of the issue of what Croce calls 'the question of the *unity of the language*' (Croce 1953: 150). As noted earlier, for Bakhtin the unitary language is a product of the action of the forces of centripetalisation: 'A unitary language is not something which is given (*dan*) but is always in essence posited (*zadan*)' (Bakhtin 1981: 270). For Croce too this issue is one which hinges upon a misrecognition of the nature of language: 'The question of the unity of language is always re-appearing, because, stated as it is, it is insoluble, being based upon a false conception of what language is.' This mistake had led the proponents of such a thesis to take up a flawed position:

> Their error consisted in transforming the manifestation of a need into a scientific thesis, the desirability, for example, of easier mutual understanding among a people divided by dialects into the philo-sophic demand for a single, ideal language. Such a search was as absurd as that other search for a *universal language*, a language posses-sing the immobility of the concept and of abstraction.
>
> (Croce 1953: 151)

This is not to say, however, that Bakhtin's position is identical to that of Croce, though at times it comes uncomfortably close. Instead Gramsci's assertion that 'the "question of the language" has always been an aspect of the political struggle' (Gramsci 1985: 187) can be seen to be analogous to many of the arguments proposed by Bakhtin. The difference is that Gramsci pushes Bakhtin's arguments to the limits by refusing to attach any ethical overtones to them. For Gramsci, unlike Bakhtin, it is the historical context that will enable us to evaluate which are to be the required forms and representations of language. Therefore although Bakhtin's preference for heteroglossia is correct in analysing particular historical examples (say, for instance, the formation of 'standard English' in the cultural hegemony of Britain), it is correct only with regard to this specific historical conjuncture. The repressive and centralising forms of unity demanded by the imperialist state offer an example of a represen-tation of a monoglossic language couched in monologic terms which need to be resisted by the privileging of heteroglossia and dialogism. But the diffuse and politically disorganised situation of early twentieth-century Italy, in which lack of common literacy amongst the national-popular mass served the interests of the governing class, requires a quite different analysis.

The fate of nations which have managed to escape from colonial rule and the historical complexities involved in such processes serve as further counter-examples to Bakhtin's automatic preferences and again stress the need for historical specificity in the analysis of such situations. The prejudice in favour of pluralism and difference may well in general be a laudable one; but it is a decontextualised judgment, since history demonstrates that forms of unity and organisation may be prerequisites before such an achievement can be attained. One example of a nation which defeated its colonial masters in a revolutionary struggle, and for which the question of the language was important, was the United States of America. After the War of Independence a significant cultural and political task for the newly liberated people was the necessity of constructing a monoglossic 'federal English' by which they would at once mark themselves off as distinct from their former masters and posit themselves as a united federal nation. As one of the most eager participants in this process, Noah Webster, argued in 1789:

> Our political harmony is therefore concerned in a uniformity of language.
> As an independent nation, our honor requires us to have a system of our own, in language as well as government.
>
> (Webster 1789: 20)

He continues:

> Besides this, a *national language* is a band of *national union*. Every engine should be employed to make the people of this country *national*; to call their attachments home to their own country; and to inspire them with the pride of national character. However they may boast of Independence, and the freedom of their government, yet their *opinions* are not sufficiently independent.
>
> (ibid.: 397–8)

Here a form of monoglossia (an American English which attempts to deny its historical links with Britain) serves the purpose of creating a positive break with British culture and, thereby, of forming an identification with America. The project, however, was not limited to external division, since it also sought to create internal unity:

> We have therefore the fairest opportunity of establishing a national language, and of giving it uniformity and perspicacity, in North America, that ever presented itself to mankind. Now is the time to begin the plan. The minds of the Americans are roused by the events of a revolution; the necessity of organizing the political body and of forming constitutions that shall secure freedom and property, has called all the faculties of the mind into exertion; and the danger of losing the benefits of independence has disposed every man to embrace any scheme that shall tend, in its future operation, to reconcile

the people of America to one another, and weaken the prejudices which oppose a cordial union.

(ibid.: 36)

The centrality of the language programme here is proof of Gramsci's assertion of its political importance; it is no coincidence that Webster links it to the organisation of the political body and the formation of the constitution which will guarantee freedom and property. In this role the language was to act precisely as the abnegator of differences which prevented union. In that task, at that time, its monoglossic function was radical rather than conservative. In the altered circumstances of the present of course the political role of American English has altered fundamentally. The relations which hold now between centripetal and centrifugal forces in respect to the spread and use of American English in the present demand a very different analysis.

Perhaps the most interesting examples of the ways in which the cultural functions of monoglossia and heteroglossia change historically are provided by the more recently liberated British colonies. Britain's African colonies were places where English was imposed as a monoglossic and monologic language. It represented the linguistic embodiment of the authority of empire, and it sought to repress linguistic otherness by relegating all other languages to the state of non-recognition as forms of language proper. As one nineteenth-century linguist put it, in a way which was unable to think outside the framework of empire, English became the language of civilisation itself:

> That language too is rapidly becoming the great medium of civilisation, the language of law and literature to the Hindoo, of commerce to the African, of religion to the scattered islanders of the Pacific. The range of its influence, even at the present day, is greater than ever was that of the Greek, the Latin, or the Arabic, and the circle widens daily.
>
> (Guest 1882: 703)

Outstripping the other empires in the reach of its ambition, the imperial language was represented as carrying its liberal and decent qualities on to the world stage in order to take its rightful place:

> English is emphatically the language of commerce, of civilisation, of social and religious freedom, of progressive intelligence, and of an active catholic philanthropy; and beyond any tongue ever used by man, it is of right the cosmopolite speech.
>
> (Marsh 1862: 23)

Another linguist saw this monoglossia developing in such a way that it would become *the* language, reducing all others to sub-linguistic status:

> It will be a splendid and novel experiment in modern society, if a

language becomes so predominant over all others as to reduce them in comparison to the proportion of provincial dialects.

(Watts 1850: 212)

And, as usual with the imposition of monoglossia, there are cultural effects too, as the same linguist continues to anticipate the time when 'the world is circled by the accents of Shakespeare and Milton'.

Such aspirations of course were nothing new, since at various times a number of different languages were posited as either the original language of Eden or the potential world language. Alexander Gil, for example, wrote in the preface to *Logonomia Anglica* (1619) of the worth of the English language:

> Since in the beginning all men's lips were identical, and there existed but one language, it would indeed be desirable to unify the speech of all peoples . . . and were human ingenuity to attempt this, certainly no more suitable language could be found.

These monoglossic representations of English indicate the force of centripetalising tendencies in the formation of cultural unity at home, and the repression of linguistic and cultural difference abroad. For the British recipients of such representations in the nineteenth century, the language stands against the historical difference of the past (in stressing national continuity), against the social divisions of the present (in praising the liberality of the social order), but for the future (in the promise of world domination). For the conservative nationalists of the day such representations were part of the creation of an hegemony in which major differences were suspended in favour of a minimal but durable unity.

There was of course another story to be told. What of the peoples upon whom this monoglossic language was imposed? How did they react to their 'liberation' into the English language? This is a question which has been posed most clearly by post-colonial theorists and writers who have lived in countries where the old imperial languages retain their privileged status. Fanon, for example, articulated this question succinctly:

> The Negro of the Antilles will be proportionately whiter – that is, he will come closer to being a real human being – in direct ratio to his mastery of the French language . . . .. Every colonised people – in other words every people in whose soul an inferiority complex has been created by the death and burial of its local cultural originality – finds itself face to face with the language of the civilising nation; that is, with the culture of the mother country. The colonised is elevated above his jungle status in proportion to his adoption of the mother country's standards.

(Fanon 1986: 18)

The contemporary Kenyan writer Ngũgĩ Wa Thiong'o takes up Fanon's analysis in his own account of linguistic imperialism. For Ngũgĩ the roots of imperial power were linguistic: 'in my view language was the most important vehicle through which that power fascinated and held the soul prisoner' (Ngũgĩ 1986: 9). To clarify his view he cites Cheikh Hamidou Kane's novel *Ambiguous Adventure*:

> On the Black Continent, one began to understand that their real power resided not at all in the cannons of the first morning but in what followed the cannons. Therefore behind the cannons was the new school. The new school had the nature of both the cannon and the magnet. From the cannon it took the efficiency of a fighting weapon. But better than the cannon it made the conquest permanent. The cannon forces the body and the school fascinates the soul.
>
> (Ngũgĩ 1986: 9)

For Ngũgĩ, then, the imposition of the monoglossic English language was a form of violence, a counterpart to the cannon-ball at the level of culture. Ngũgĩ's response to this is to reject English altogether, seeing it as inevitably tainted with the venom of imperial subjection: 'This book, *Decolonising the Mind*, is my farewell to English as a vehicle for any of my writings. From now on it is Gĩkũyũ and Kiswahili all the way' (Ngũgĩ 1986: xiv). In a sense, however, Ngũgĩ repeats Bakhtin's mistake of thinking of a form of language in static, absolutist terms. For while English was indeed the violent weapon of the imperialists, its status is not inevitably fixed to that particular historical moment. Indeed other contemporary African writers have taken a different position, seeing English as problematic but usable. Chinua Achebe, for example, in an essay entitled 'English and the African writer' poses the question:

> The real question is not whether Africans *could* write in English but whether they *ought to*. Is it right that a man should abandon his mother-tongue for someone else's? It looks like a dreadful betrayal and produces a guilty feeling.
>
> (Mazrui 1975: 223)

He responds to the question: 'But for me there is no other choice. I have been given this language and I intend to use it' (ibid.). Yet this is not a fatalistic surrender to domination by a monologic and monoglossic form of the English language. Rather, Achebe's stance is to take the language he was 'given' and to dialogise it, to make it heteroglot, to make it bear the weight of difference, to open up its closed borders: 'I feel that the English language will be able to carry the weight of my African experience. But it will have to be a new English, still in full communion with its ancestral home but altered to suit its new African surroundings' (ibid.).

The sense of guilt, betrayal, shame and alienation which are the consequences of an imposed language is of course a relatively common theme in modern literatures in English. Perhaps the *locus classicus* is to be found in Joyce's portrayal of Stephen Dedalus's encounter with the English dean of studies in *A Portrait of the Artist as a Young Man*. In it the young Irishman and the figure of English authority discuss the propriety of the word 'tundish', in relation to 'the best English'. The dean indicates that it is an Irish word, or at least a dialect word, certainly a non-standard word, and thereby reduces the young Irishman to silence. Stephen reflects upon the conflict:

> The language which we are speaking is his before it is mine. How different are the words *home*, *Christ*, *ale*, *master*, on his lips and on mine! I cannot speak or write these words without unrest of spirit. His language, so familiar and so foreign, will always be for me an acquired speech. I have not made or accepted his words. My voice hold them at bay. My soul frets in the shadow of his language.
>
> (Joyce 1960: 189)

The monoglossic language, at once familiar and foreign, necessary but felt to be alien, carries with it the force and violence of colonial oppression. It does not produce absolute silence but presents the colonial subject with a problem: how to engage in that language without, in using the oppressor's language, reinforcing one's own dispossession. One possible answer of course is to take the monoglossic nature of that language as something which is absolute and cannot be altered. In that case perhaps the only recourse is to turn to the language which has been subjugated; for Stephen this would be Gaelic, for Ngũgĩ Gĩkũyũ. But there may be problems with that answer too, as we shall see later. In fact what Joyce, and, later, Achebe do instead is to recognise the provisional status of the particular form of monoglossia with which they are faced; to see it as not absolutely rigid and exclusive; to challenge its borders and limits and eventually to break through them. By dialogising the authority of the language, by relativising its status, by opening it up to linguistic and cultural difference, these writers take part in the process of making it reveal its heteroglot nature. For as Heaney observes of Joyce: 'his achievement reminds me that English is by now not so much an imperial humiliation as a native weapon' (Heaney 1978: 40). Joyce, like many of the major modernists, took the English language and made it new. And this is a process which continues to the present. Consider, for example, Agard's sarcastic apostrophe to the cultural and linguistic establishment, which turns on his re-working of racist stereotypes, in 'Listen Mr Oxford Don':

> Me not no Oxford don
> me a simple immigrant

from Clapham Common
I didn't graduate
I immigrate . . .
I don't need no axe
to split/up yu syntax
I don't need no hammer
to mash/up yu grammar . . .
So mek dem send one big word after me
I ent serving no jail sentence
I slashing suffix in self-defence
I bashing future wit present tense
and if necessary

I making de Queen's English accessory/to my offence.

(Allnutt *et al.* 1988: 5–6)

Here the language is embraced by Agard, turned to his own purposes
and used in a way which refuses various types of prescription. It may also
be read as an ironic comment on Jakobson's definition of poetry as
organised violence upon language. This process, of refusing to be
silenced by the master language, is then a common topic in post-
colonial literature. And the attitudes towards it vary from writer to
writer. One thing which is clear, however, is that from this conflict there
has arisen a new set of literatures, written in new languages, which refuse
monoglot and monologic forces. One of the clearest statements of this is
given by Nichols in her 'Epilogue':

I have crossed an ocean
I have lost my tongue
from the root of the old
one
a new one has sprung

(Nichols 1990: 87)

It is important in such debates to resist images of those who have been
colonised, or subjugated in other ways, as passive recipients of the
dictates of their masters. Surely *that* is the colonial fantasy. For it may
well be that their re-invention of the master tongue offers new and
imaginative uses of language, scored through with heteroglossia and
difference. On considering major literature of the recent past, we may
want to alter Caliban's protest in *The Tempest*. Caliban answers Miranda's
argument that she had 'liberated' him into language by saying: 'You
taught me language, and my profit on't/Is, I know how to curse.' We
might rather have a latter-day Caliban say: 'You taught me language,
and my profit on't/Is I know how to write major novels, drama and
poetry.'

CONCLUSION

The force of the examples which we have considered is not intended to discredit the validity of Bakhtin's theoretical distinctions but to demonstrate the necessity of developing them further in order to exploit fully their significance for the study of language in history. The examples show how the highly abstract form and ethical tone which attach to these concepts in Bakhtin's work serve as an impediment which can only be eradicated by specific historical analyses which take into account the relative state of the differing forces holding at any particular moment. This is important for the study of language in history, since it means that this field, while necessarily employing these concepts, will have to do so in a way which demonstrates a clear view of the historical and political contexts to which they are related. In turn this reveals a need to pay attention to the question of power and its distribution. For although Bakhtin is correct in arguing that there is a constant conflict between centripetal and centrifugal forces in language, it sometimes appears as though this conflict takes place without historical cause and to little historical effect. And indeed on occasion Bakhtin's favouring of the constantly shifting, non-iterable and heteroglot aspects of language sounds closer to Croce than to his theoretical and political opponent Gramsci, nearer to a conception of language as scored through with poetic rather than political significance. As the differing examples above demonstrate, however, the struggle between monologism and dialogism, and that between monoglossia, polyglossia and heteroglossia, is not simply a conflict of linguistic tendencies and effects but a conflict in which what is at stake is precisely forms of representation and self-representation which are closely linked to power. The political status of any particular form of language cannot be read off an abstract schema in advance, since it depends upon the historically specific forms of power which it engenders. It is this that students of language in history can take from Bakhtin's work.

Chapter 3

Wars of words
The roles of language in eighteenth-century Britain

'Riches and Poverty, Love and Hatred, and even Life and Death are in the Power of the Tongue.'

(Wilson 1724: 36)

VERBAL VIOLENCE

Eighteenth-century Britain was fascinated by language; from Universal Grammarians to elocution masters; from defenders of Latin to upholders of English grammar; from literary practitioners to their aristocratic patrons; from religious zealots to working-class campaigners for suffrage. The English language, as perhaps never before, became subject to various kinds of scrutiny, the object of the gaze of science, literature, politics and philosophy. One pamphlet purporting to tell the truth about the history of the English language was followed by another denouncing it as nonsense. A tract claiming to advance a non-partisan account of the means of reforming the language was attacked in reply as merely a piece of party-political propaganda. Academies of the language were suggested and rejected. Grammar books describing themselves as comprehensive were ridiculed for their limited scope. Spelling-books contradicted spelling-books; and one was produced of a size deliberately to fit in a woman's pocket. Elocution texts – perhaps the most intemperate of all – attacked each other viciously on grounds which ranged from a tendency to undermine the political unity of the kingdom, to deliberate attempts to corrupt the morality of women. It was, in all its various ways, a great feast upon language; but how are we to make sense of it, to decode it, to read it in terms of language in history, as signs of the times?

Bakhtin's idealist account, discussed earlier, saw the rise of the vernaculars in this way:

> the complex and multi-leveled hierarchy of discourses, forms, images, styles that used to permeate the entire system of official language and linguistic consciousness was swept away by the linguistic revolutions of

the Renaissance. European *literary* languages – French, German, English – came into being while this hierarchy was in the process of being destroyed.

(Bakhtin 1981: 71)

The vernaculars were liberated, set free from the dominance of Latin, according to Bakhtin. And it is clearly true that in one sense in the post-Reformation period there was a 'triumph of the English language' (Jones 1953). The crucial conjunction of the rise of Protestantism with the technological advance of print capitalism had, as Anderson describes, tied the language firmly to the nation and thereby massively enhanced its status (Anderson 1983). In Bakhtin's terms a situation of polyglossia, in which Latin was the dominating language, had been replaced by one of monoglossia, in which the English language held sway. What is more, the forces of centripetalisation, here embodied in the English state, the Protestant religion, and print, had been victorious in establishing recognisable forms of the English language as central and stable. At the level of writing this could be seen in the appearance of the King James Bible (1611), which was produced precisely out of that concatenation of state, religion and print. At the level of speech this stability had also been produced by means of the operation of political and social prestige. Evidence for this is offered in Puttenham's *Arte of English Poesie* (1589), in which, after rejecting various forms of the language as unsuitable, he then defines for the poet the form which is 'the natural, pure and most usual of all his country'. On this account, he says, 'the poet shall therefore take that usual speech of the court, and that of London and the shires lying about London, within lx miles, and not much above' (Puttenham 1936: 144–5). There was then, as Bakhtin would have it, a stable language free from the yoke of Latin, liberated into existence in its own right.

Yet if Bakhtin's account were accurate, why should a major English political and philosophical theorist such as Hobbes write in Latin in order to enhance his European status? More puzzlingly, why should his close successor in both those traditions, Locke, compose his major work, the *Essay Concerning Human Understanding* (1690), in English? Not only that, why should Locke assert that 'if a gentleman be to study any language, it ought to be that of his own country' (Locke 1823: 156)? If the question of the status of the English vernacular had been settled in the way Bakhtin suggests, why should these near-contemporary theorists differ on the question of which language it was in which they would set their work?

The question is more than one of personal choice, since if the vernacular really had achieved high status, then why does Swift complain

that our Language is extremely imperfect; that its daily Improvements are by no means in proportion to its daily Corruptions; that the

Pretenders to polish and refine it have chiefly multiplied Abuses and Absurdities; and, that in many Instances, it offends against every part of Grammar.

(Swift 1957: 6)[1]

Nearly half a century later why does the lexicographer Johnson admit that when he undertook his task he found English speech 'copious without order, and energetic without rules: wherever I turned my view there was perplexity to be disentangled, and confusion to be regulated' (Johnson 1806: II, 33). Again, why does the grammarian Lowth, consciously echoing Swift, though in fact making a different point since he argues that it is practice rather than the language itself that presents the problems, claim that even in the speech of 'the politest part of the nation' and in the writings of 'the most approved authors', the language 'often offends against every part of grammar' (Lowth 1762: iv)?

If this is the English language in triumph, then there are clearly problems. However, rather than presenting us with insuperable difficulties for our theoretical model, the opinions cited above in fact offer a vindication of the re-reading of Saussure and Bakhtin. For they point to the fact that in order to understand language in history we have to read the debates, claims, and representations carefully and in relation to the history in which they are set, and of which they form a part. The revised reading of Saussure and Bakhtin not only alerts us to the contextual interrelation of language and race, nation, political history, institutions and literature; it warns us also that these interrelations are constantly shifting, contested, won and lost; that is, that they are dialogic, forever at stake, and always up for grabs. The English language then: one day triumphant, the next a dead loss. Superior to all other languages; a mongrel of a language in need of reformation. At one point polyglot, anxiously looking over its shoulder at the dominance of Latin; at another celebrating its independence and status as a pure language. At a later point perhaps struggling to maintain its monoglot absolutism against the heteroglot cacophony of voices from within; voices which it attempts to exclude, as we shall see.

What we will find in our reading of the roles of language in eighteenth-century Britain is a series of wars of words. War with words, war against words, war over words, war for the right to the power of words. We will attempt to trace the shifting ways in which language is related to questions of national identity, political history, the status of the colonies, the construction of the public sphere, regionality, gender and social class. We will discover centripetal forces struggling against the centrifugal, the monoglot against the heteroglot, in a logomachy in which a great deal was at stake. What was the prize? The right to say who could enter and speak, who was to be excluded, who could be allowed in, if only on strict terms, what could be said, and what was forbidden, how things could be spoken, and how not. For women of all classes, for the poor and dispossessed, for the internal foreigners of the regions, for the Scots, the Irish, the Welsh and the Cornish (the last Cornish speaker is held to have died in 1777), and for colonial subjects, what was at stake were the proto-patterns of exclusion and difficulty, the forms of silencing, which, it will be claimed, have a long and continuing history.

It may seem as though it is an exaggeration to describe the processes described above as a war, an overblown piece of rhetoric perhaps. Yet there are two points to support such an account. The first is that the linkage of language and war was a very common trope in the eighteenth century. And perhaps the dominance of war imagery in *any* context in eighteenth-century Britain is unsurprising, since after the Act of Union in 1707 which conjoined Scotland to England and Wales, Great Britain was at war with France, only one of its enemies, for a grand total of thirty-seven years between 1702 and 1802. The second point includes and extends the first. It is evidently the case that the claim for the predominance of figurations of war is not often encountered in standard histories or theoretical accounts of the period, though recent work has challenged this. The age following the 'Glorious Revolution', the 'Age of Reason', the 'Age of Enlightenment', the age of 'Cosmic Toryism' is not often set against or understood in terms of the backdrop of war. The contention here, however, is that this is precisely the context in which the texts considered below are set. And this is the point that develops the first: it is a society at war abroad *and* at home. Such a depiction, of course, does not quite fit with one of the most important theoretical accounts of eighteenth-century Britain, that rendered by Habermas in his sketch of the emergence of the public sphere (Habermas 1989). Tracing the defeat of absolutism and the social conflict which that process had engendered, Habermas points to the gradual emergence of a consensual public sphere, a more democratic and accountable social formation which owed more to Locke than to Hobbes. However, although there are real strengths to his now classic account, it must finally be said that in detail the evidence supports a much more fragile, contested and acrimonious process in the establishment of the new sphere of political and public activity. It is true that the bourgeois public sphere did force a greater degree of political accountability and responsibility, demanding justification before a public exercising its reason, than had ever existed previously. But its silences, exclusions and often desperate attempts at self-demarcation tell a different story from that of a gradual emergence into consensual public discussion amongst the free.

Take, for instance, the work of James Thomson, the ambiguity of which is pointed up by Colley in her analysis of his most popularly

enduring ode of 1740 'Rule, Britannia' (Colley 1992: 11). Thomson's
major achievement is *The Seasons* (1746), and at its heart lies this
panegyric to the settled 'Island of Bliss':

> ISLAND of BLISS! amid all the subject seas,
> That thunder round thy rocky Coasts, set up,
> At once the Wonder, Terror and Delight,
> Of distant Nations; whose remotest Shore
> Can soon be shaken by thy Naval Arm,
> Not to be shook thyself, but all Assaults
> Baffling, like thy hoar Cliffs the loud Sea-Wave.
>
> O THOU! by whose almighty *Nod* the Scale
> Of Empire rises, or alternate falls,
> Send forth the saving VIRTUES round the Land,
> In bright Patrol: white *Peace*, and social *Love*,
> The tender-looking *Charity*, intent
> On gentle Deeds, and shedding Tears thro' Smiles.
>
> (Thomson 1981: 132)

What more pleasing encomium, what more gentle description, of the
imperial power, victorious abroad and settled at home? And yet, when
we read carefully here, what we find is *not* bliss. In relation to the empire
abroad, what we discover are 'subject seas', and the 'Wonder, Terror and
Delight,/Of distant Nations'. We note the power of the 'Naval Arm'
pitted against the threat of 'all Assaults'. And we are told that imperial
power and status depends upon the '*Nod*' of the Almighty, a nod which
was not always taken for granted in eighteenth-century Britain.

If the status of the victorious imperial nation is precarious, then the
situation at home is even worse. For what we find within the borders of
the nation, by default, is a description of a far from settled and happy
land. What the second stanza performs is not an appraisal but an act of
hope; the nation at ease with itself is not so much described here as
invoked. There is no consensual social harmony: 'white *Peace*', 'social
Love', 'tender-looking *Charity*', 'gentle Deeds', 'shedding tears thro'
Smiles' are asked for rather than taken as already given. But this
invocation is predicated upon the fact that these 'saving VIRTUES' do
not as yet exist in the nation, since why else ask the Almighty to bring
peace and harmony to a land which knows these qualities already?

Thomson's lines indicate to us a nation at war abroad, rapaciously
gathering and defending its empire. Yet they show us too, and more
importantly for our reading here, a nation at war with itself; a nation
needing saving virtues, or to put it in an abrupt way, a nation needing to
be saved. From what was it that the nation needed to be saved; and for
what was it to be saved? From whom was it to be saved; and for whom

was it to be saved? Most significantly, how was it to be saved? These questions, and others like them, are crucial in looking at the relations between language and history in the eighteenth century. Their place in the internal warfare that took place in this historical context will be the subject-matter of this chapter. In it there will be a focus upon a number of different debates to show just how furiously these questions were fought out, and precisely what it was for which these battles were fought.

READING LANGUAGE, READING LITERATURE, READING HISTORY

One of the central texts in language debates of the period is Swift's *Proposal For Correcting, Improving and Ascertaining the English Tongue* (1712), also one of the few known to a general readership. Often dismissed as a minor piece, it is in fact an important intervention, by means of a specific reading of a linguistic and literary tradition combined with an answer to the problem of linguistic change, in the political history of the period. That Swift saw the *Proposal* as a document of major importance is undoubted; it is the only prose piece he ever signed. Yet the piece has more general significance, for it has claims – and articulates them clearly and boldly – to a more elevated status. It begins with what at first sight seems to be an exaggerated claim: that although not of such immediate benefit as resolving the National Debt or expanding colonial trade, in the future the project embodied in the *Proposal* will be as advantageous as both. In fact the linking of language texts to trade and colonialism was not quite as unusual as it appears. Lane, in his *Key to the Art of Letters* (1700), quotes without reticence from a poem dedicated to him by an admirer of his work:

> Yours is the triumph sir, to prove our words,
> No less design'd for Conquest than our swords.
>
> (Lane 1700: xv)

Words and swords were allies in the same campaign. Greenwood, Swift's contemporary, wrote in relation to language change that 'the laws of foreign Conquests usually extend to letters and speech, as well as Territories' (Greenwood 1711: 16). Nonetheless Swift's assertion is remarkable: that a tract on the defects (and their remedies) of the English language could be as important as economic and imperial development. However, it is a claim which when viewed contextually does merit the status Swift accords it; and it is certainly the case that Swift's political opponents thought so. For the *Proposal*, as Oldmixon, the chief of his antagonists, saw, was not simply an essay to reform language but an attempt to make the reform of language the vehicle for social and political change.

The concern demonstrated by Swift's pamphlet for its own political importance is signalled by his use of a significant analogy: the linking-together of the language and the civil and religious constitution. Again, this was to become a common figure in the eighteenth century, perhaps most typically in Johnson's plea in the *Preface to the Dictionary*: 'tongues, like governments, have a natural tendency to degeneration; we have long preserved our constitution, let us make some struggles for our language' (Johnson 1806: II, 64). As Barrell has shown, this concatenation is politically resonant, particularly in relation to the theoretical links which are made between language, law and government (Barrell 1983: 148–54). Swift's use of the analogy is politically important too, though in a quite specific way. For just as he attacks those 'who would not have us by any means think of preserving our Civil or Religious Constitution, because we are engaged in a war abroad' (Swift 1957: 5–6), likewise he dismisses those who would postpone any reform of the language to a time of peace. Simply by mentioning the two projects in this way Swift accords enormous significance to linguistic reform. Moreover, the *Proposal* is also linked to the constitution in that its aim is to deliver peace, and thus the fact that it is written in a time of war enhances rather than diminishes its importance. The *Proposal* then is eirenic and sets out to find ways of avoiding the language of the Civil War which had beset the English seventy years earlier. As with the Académie Française, one of whose original aims was declared by Louis XIII to be 'to remedy those disorders which the Civil Wars . . . have brought into [the language]', the *Proposal* sought to engender peace by stabilising the language and thus facilitating what Swift calls 'knowledge and politeness' in the social order (Kelly 1984: 60). Echoing Locke's attempt to determine language in the *Essay Concerning Human Understanding* (1690), and in particular its aim of finding the way to 'knowledge, truth and peace' (Locke 1975: 512), Swift's work intends to reform the language in order to create a proper vehicle of communication. Once stabilised, the language can then become the medium of social conversation, the untroubled area in which opinions, beliefs and ideas can be exchanged freely and openly in the public sphere without the danger of 'enthusiastic jargon' and sentiment. The process of stabilisation, later to be called standardisation, would thus be a remedy to that war-like state of language and society in which polite conversation, 'so useful and innocent a Pleasure, so fitted for every Period, and Condition of Life, and so much in all Men's Power', had become 'so much neglected and abused' (Swift 1957: 88). Language would then be restored to its rightful use, 'the great Instrument, and common Tye of Society', as Locke had described it (Locke 1975: 402).

Swift's aim appears to have been to create the language in which rational, free and non-partisan discussion could take place. However, the *Proposal* is in fact a highly charged political document, though its politics are complex. First, there is the overt Tory slant: the essay is dedicated to Robert Harley, earl of Oxford, Tory Prime Minister. And there is a direct attack upon the Whigs in the appraisal of the earl of Oxford as the 'very wise and excellent Man' who saved the country from ruin by a *'foreign War*, and a *domestic Faction'* (Swift 1957: 18). The second political implication of the *Proposal* flows from the way in which Swift intends to reform the language. He suggests what is in effect an academy:

> In order to reform our language; I conceive, my Lord, that a free judicious Choice should be made of such Persons, as are generally allowed to be best qualified for such a Work, without any regard to Quality, Party, or Profession.
>
> (ibid.: 13–14)

The idea of an academy was not an unusual one in the eighteenth century: it was proposed by Dryden, Defoe, Addison and Wilson (anonymously in 1724). Moreover there were already academies in existence in Europe: the Accademia della Crusca was set up in 1582, and the Académie Française, modelled on the Italian institution, had been constituted in 1635. Swift's suggestion, therefore, for non-partisan membership of the academy appears to be founded upon simple meritocracy. However, once again here the *Proposal* engages directly with politics. For in the simple act of suggesting an academy, Swift was bound to alienate the Whigs. As with most appeals for open, untendentious debate according to the principles of reason, there is a hidden agenda. The Whigs were alienated by Swift's essay for two reasons. First, the academy was identified, to Whig eyes at least, with France, and thus with the Stuart claimants to the monarchy; and, second, it had been instituted by Cardinal Richelieu (who signed its statutes and rules), an aristocratic Catholic. The Whig response was as predictable as it was fierce, and came principally from Oldmixon. He declared that the Tories would

> not only force their principles upon us, but their language, wherein they endeavour to ape their good friends the French, who for these three or fourscore Years have been attempting to make their Tongue as Imperious as their Power.
>
> (Oldmixon 1712: 2)

The perception of the political threat was clear: 'He has imposed upon us already the Court Stile of France, and their Politicks would soon come after it' (ibid.: 30).

The idea of an academy re-appeared in the 1750s. George Harris, anonymous author of *Observations upon the English Language in a Letter to a Friend* (1752), calls for an academy to be backed up by legislation:

> Sometimes I imagine that a Grammar and a Dictionary, published
> under the auspices of an Academy, would not sufficiently ascertain our
> language without the assistance of the legislature . . .. I can not but
> esteem the English language to be of such consequence to Englishmen
> in general, that a proper Act, for the Improvement and Preservation
> of it, would do honour to an English Parliament.
>
> (Harris 1752: 13)

Harris is in fact referring to orthography rather than speech, but once
agreed by the Academy, he maintains,

> it should be enacted by the Authority of Parliament, that the new
> regulations in spelling should from thenceforth be strictly adhered to
> in printing in all English Bibles, Common Prayer Books, Books,
> Pamphlets, Newspapers etc, under a most severe penalty to be levied
> upon every printer and publisher who shall purposefully offend.
>
> (ibid.: 14)

Such draconian measures were of course much more strict and rigid
than those proposed by Swift. In Harris's plea Bakhtin's theoretical
centripetal forces are embodied in the most stark way: the strictures of
a centralised academy, supported by Parliamentary legislation, and
backed by the threat of severe punishment. This is another reason,
again politically resonant, why the idea of an academy failed, for it
smacked too much of authoritarian dictates, pronounced from on high
and maintained by threat. To put it another way, to eighteenth-century
English thinkers it smacked too much of French political life and society.
Thomas Sheridan makes the point succinctly. Comparing Britain to
France, he claims that an academy, or society as he calls it here, would
not work in Britain by dint of 'our constitution, and the genius of our
people'. France, however, was different:

> The endeavours of such a society, in arbitrary government, under the
> faction and countenance of an absolute prince, may be crowned with
> success; but the English have no idea of submitting to any laws to
> which they do not give their own consent.
>
> (Sheridan 1756: 368)

The English: free-thinking, independent, able to engage in rational
discussion in order to produce a consensus, and by dint of the fact
that they consented, able to obey laws in good faith; the French: subject
to the arbitrary whim of their leaders, restricted by the absolutism which
the English had cast off a century previously, cringing and dependent on
others to decide for them. Johnson summed it up:

> If an academy should be established for the cultivation of our stile,
> which I, who can never wish to see dependence multiplied, hope the

spirit of *English* liberty will hinder or destroy, let them, instead of compiling grammars and dictionaries, endeavour, with all their influence, to stop the licence of translators, whose influence and ignorance, if it be suffered to proceed, will reduce us to babble a dialect of *France.*

(Johnson 1806: II, 64)

An academy in Britain was a non-starter since the self-representations of English liberty could not allow such a dictatorial idea to be realised. Swift's appeal for a non-partisan academy to fix the language ran into the hopeless contradiction of the English self-image of the age. Custom rather than law, precedent rather than rational change, were to be the guiding principles, though these axioms masked a whole series of arbitrary rules, exclusions and orders within Britain, as we shall see.

Though the idea of an academy was an impossibility, Swift's pamphlet reverberates with various other political and historical points. One such is Swift's masterly reading of language and history together: history forging changes in language, language bringing about difference in history. For example, although not the first to do so, since like many others in the eighteenth century his version of English linguistic history is deeply indebted to Wallis's *Grammatica linguae Anglicanae* (1653), Swift is an important figure in the process by which the history of a language is traced in conjunction with the history of the group which used it. In fact his essay can be read as an early example, pre-dating Herder, of what was to become known as cultural nationalism, which will be discussed at length later. In the *Proposal*, Swift establishes the fact that linguistic history can only be explained by reference to political history. And he does this in order to be able to draw lessons from both fields of historical knowledge. Regarding the decay of Latin, for example, he claims that there were many reasons for it:

As the Change of their Government into a Tyranny, which ruined the Study of Eloquence; there being no further Use or Encouragement for popular Orators: Their giving not only the Freedom of the City, but Capacity for Employments, to several Towns in *Gaul, Spain,* and *Germany,* and other distant Parts, as far as Asia; which brought a great Number of foreign Pretenders into *Rome*: The slavish Disposition of the Senate and People . . .. Not to mention those Invasions from the *Goths* and *Vandals,* which are too obvious to insist on.

(Swift 1957: 8)

What Swift does here is to use the historical vicissitudes of a language as a way of reading the moral and political fortunes of its speakers. Here heteroglossia brings about imperial downfall. In other words, he uses the language as a means to facilitate the construction and reading of a history. This is significant in that it allows a number of judgments to take place under the guise of a critique of language. For not only is the language to be evaluated – richness and eloquence set against corruption and decay; it is also the case that both the nation and history itself are to be understood from this perspective. Thus, when Swift turns his attention to the English language his reading of its history becomes automatically a construction of the history of the English nation and people. In fact his account is an early example of political literary criticism in which the highpoints of the language correspond perfectly to the highpoints of the literary tradition and thus, by corollary, to the major political achievements of the English nation itself. It is worth quoting at length:

> The Period wherein the *English* tongue received most Improvement, I take to commence with the Beginning of Queen *Elizabeth's* reign, and to conclude with the great Rebellion in Forty-two. It is true, there was a very ill Taste both of Style and Wit, which prevailed under King *James* the First; but that seems to have been corrected in the first Years of his Successor; who among many other Qualifications of an excellent Prince, was a great Patron of learning. From that Great Rebellion to this present Time, I am apt to doubt whether the Corruptions in our Language have not, at least, equalled the Refinements of it; and these Corruptions very few of our best Authors in our Age have wholly escaped. During the usurpation, such an Infusion of Enthusiastick jargon prevailed in every writing, as was not shaken off in many years after. To this succeeded that Licentiousness which entered with the *Restoration*; and from infecting our Religion and Morals, fell to corrupt our Language.
>
> (ibid.: 9–10)

A perfect match is achieved: as the political state of the nation declines (signalled in this account by regicide and the English Revolution), likewise the language suffers corruption and decay. At one level this can be taken as a fairly crude attempt to intervene in history, as it rapidly becomes an account of the golden age, 'the period wherein the English tongue received most improvement' and in which those political and moral standards were set up from which the nation has been falling off ever since. At another level, however, and ignoring for a moment the specifics of this reading, this is a more sophisticated attempt to intervene historically since it sets up an ideological framework, at a fairly abstract level, whose effect has continued to be felt. For at this other level what Swift's *Proposal* does is to weave a powerful and enduring web of forces which have been so crucial to the English historical experience. Put simply, what the essay does is to articulate what James Joyce in an entirely different context was later to call the triple net of nationality, language and religion. All three of these forces are centripetal, as they attempt to organise a form of monoglossia which can see nothing beyond its own limits. The ideological significance of this triple net in eighteenth-century English national consciousness cannot be overestimated.

Swift was not the only writer of the period, to read the literary and linguistic history as an index of the nation's fortunes, nor was the period unique in this trope. Welsted, writing on 'The State of Poetry' in 1724, comments:

> It is not, unless I am mistake, much more than a Century, since *England* first recovr'd out of something like Barbarism, with respect to its State of Letters and Politeness: The Great rude Writers of our Nation, in early Times, did indeed promise what the *English* Genius would one day be capable of, when the Refinement of our Language, and other Improvements, might afford favourable Opportunities for the exerting of it; and at the *Restoration* it was, that Poetry and polite Arts began to spring up: In the Reign of *William* the Third, the Founder of *English* Liberty they acquir'd great Strength and Vigour, and have continued to thrive, gradually, down almost to our Times.
>
> (Durham 1915: 357)

The political stress of this argument is as clear as that of Swift. But perhaps the best example of this reflex of reading of language, literature and history together is a criticism of Milton by Bayly: 'Milton may be followed in some particular spellings, but not in general; who is as monstrous in literal as in political freedom' (Bayly 1772: xii). The history of the language was thus figured as the index of the nation's fortunes.

A distinct way in which Swift treats significant worries about language and history in the period appears in the *Proposal*'s long treatment of the dangers and problems caused by linguistic mutability. This was a common complaint at the time and became one of the factors in the campaign for language standardisation. It was a problem for writers, many of whom saw the fact that the language changes historically as a positive threat to their fame and reputation. Even Oldmixon, Swift's Whiggish opponent, agrees that this is a problem and cites Edmund Waller:

> But who should hope his lines should long
> Last, in a daily changing tongue? . . .
> Poets that lasting Marble seek
> Must write in Latin or in Greek;
> We write in Sand.
>
> (Oldmixon 1712: 25–6)

In *The Seasons* Thomson eulogises Chaucer's art, claiming that it 'shines thro' the Gothic Cloud/Of Time and Language o'er thy Genius thrown'

(Thomson 1981: 132). But later in the century Sheridan indicates the same problem and appeals to his patrons: 'suffer not our Shakespeare, and our Milton, to become two or three centuries hence what Chaucer is at present' (Sheridan 1756: ix). Yet the problem was not one which was restricted to literary authors, for, as Swift pointed out, it was a problem which beset all writing and therefore, importantly, called into question the very writing of history itself. Again Sheridan, who is close to Swift in many respects, puts the matter concisely:

> How many British heroes and worthies have been lost to us; how have their minds perished like their bodies . . .. England has never wanted proper subjects, but historians; and historians will not be found 'till our language be brought to a fixed state and some prospect of duration be given to their works.
>
> (ibid.)

In fact it is this concern that forms the core of the *Proposal*; for the aim is to stabilise the language by standardising it, thereby preventing diachronic change and ensuring that it can be reliably fixed for ever. Swift's recommendation of the essay to his patron, the Prime Minister, makes this point clear:

> Your Lordship must allow, that such a Work as this, brought to Perfection, would very much contribute to the Glory of Her Majesty's Reign, which ought to be recorded in Words more durable than Brass, and such as Posterity may read a thousand Years hence, with Pleasure ás well as Admiration.
>
> (Swift 1957: 16–17)

'Words more durable than brass' is a good definition of the material of an ideal monoglossia; a language which will last a thousand years. Swift's intention then is to fix the language in order that history can be recorded faithfully once and for all, and thus to ensure that Queen Anne's reign shall be available to readers of history at all future points. To stress the significance of the point to his patron, Swift adds:

> But at the same Time, I must be so plain as to tell your Lordship, that if you will not take some Care to settle our Language, and put it into a State of Continuance, I cannot promise that your Memory shall be preserved above an Hundred Years, further than by imperfect Tradition.
>
> (ibid.: 17)

This is the ultimate threat: unless the language is settled and fixed, not even the historical record of the Prime Minister's achievements can be guaranteed. The clear concern here is that linguistic mutability brought about by the passage of time will undermine the transmission of history;

the narratives of history, the 'memories' of the past, will not be under any guarantee of successful communication to the future. However, it was not simply Swift's desire to be historiographer royal that led him to voice this concern about the problematic relationship between language and history; since, as an acute political observer, and Tory in Whiggish times, he was aware of the importance of ensuring that language and historiography played a central role in the formation of 'tradition'. He saw the need to make sure that the values of the present were encased in a language which would guarantee their successful transmission. At this level then the essay can be read as an attempt not merely to fix the language for future users, but to try and ensure that particular values, forms of social life, preferences and exclusions, traditions in the most general sense, could also be fixed for the future. Swift's proposal then is our first example of the war for history which is fought in words.

SUPERIOR LANGUAGE, SUPERIOR NATION

Swift's tactic of reading the history of the nation through the history of the language is not one which his contemporaries and successors neglected, though they did adapt it. Indeed they took it on as a symptomatic mode of reading in a highly political way. For rather than simply reading language and history in terms of the past, as Swift had in his linguistic and literary history, they applied the principle to the present. This meant that it was necessary first to establish the link between language and nation at a theoretical level; and it is with that linkage that we can start. It is often asserted that Herder was the first to proclaim this link, and that his idea was taken into German Romanticism and eventually transposed into the various forms of cultural nationalism which arose across Europe in the nineteenth century. Herder's formulation has in fact been traced back to the work of Harris in his *Hermes* (1751), in which he declares: 'we shall be led to observe how Nations, like single men, have their *peculiar* Ideas; how these *peculiar* Ideas become THE GENIUS OF THEIR LANGUAGE' (Harris 1751: 407). Aarsleff (1992: 147ff.) on the other hand cites Condillac as the source. Whatever its origin, this interrelation of nationality, mentality and language is crucial to the modern history of Western Europe and its colonies. At specific times it served the purposes of radical resistance movements opposing systems of domination and thus functioned dialogically; at other times it became the tool of racism and refused difference in the name of an absolute and monologic self-confidence.

There were in fact earlier examples of this conjunction of language and nation. Oldmixon writes: 'For every age, as well as every Nation, has its different manner of Thinking, of which the Expression and Words will always have a relish' (Oldmixon 1712: 26–7). Bailey offers this dictionary definition of a language in 1730: 'Tongue or Speech, a set of Words upon which a particular Nation or People are agreed, to make use of to express their Thoughts' (Bailey 1730). And Buchanan, writing later in the century, takes this theoretical point as given. In order to explain the fact of different languages, he cites 'the distinguishing Character and Genius of every Nation' (Buchanan 1762: 73).[2]

Whatever be the source of this idea, the linkage of language and nation became particularly important in mid- to late eighteenth-century Britain. As the recently united nation strained under various forms of historical pressure, the need for a cultural cementation of the newly created unit was clear. Sheridan writes of the differing elements of Britain, by which he means the Scottish, the Welsh and the Irish,

> who spoke in tongues different from the English, and who were far from being firmly united with them in inclination, and of course were pursuing different interests. To accomplish an entire union with these people, was of the utmost importance to them, to which nothing could have more effectually contributed, than the universality of one common language.
>
> (Sheridan 1756: 213)

The new nation, Britain, was an uneasy amalgam of four distinct nations, and thus needed to be consolidated at the level of language. However, combined with this situation of polyglossia, in which there were at least four different languages hierarchically related, there was also the complicating factor of internal difference within the main language:

> even in England itself for want of such a method, there were such various dialects spoken, that persons born and bred in different and distant shires, could scarcely any more understand each others speech, than they could that of a foreigner.
>
> (ibid.: 214)

This internal stratification of English evidently produced problems for the creation of the nation as an imagined community; since by the logic of cultural nationalism the members of the community have all to be able to communicate with each other by means of the one thing which they, and only they, share: the language. Thus one of the driving forces of the language reformers in the latter part of the century was the impulse to create this monoglot language by eradicating the heteroglot elements from English:

> it cannot be denied that an uniformity of pronunciation throughout Scotland, Wales and Ireland, as well as through the several counties of England, would be a point much to be wished; as it might in great

measure destroy those odious distinctions between subjects of the
same King, and members of the same community, which are ever
attended with ill consequences, and which are chiefly kept alive by
difference of pronunciation, and dialects; for these in a manner
proclaim the place of a man's birth, whenever he speaks, which
otherwise could not be known by any other marks in mixed
societies.

(Sheridan 1762: 206)

Linguistic difference clearly had important national and social implications. The fear was that heteroglossia meant disunity, encouraged independence and, as Swift had argued of Latin, indicated a desire not to be
counted as one of His Majesty's subjects and pointed to a refusal of the
polite social etiquette of the emerging public sphere. Sheridan's estimation of the danger was clear:

there never was a language which required, or merited cultivation
more; and certainly there never was a people upon earth, to whom a
perfect use of the powers of speech were so essentially necessary, to
support their rights, privileges, and all the blessings coming from the
noblest constitution that ever was formed.

(Sheridan 1780: i)

His own particular remedy for this ill was brilliantly opportunistic. He
proposed that the clergy should be taught pronunciation in order that
they could then act as the medium by which it could be propagated.
They would be particularly effective since 'it is part of the duty of every
person in the nation to attend divine service at least one day in the week'
(Sheridan 1756: 247). Church, state and the principles of elocution are
yoked together in an attempt by centripetalising forces to bring about a
new linguistic and historical order.

As with any successful act of hegemony, however, the attempt was not
simply a coercive one. Rather, those being asked to renounce their
linguistic differences in order to speak 'nationally' were assured that
what they would receive in return would be worth the price. Their
reward was the English language, a 'commodity' praised throughout
the eighteenth century in a series of clear attempts to gain for it the
status which Bakhtin presupposed it had already achieved. At the start of
the century the ancient–modern debate was played out in the sphere of
language in relation to the question of whether English or Latin grammar should be taught. This question, which recurs constantly in our
period, is one of the focal points for a defence, and often encomium, of
the English language. Lane, for example, comments that 'the English
tongue is as capable of all the arts and elegancies of Grammar and
Rhetorick, as Greek or Latin, or any other language of the world,

whether antient or modern' (Lane 1700: iv). The keyword here is 'capable', since as with many of the early defences of English in the period the assertion is tentative and stresses the fact that English has as yet been 'neglected and uncultivated'. Later in the century, however, when the debates around nationality became much more pointed, and thus when the language assumes a higher importance, estimations of the value of the language become more confident and assertive. Sheridan regards a 'uniformity of pronunciation' as part of the national and patriarchal heritage:

> Thus might the rising generation, born and bred in different Countries, and Counties, no longer have a variety of dialects, but as subjects of one King, like sons of one father, have one common tongue. All natives of these realms, would be restored to their birthright in commonage of language, which has been too long fenced in, and made the property of a few.
>
> (Sheridan 1761: 36)

So confident were the appraisals of the language that it was seen, no doubt under the influence of imperial growth, as a potential world language:

> Upon the whole, were our language to be studied and cultivated, we should find, that in point of giving delight, it would not yield to those of antiquity; and that it is much better fitted for universal use . . ..
> Nothing but the most shameful neglect in the people can prevent the English from handing down to posterity a third classical language, of far more importance than the other two.
>
> (Sheridan 1756: 367)

Towards the end of the century, however, the comparative stance is taken less towards Latin and Greek than towards the modern European vernaculars with which the English language was held to be in competition. There was of course no real comparison to be made; English simply made good the deficiencies which other languages were unfortunate enough to have. In such figurations the vernacular languages stood as representations of the national identities of their speakers, and as such there could be no real question as to whether the non-English-speaking British subjects, including those who did not speak the approved form of the language, would wish to adopt English as their superior and unifying tongue. The rhetoric is mellifluous:

> The Italian is pleasant, but without sinews, like a still fleeting water; the French delicate, but even nice as a woman scarce daring to open her lips for fear of spoiling her countenance; the Spanish is majestical, but runs too much on the *o*, and is therefore very gutteral and not very

pleasant; the Dutch manlike, but withal very harsh, as one ready at
every word to pick a quarrel.

Now we in borrowing from them, give the strength of consonants to
the Italian, the full sound of words to the French, the variety of
terminations to the Spanish, and the mollifying of more vowels to
the Dutch: and so like bees, we gather the honey of their good
properties, and leave the dregs to themselves.

(Peyton 1771: 29)

Compared with English, French was 'flimsy', Italian was merely 'neat',
Spanish 'grave', Saxon, High Dutch 'Belgic' and the Teutonic tongues
were natively 'hoarse' and 'rough' (Lemon 1783: vi). Given the poor
choice on offer, who would not choose a language 'as lofty and manly, as
those are truly brave who speak it'? (Buchanan 1757: xvi). The language,
reflecting the nation, was surely worth the price of renouncing region-
alisms, provincialisms, vulgarisms, dialects, and all those other forms of
heteroglot difference. For 'as England is the *Land of Liberty*, so is her
Language the *Voice of Freedom*' (Lemon 1783: vii). Compared to this the
other languages of Britain could only appear inferior and restrictive:
'And how can the greatest wit find clear and fit words in a language that
hath them not? What orations could Tully or Demosthenes have made in
Welsh?' (Wilson 1724: 36).

English then was the language which would unite the nation and serve
its interests: 'it will answer the honest ends of life, and we may live, and
fight, and trade with it as it is' (ibid.: 25). Fighting and trading were
certainly the ways of the British empire, and it is unsurprising to find that
the identification of a postulated national identity with the language, and
vice versa, extends to the nation's colonial activities too. English, wrote
Sheridan, should be rendered easy 'to all inhabitants of His Majesty's
dominions, whether of South or North Britain, of Ireland, or the other
British Dependencies' (Sheridan 1780: i). The language, if properly
cared for and refined, could act in the same manner as the classical
languages, as the vehicle for the civilising mission of colonialism:

Were we as industrious in improving and cultivating our language, as
the Greeks and Romans were . . . we might have as learned Leaders
and Commanders both by sea and land as they had who by their
Learning, Civility and Eloquence in their mother tongue, inlarged
their Dominions no less than by their arms: The barbarous Nations
being, as it were, ambitious to be conquered by such brave and
generous enemies, who fought rather to subdue their barbarity, and
civilise their Manners, than to enslave their Persons, or ruin their
Countries . . . .. And since it pleas'd God to convey Christianity into
the Isle of Great Britain, on the wings of these learned languages,
which are now dead, ought not the *British* Christians, in a grateful

sense of such goodness, to polish, refine and enrich their living language with all excellent knowledge, were it for no other end but to carry the Christian religion to other barbarous and wretched nations, who for want of Learning and Virtue, are but a kind of more savage beasts?

(Lane 1700: xix)

Here is the colonial fantasy captured in an image of language some twenty years before Defoe fictionalised it. In Defoe's version, one of the barbarous nation, 'Friday', is indeed ambitious to be conquered, and given language, by such a brave and generous man as Crusoe. He places his head willingly under Crusoe's foot and is immediately taught words from the language of civility and eloquence: 'first, I made him know his name should be Friday, which was the day I saved his life; I called him so for the memory of the time; I then taught him to say "Master", and then let him know that was to be my name' (Defoe 1972: 206). Crusoe says 'name' of course, when he means social position. Until civilised by the gift of the English language, Friday is as an infant (*in fans*, without speech), and can only offer thanks by means of dumb signs:

When he espied me, he came running to me, laying himself down again upon the ground, with all the possible signs of an humble, thankful disposition, making a many antic gestures to show it.

(ibid.: 206)

For the purposes of colonialism, the slave had to be brought to speak his master's language, thus gaining what Lane had termed 'Learning and Virtue'. Or, as Crusoe puts it, in rather more stark words:

I was greatly delighted with him, and made it my business to teach him everything that was proper to make him useful, handy, and helpful; but especially to make him speak and understand me when I spoke.

(ibid.: 210)

In this section we have tried to further the analysis which we began by looking at Swift's *Proposal*. Swift's reading of linguistic history as indicative of the nation's past has been extended here to demonstrate how the English language was used to represent, and help create, the nation's sense of its identity. Its function was not merely to act as an agent of unification for the nation, but to evince national superiority by the very nature of its language. English speakers were made to feel that they shared in something of genuine value each time they opened their mouths or raised their pens. For this was not merely an imagined community, but an imagined community of superiority. However, the phrase 'opened their mouths or raised their pens' should give us pause for thought. For not all British subjects were literate, and in our next section we will address the question of whether this community was quite as linguistically equal as it was represented. By considering at the level of language the constitution of what Habermas (1989) called the bourgeois public sphere, we will start to see how both language and history were heavily stratified; how forms of heteroglossia of various sorts were to be banished or silenced, proscribed and prescribed.

THE BOURGEOIS LINGUISTIC SPHERE

The story of the emergence of the bourgeois public sphere rendered by Habermas, though subject to a good deal of revision, is still a useful historical and sociological account of the social developments of our period. In his history, Habermas identifies the appearance of the bourgeois public sphere in Britian as the result of the confrontation between the absolutist state and the newly emergent bourgeois class. In Britain the new deal ushered in by the Glorious Revolution of 1688 confirmed the restriction of the independent power of the monarchy and the consolidated status of the newly visible class. The historical settlement, characterised principally by the increased economic and political power of the bourgeoisie, had the effect of engendering a new form of discursive organisation in British society, the bourgeois public sphere. In opposition to the authoritarian politics of France – and we have seen how contemporary English writers on language responded to that model – the bourgeois public sphere was the space in which free, bourgeois subjects met and conversed, exercising their rationality and judgment. Its institutions were the coffee houses, the periodicals and journals, and the gentlemen's clubs, sites where consensual and polite rational discussion took place for mutual benefit. As Swift put it,

> To discourse, and to attend,
> Is to *help* yourself, and Friend.

> (Swift 1966: 633–4)

One of the consequences which the emergence of the new sphere brought about was, as Eagleton (1984) has traced, the rise of literary criticism, a mode of discourse in which various forms of social judgment can be passed without ever entering directly into the language of politics, or 'enthusiastick jargon' as Swift dismissively described it. The appearance and development of such a discourse was part of the process by which the newly empowered class created a cultural and social identity for itself. And it is this that becomes the main function of the bourgeois public sphere: to forge a space for the creation, consolidation and dissemination of specific cultural practices, distinct from those of other social groups, by which the bourgeoisie could be identified. As Eagleton has put it, the principal task which is carried out in this sphere 'is one of class-consolidation, a codifying of the norms and regulating of the practices whereby the English bourgeoisie may negotiate an historic alliance with its social superiors' (Eagleton 1984: 10). We shall see later how codified and imperative some of these norms became, but first we have to trace the effects of the emergence of the new sphere on attitudes to, and representations of, the English language.

Eagleton, following Habermas, cites literature and literary criticism as the key locations in the formation of the identity of the bourgeoisie at a cultural level. In this space the bourgeoisie spoke to itself, told itself narratives, created histories, forged a culture. Eagleton characterises this as 'the cementing of a new power bloc at the level of the sign' (ibid.: 14). This is an accurate account of the particular form of this historical development; yet if literature has been shown to be one of the key sites of the formation of the new cultural identity of this class, the material of that medium has so far been neglected. For if the new political settlement was cemented at the level of the sign, then it is evidently the case that language itself would come under the most close scrutiny and fierce contestation. And in the work of many eighteenth-century writers on language we see precisely that: the process of bourgeois self-identification, at the social, political and cultural levels, by means of language; a process which depends quite as much on the construction of social 'others' as it does upon the identification of who, or what, the bourgeoisie was. It is that process that we will attempt to describe in this and the following sections.

The debate between the upholders of Latin against English, and vice versa, which was referred to earlier, was heavily politically loaded in the eighteenth century. Gentlemen, it might have been said, preferred Latin. For this was a highly contentious argument which ranged from Locke's defence of both languages, in their appropriate contexts, to the Leeds Grammar School case early in the next century (Smith 1984: 16), in which grammar schools were legally obliged to teach Latin and Greek. Locke's treatise on education is an important starting-point, since it presents clearly views which were to become the reference points for debates later in the century. Locke had argued that 'if a gentleman be to study any language, it ought to be that of his own country' (Locke 1823: 156). However, it is important to note that when he uses the term 'study' here, he means the grammatical or rhetorical study of the language. As far as considering language, or languages, in general is concerned, Locke articulates views which were both commonplace and highly political. Locke, like many in the eighteenth century who followed him, saw the teaching of language as connected clearly to the social position of the student. He complains:

Can there be anything more ridiculous, than that a father should waste his own money, and his son's time, in setting him to learn the Roman language when, at the same time, he designs him for a trade . . .? Could it be believed, unless we had every where amongst us examples of it, that a child should be forced to learn the rudiments of a language, which he is never to use in the course of life that he is designed to, and neglect all the while the writing a good hand, and casting accounts, which are of great advantage in all conditions of life, and to most trades indispensably necessarily? But though these qualifications, requisite to trade and commerce, and the business of the world, are seldom or never to be had at grammar schools; yet thither not only gentlemen send their younger sons intended for trades, but even tradesmen and farmers fail not to send their children, though they have neither intention nor ability to make them scholars.

(ibid.: 152–3)

Latin, an unnecessary accomplishment for the various ranks of the bourgeoisie, is to be replaced by the language which will help in the quotidien round of trade and commerce. What then of Latin? Locke is clear upon this too: 'Latin I look upon as absolutely necessary to a gentleman' (ibid.: 152). Later in the treatise he asserts rather defensively: 'I am not here speaking against Greek and Latin; I think they ought to be studied, and the Latin at least, understood well, by every gentleman' (ibid.: 182). The same principles are articulated later in the mid-century by Buchanan, who often echoes Locke, in his recommendation of the utility of his etymologies. He argues that they will 'in a great measure supply the want of Latin to the Fair Sex, and prove very advantageous to Boys who are to be put to Trades' (Buchanan 1753: xii). Again reinforcing Locke's position, he denies that he denigrates the classical languages:

The knowledge of these are absolutely necessary for some Professions in Civil Life, as well as for Persons intended for the Service of the Church: But the far greater part of Mankind have need of no language other than their own, to carry on their several Arts and Professions.

(ibid.: xiv)

This association of Latin with the learned and leisured, and the vernacular with the mercantile class, is extended in the early part of the century to the teaching of grammar itself. One writer of the period defends the teaching of grammar to 'the Nobility and Gentry (whose children need learning most, and in whom it would be most beneficial to Mankind)' (Lane 1700: viii). We can trace here attitudes to the Latin and English languages which are evidently based on political and cultural presuppositions. In these early examples it is Latin, the language associated with the aristocracy, that holds sway. Yet in a way which mirrors the shifting relations and antagonisms between the aristocracy and the bourgeoisie throughout the eighteenth century, relations which are never fully resolved in either direction, there is a distinct move away from Latin and towards the study of English as the bourgeoisie gains in confidence and status. There is, in fact, that movement towards the vernacular which Bakhtin was to assert had taken place much earlier.

Even in the early part of the century dictionaries had been written and intended for the newly empowered bourgeoisie, though at that point members of that class were still figured as outsiders. Bailey's *Universal Etymological Dictionary*, for example, was intended 'as well for the entertainment of the Curious as the Information of the Ignorant, and the benefit of young Students, Artificers, Tradesmen and Foreigners' (Bailey 1721: title). Later the *New English Dictionary* of Dyche and Pardon was not dedicated to Locke's 'gentlemen', but 'peculiarly calculated for the use and improvement for such as are unacquainted with the learned languages' (Dyche and Pardon 1735: title). Rapidly, however, the note of condescension alternating with defensiveness in the titles of such works is superseded. In its place there starts to appear a note of confidence, an assuredness which permeates the growing number of texts which are addressed explicitly to a bourgeois audience. Thus Fisher composes *The Instructor: or, Young Man's Best Companion* with the aim of inculcating 'the first step of forming the young man's mind for business, viz. The being instructed in, and acquainted with our Mother Tongue, viz. English' (Fisher 1740: iii). Just as Defoe's novels have been read as the fictionalised depiction of bourgeois virtue, here we begin to see its codification in language texts. *The Instructor* contained 'Spelling, Reading, Writing, and Arithmetick', as well as 'instructions to write variety of Hands', 'Merchants Accounts,' 'The Practical Gauger', to which is added 'The Family's Best Companion, With Instructions for Marking Linen, how to Pickle and Preserve, to make divers sorts of Wine; and many Plaisters and Medecines, necessary to all Families' (ibid.: title). 'All Families' is a revealing phrase, for this is a text which reveals the limitations of the public sphere: 'all families' refers to all bourgeois families.

The shift towards the vernacular becomes most pronounced in the mid- to latter part of the century. And it is at this point that we begin to hear the clear calls for English grammar schools. Martin, noting that 'an English grammar school, is a Thing unheard of in our Nation', asserts that English, 'compounded and irregular as it is, does still admit of *Grammar*, and is subject to the *Rules of Construction*, as much as any other' (Martin 1754: v–vi). Farro, in a far more confident display, intends the achievement that 'every *Female Teacher* in the British dominions may open an *English Grammar School* (Farro 1754: title). His aim, he declares, is

> That Britannia's sons in general may be universally benefited, and improved, by this grammar and vocabulary; and perfectly enabled to understand the true state of their excellent mother tongue, to the glory of the omnipotent God, the indelible honour of their country; adjoined to the highest renown for themselves; far excelling the sons of ancient Rome and Athens.
>
> (ibid.: xix)

Consequent upon the consolidation of the bourgeois public sphere the argument over the status of the classical and vernacular languages had moved on. Rather than Latin exerting dominance in a context of polyglossia, it was English that was beginning to become the hegemonic tongue:

> The importance of an English education is now pretty much understood; and it is generally acknowledged, that, not only for ladies, but for young gentlemen designed merely for trade, an intimate acquaintance with the Proprieties, and Beauties of the English Tongue, would be a very desirable, and necessary Attainment, far preferable to a smattering of the learned languages.
>
> (Ash 1761: iii)

Buchanan, maintaining the distinction made by Locke, reiterates the same point but with a distinct inflection. He cites

> a certain Alderman of a Country corporation, [who] took it highly ill that some Mechanics sent their sons to a Latin School, before they put them to Trades; for what else, says he, can we, Gentlemen, do for our sons?
>
> (Buchanan 1769: xvii)

Buchanan's comment on this is revealing, for rather than noticing the apparent blurring of class relations, he simply says that the tradesmen are 'wasting their children's time to no manner of purpose'. The children of tradesmen, he dictates, ought 'to learn to write their own language correctly'; but in an interesting shift he also adds that

> youths of distinction, and all designed for the Pulpit, Bar, Physic and other genteel Professions requiring a liberal Education, ought to lay the foundation of Grammar in that of their own tongue.
>
> (ibid.: xvii)

This leads Buchanan to a radical appeal, and one which is echoed in the early nineteenth century in Cobbett's campaign for the empowering effect of grammar:

> We have Latin Grammar schools in most incorporate towns; but we
> have not a professed English Grammar school in all Britain; not-
> withstanding, that take the youths of the United Kingdom in gen-
> eral, hardly one of a hundred requires a Latin education; though
> those of all ranks require an English one. English Grammar ought to
> be taught in every Latin school: And there ought to be a Master for
> the English language in each of those seminaries of Westminster,
> Eaton, etc.
>
> (ibid.: xxiii)

By the end of the century the argument was almost clinched, though, as
Cobbett proclaimed, the status of the classical languages was in particular circumstances designed to maintain the deepest form of class
division. Entrance to the bar, for example, cost the princely sum of
£500 if the candidate did not have the classical languages (Smith
1984: 1). Despite this, a shift had taken place in the relations between
the vernacular and the 'learned' languages. We can see this, for example,
in the attack made by Withers upon the mercantile classes. He creates
the figure of an ignorant merchant:

> As to your learning, and your Grammar, and all that, what Good will
> it do to me? I have often heard Alderman Leatherhead say as how
> Riches is the Main Chance; and it is true enough for the Matter of
> that, for what is a Man without money?
>
> (Withers 1789: 4–5)

The scorn of the attack is unmistakable, but so is the recognition that the
bourgeois public sphere had been cemented. Withers notes:

> The importance of a correct Mode of Expression in *Business* is
> sufficiently obvious. SHOPMEN, CLERKS, APPRENTICES, and
> all who are engaged in the Transactions of commercial Life, may
> be assured that the acquisition will procure them Respect, and be
> highly conducive to their Advancement in Life.
>
> (ibid.: 30)

In this respect at least, the bourgeois sphere of trading and business
had the same requirements as those professions which had previously
been restricted: 'In the Pulpit, the Senate, at the Bar, and in all
Public Assemblies, it is necessary to speak with Purity and Elegance'
(ibid.).

The growth and development of the bourgeois public sphere then
stimulates the new interest in the vernacular as the vehicle of social and
political life. In another assertion which explicitly though falsely equates
the bourgeoisie with the population at large, Walker claims that the
language should be studied, since

It is the privilege of every Englishman from the greatest to the meanest, if an Englishman possessing such privilege, can be said to be mean, to be occasionally the judge of the life and fortune of his fellow citizens. It is his happiness to have a voice in forming those laws he is governed by, and his still greater happiness to have the application of those laws open to the freest and most unbiased discussion.

(Walker 1774: 26–7)

Walker's description may well serve as an accurate account of the activities and rights of the privileged bourgeoisie, but it is wholly inaccurate as a description of the rights of *every* English man and woman.

This reservation notwithstanding, there is throughout the century a considerable stress on the importance of language itself, one which can be traced not least to the tremendous influence of Locke's *Essay*. Wilson comments:

Words are the Images of our Thoughts, the landmarks of all Interests; and the Wheels of our Human World are turned by them. They move Interests that are greater than Mountains, and many a time have subdued kingdoms.

(Wilson 1724: 36)

Social and political life comes to be seen as dependent upon the proper use of language in the public sphere. For Sheridan the very institutions of the state itself were at risk, unless protected by the power of words:

it must be obvious to the slightest enquirer, that the support of our establishments, both ecclesiastical and civil, in their due vigour, must in a great measure depend upon the powers of elocution in public debates, or other oratorical performances, displayed in the pulpit, the senate-house, or at the bar.

(Sheridan 1759: 4)

What is more Sheridan claims that it is acknowledged that 'a general inability to read, or speak, with propriety and grace in public, runs thro' the natives of the British dominions' (Sheridan 1762: 1). Of course as an elocution master this is the sort of thing that Sheridan would say, since if there were not such linguistic difficulties then there would be no requirement for practitioners of his trade. But the problem which he describes is not an imaginary one; throughout the century defenders of the vernacular had worried over which version of it was the best. Which was to be the identifiable form which would act as the medium of the public sphere? That is to say, which of the different forms was to be elevated to the status of monoglossia? Again Locke gives us indications of a preference which was to become common. Arguing against the general learning of grammar by children, Locke argues instead for tuition by example:

> Languages were not made by rules or art but by accident and the common use of the people. And he that will speak them well, has no other rule but that; nor anything to trust but his memory, and the habit of speaking after the fashion learned from those that are allowed to speak properly.
>
> (Locke 1823: 160)

Precedent rather than rule is to be the guiding factor in the young child's education, imitation of the speech of the people who are 'allowed to speak properly'. There is a significant separation here of course between the 'common use of the people' which creates language, and proper speech, the form which is to be mimicked. And the gap between these two forms of the language was as great as any of the class barriers which were set up around the bourgeois public sphere.

That this question of using the language 'properly' was immensely important in Britain in the eighteenth century is undoubted. In the mid-century for example, one writer asks, 'what can reflect more on a Man's reputation for Learning, than to find him unable to pronounce or spell many words in common use' (Martin 1749: iv). The problem of course was which form was it to be? Where was it to be found? Who spoke it? There are numerous answers to those questions, and others like them, which have been circulating in British society for almost three hundred years. There are two definitions of proper English from this period, however, which will serve to demonstrate the way in which the bourgeois linguistic sphere emerges at this time, and the success of the construction. In 1701 Jones defined the language in these terms: 'English speech is the Art of signifying the Mind by humane Voice, as it is commonly used in England, particularly in *London*, the *Universities*, or at *Court*' (Jones 1701: 1) This definition of 'common use' echoes that of Puttenham, which was cited earlier: 'the usuall speach of the Court, and that of London and the shires lying about London within lx. myles and not much above'.[3] Compare these two definitions with that of 'national or general use' rendered by Campbell in 1776:

> In every province there are peculiarities of dialect, which affect not only the pronunciation and accent, but even the inflection and combination of words, whereby this idiom is distinguished from that of the nation, and from that of every other province . . .. This is one reason, I imagine, why the term *use* on this subject is commonly accompanied with the epithet *general*. In the generality of provincial idioms, there is, it must be acknowledged, a pretty considerable concurrence both of the lower and middle ranks. But still this use is

bounded by the province and always ridiculous. But the language properly so called is found in the upper and middle ranks, over the whole British Empire. Thus though in every province they ridicule the idioms of every other province, they all vail to the English idiom and scruple not to acknowledge its superiority over them.

(Campbell 1776: I, 353–4)

The language is no longer that of the court, the universities or anywhere so unspecific as 'London'; instead it is the language of a specific social group. The bourgeois linguistic sphere had found its voice.

WELL FASHIONED: PATROLLING THE BOUNDARIES OF LANGUAGE AND THE BODY

This new, central form of the language which was forged in the eighteenth century was a type of monoglossia, and, like all monoglot forms, it had to be strictly policed in order to be sustained against threats from outside. Such threats to the preservation of the 'purity' of the language took various forms. One was the introduction of 'foreign words', which Johnson attacks in the significant discourse of political and national identity: 'some of them are naturalised and incorporated, but others still continue aliens, and are rather auxiliaries than subjects' (Johnson 1806: II, 7). Johnson, who dedicated the *Plan of an English Dictionary* to the earl of Chesterfield on the grounds that Dormer had concerned himself with the dictionary project as well as 'with treaties and with wars' (ibid.), saw himself in fact precisely as a guardian of the language. Using the discourse of warfare, he compares himself to one of Caesar's soldiers, looking on the language as they had perceived Britain:

> as a new world, which it is almost madness to invade. But I hope, that though I should not complete the conquest, I shall at least discover the coast, civilise part of the inhabitants, and make it easy for some other adventurer to proceed further, to reduce them wholly to subjection, and settle them under laws.

> (ibid.: II, 29)

What, or who, was it that needed to be 'civilised', 'reduced', to suffer 'subjection' and to be brought under the rule of law? We shall see in this and the following section that it was not in fact words alone that were to be so controlled, but particular social groups.

Johnson, self-figured as a colonial soldier discovering the coast (the *natural* boundary) of the language, patrolled the border and excluded the words of a particular class. Yet the policing was meant not merely to be exclusive but to watch over and regulate the behaviour of those who belonged. By using Bourdieu's theoretical term 'habitus', we shall see

how the bourgeois public sphere was policed internally and thus consolidated both in language and behaviour at a level of extremely precise
detail. By 'habitus' Bourdieu means a system of dispositions which acts as
'the principle of generation and structuration of practices and representations which can be objectively "regulated" and "regular"' without
being reducible to a set of rules (Bourdieu 1977: 72). These dispositions, though not absolute (no one is forced to act in accordance with
them, but doing so is usually constructed as being in the best interests of
the individual), are normative and derive from forces and structures
which exist in the context in which the dispositions are picked up. The
emergent class formation in eighteenth-century Britain is interesting in
this respect, since we can see clearly here the forging of a new habitus in
relation to a new historical situation.

The set of dispositions is inculcated, according to the social location of
the individual, by means of a formation of overt and covert modes of
training which aim to produce specific effects. These might range from
the correction of a perceived speech fault to the order not to speak with
your mouth full. Again, depending on the place of the individual, these
modes will be structured in the sense that they are geared towards
enabling the individual to function 'properly' in their social position.
They furnish the subject with what Bourdieu calls 'practical sense', that
is, the feel for what is right in particular contexts. Importantly, they lead
the individual to act in specific ways, but they do not determine them.

Bourdieu cites two particularly significant aspects of this process. The
first is the inculcation of linguistic habitus; which might reductively be
summarised as the way in which, say, working-class people learn to
sound like the working class (in terms of vocabulary, accent, tone, and
so on). The second is what Bourdieu calls 'bodily hexis', which he
describes as 'political mythology realised, *em-bodied*, turned into a permanent disposition, a durable way of standing, speaking, walking, and
thereby of feeling and thinking' (Bourdieu 1990: 69–70). That is to say,
the practices by which, say, the *petits bourgeois* learn how to look and act
like the *petits bourgeois*. More abstractly, and to use a different vocabulary,
this is ideology made incarnate, the authoritative word made flesh.

Bourdieu's argument then is that each individual's linguistic and
corporeal actions are thoroughly historicised and comprehensible only
in terms of a constant set of negotiations between structures which exist
externally, such as economic relations, and the dispositions which an
individual has. For example, the negotiations which take place when a
person attends an important interview: the adjustment of clothes, voice,
manners, and so on. He claims that this whole process, which he
describes as the practice of symbolic power and violence, is not usually
overt and directly oppressive but rather subtle, quiet, quotidien and
barely susceptible. In a sense it is a theory of how we come to police

ourselves. One way of thinking about this is to consider the injunctions delivered to children about how to eat, how to stand, not to put hands in pockets, to speak when spoken to, and all the other minor behavioural restrictions. These are not in themselves violent acts; but Bourdieu's point is that they act to produce a certain set of practices and beliefs throughout an individual's life. The importance, and symbolic violence, of such dispositions can be seen, for example, in a case such as that in which rather than being told to speak when spoken to, a working-class child is told to be polite and respectful towards her or his 'betters'. Behind such apparently innocuous commands there is a whole history of social presuppositions and future programming.

Bourdieu's point then is that this process takes place at a local, individual and often familial level. And this is certainly the case. Elocution lessons, for example, are now relatively rare in schools, and perhaps this is because their function is now performed, and executed more effectively, by the family. However, although Bourdieu's account is interesting, it is in some respects ahistorical. Just to use the example of elocution lessons, we have seen in the chapter so far that they were not always conducted in the private sphere. That is to say, Bourdieu's account supposes that the production of lingusitic habitus and bodily hexis has always continued in the same way. But this may well not always have been the case. In this section then we will examine how at a time of historical crisis, here the emergence of the bourgeois public sphere, this process of production was much more sharply open and contested. To put it another way, we will look at how the bourgeois public sphere was internally policed.

Locke, as ever in the eighteenth century, gives the key to the construction of English codes of language and behaviour. To avoid 'ill-breeding', Locke recommends:

> first, a disposition of the mind not to offend others; and secondly, the most acceptable and agreeable way of expressing that disposition. From the one, men are called civil; from the other, well fashioned.
>
> (Locke 1823: 134)

Our interest here is in the latter, for although the first is preferable, the second is, after Machiavelli, the more possible. In this respect we see the emergence of Bourdieu's 'habitus':

> that decency of gracefulness and looks, voice, words, motions, gestures, and of all the whole outward demeanour, which takes in company, and makes those with whom we converse easy and well pleased. This is, as it were, the language whereby that internal civility of the mind is expressed; which, as other languages are, being very

much governed by the fashion and custom of every country, must, in the rules and practice of it, be learned chiefly from observation, and the carriage of those who are allowed to be well-bred.

(ibid.: 134)

This is the perfect exemplification of Bourdieu's theory: language and manners designed to make everyone comfortable and secure in their place. A model of social behaviour, moreover, based on the demeanour of the 'well-bred', the aim of which is to secure everyone else in their place: to know it and stay there.

How then was Locke's account of behaviour as a semiotic code which had to be learned (formulated, along with the theory of the arbitrariness of the sign, some two centuries before Saussure) taken up in the eighteenth century? How was the inculcation of the code managed in the period, how did the policing take place? Against Bourdieu's view that this process is quiet and mostly hidden, we can see that in the eighteenth century it was anything but. This is to be explained by the very novelty of the historical situation; for what we see in this period is *this* particular system of dispositions being formulated and set out for the first time. In later periods, say in the nineteenth century, the code was effective enough to work in an occluded manner. At that point language and the body were indeed covered by highly complex discursive restrictions; 'white meat' and 'dark meat', for example, derive from this period and its refusal to name the bodily parts (or at least the breast and legs) of even dead chickens. But in the eighteenth century the code was still in the process of being organised and disseminated. The retreat to the family does indeed arrive later, and as mentioned earlier may well have been more effective, but in our period the code was being hawked and shouted from street corners and rooftops.

We have noted already the way in which language teaching became of such importance in the century in terms of the demarcation of bourgeois social space and the linguistic habitus required to in-habit it. For some middle-class schoolchildren inculcation of the habitus was conducted by a process which we might call that of discipline, punishment and education. Fenning tells of the method which he has used in his peda-gogical career:

the whole School was divided; and such of the Pupils as were fit to spell Words of three, four, or five Syllables, stood next my Right-Hand, according to their Order in Learning, and the others, who were to try at Monosyllables, stood in a Row at my Left; then I proposed a Word to the Head-Boy, (as we call him) if he spelt it he kept his Place, and then I immediately told him the Meaning of the Word – If he spelt it not, I went to the second, third, fourth, fifth, &c. asking the same Word, which if he spelt right, I commended, and after telling him the Meaning, I demanded him into the first Boy's Place, which he received with a Smile, and seemed proud of.

(Fenning 1767: viii)

Rewards and punishments went hand in hand in the whole process of giving children the orthographic and semantic skills required for their social position:

Then about 10 Minutes before School was done, I proposed three hard or technical Words, which I called Prize Words, and whoever spelt the first, I gave a Penny to, or two Sheets of good Paper; and then he went and sat down, while I proposed the next Word; and whoever spelt it had a Half-Penny or a whole Sheet of Paper; and the third Boy had a whole Slate-Pencil.

(ibid.)

We have already seen the way in which linguistic habitus became a question of great importance in our period. In this section then we can concentrate on the way in which a bodily hexis was created to accompany it: words and gestures united to good social effect.

The bodily language of civility was as strictly ruled as the language of public discourse. Taking his lead from Locke, Sheridan saw both as the distinguishing criteria of humanity: 'it is in the power of man, by his own pains and industry, to forward the perfection of his own nature' (Sheridan 1762: 106). Words, tones, accents and gestures were the media by which humanity demonstrated its uniqueness as a species, and also the means by which the several strata of that species were to be differentiated. Mason, writing in the mid-century, turned to Cicero and Quintilian as classical models of rhetoric in order to teach 'the art of managing the voice, and gesture, in speaking' (Mason 1748: 4). He sets out in detail the position which should be adopted by the head when expressing particular emotions. The head

should generally be in an erect posture . . . it should always be on the same side with the Action of the Hands and Body, except when we express an abhorrence, or a refusal of anything, which is done by rejecting it with the right hand and turning away the head to the left.

(ibid.: 39)

In a somewhat brusque declaration, the anonymous pamphlet on *Some Rules for Speaking and Action* had stated: 'the mouth should not be writh'd, the lips bit or lick'd, the shoulders shrugged, nor the belly thrust out' (Anonymous 1716: 14). Later in the century, however, the strictures were to become much more organised and to be given an intellectual justification. In Sheridan's estimation the most important writing of the period was Locke's *Essay Concerning Human Understanding* and his own tracts and discourses. Locke had solved the problem of the determination of the meaning of words, while Sheridan offered the answer to the problem of its transmission. There were, he claimed, two different orders of language:

> The one, is, the language of ideas; by which the thoughts pass in a man's mind, are manifested to others; and this language is composed chiefly of words properly ranged, and divided into sentences. The other, is the language of emotions; by which the effects that these thoughts have upon the mind of the speaker, in exciting the passions and affections, and all manner of feelings, are not only made known, but communicated to others; and this language is composed of tones, looks, and gestures.
>
> (Sheridan 1762: 132)

Gesture, described by Sheridan as the 'hand-writing of nature', was a powerful semiotic system. Of hands, he writes:

> everyone knows that with them we can demand, or promise; call, dismiss; threaten, supplicate; ask, deny; show joy, sorrow, detestation, fear, confession, penitance, admiration, respect; and many other things now in common usage.
>
> (ibid.: 116)

Such power needed to be carefully prescribed, and the dictates of both Sheridan and Walker demonstrated the precision that was required. Walker, for example, describes how the self-fashioning needed for the expression of joy,

> when moderate, opens the countenance with smiles, and throws as it were, a sunshine of delectation over the whole frame: when it is sudden and violent, it expresses itself by clapping the hands, raising the eyes towards heaven, and giving such a spring to the body as to attempt to make it mount up as if it could fly.
>
> (Walker 1781: 272)

Pity required 'tenderness of voice', 'pain in the countenance', 'gentle raising and falling of the hands and eyes', and the following facial arrangement: 'the mouth is open, the eye brows are drawn down, and the features contracted or drawn together' (ibid.). Fear is sketched as unerringly as in any Gothic novel (for which presumably the elocution books acted as, so to speak, manuals):

> fear violent and sudden, opens wide the eyes and mouth, shortens the nose, gives the countenance an air of wildness, covers it with deadly paleness, draws back the elbows parallel with the sides, lifts up the open hand with the fingers spread, to the height of the breast, at some

distance before it, so as to shield it from the dreadful object. One foot is drawn back behind the other, so that the body seems shrinking from the danger, and putting itself into a posture for flight.

(ibid.)

The bourgeois public sphere may well have needed policing in order to protect it from the language of the barbarians at the gates. But it needed quite as much discipline in order to control the behaviour and activities of those who dwelled within. The two sets of practices were contemporaneous and coterminous.

SWALLOWING THE MASTER'S TONGUE

Women constituted one group which presented particular problems in this process of social consolidation; and their treatment in relation to language is complex and intertwined again with questions of social class. Locke cited women in support of his claim that language is best learned by imitation rather than rote:

persons of quality of the softer sex, and such of them as have spent their time in well-bred company, show us, that this plain natural way, without the least study or knowledge of grammar, can carry them to a degree of elegancy and politeness in their language.

(Locke 1823: 160)

The qualifications 'persons of quality', acquainted with 'well-bred company' indicate that Locke had a specific class of women in mind. And it is presumably to the same group that Swift refers in the *Proposal*, when he asserts that the reform of the language should be left rather 'to the Judgment of the Women, than of illiterate Court-Fops, half-witted Poets, and University Boys'. Women, says Swift approvingly, 'do naturally discard the Consonants', as men drop the vowels. Claiming to have proved this by experiment, he concludes:

although I would by no Means give Ladies the Trouble of advising us in the Reformation of our Language; yet I cannot help Thinking, that since they have been left out of all Meetings, except Parties at Play, or where worse Designs are carried on, our Conversation hath very much degenerated.

(Swift 1957: 13)

Later in the century this association between gender and class is sustained. Arguing, by direct comparison with Jourdain in Molière's *Le Bourgeois Gentilhomme*, Baker cites a working-class woman who speaks 'generally speaking, very properly'. He postulates an hypothetical situation in order to illustrate the distinction between speaking properly and having grammatical knowledge:

> If a Man were with a serious Countenance to ask a Servant-Wench, that is standing at a Door, what a Noun Adjective is, and whether such a Verb governs a Dative or an Accusative Case, she would conclude him to be out of his Senses; and would perhaps run frightened into the House, and tell her Mistress that a Madman was going to do her a Mischief.
>
> (Baker 1770: xv)

The claim that she speaks 'very properly', however, is immediately withdrawn by the author, in a rhetorical flourish in which gender is overidden by class:

> and if she often talks false English, it is owing not so much to her being unacquainted with Grammar as to the low company she has kept. Women of polite Education, who are used to good Company, though they have studied Grammar no more than this Servant-maid, talk, if not quite correctly, yet more correctly than such Men in ordinary life as have passed some Years at a Latin-school.
>
> (ibid.: xv)

Although these arguments in favour of women learning 'proper English' by means of imitation rather than instruction were common, they were in fact far outweighed in the period by denunciations of the neglect of the formal education of women. Such attacks were particularly sharp when they concerned the lack of instruction in the English language. Lane commented in 1700 that grammar was 'universally necessary and useful to all persons of whatever Quality, Condition or Sex' (Lane 1700: vii). And his appeal for the teaching of the language to women in particular was repeated variously throughout the century, most vociferously by Buchanan in this ringing condemnation of the refusal of such an education:

> It is greatly to be lamented that the Fair Sex have been in general so shamefully neglected with regard to a proper English education. Many of them, by the unthinking part of Males, are considered and treated rather as Dolls, than as intelligent social Beings.
>
> (Buchanan 1762: xxix)

Sheridan the playwright, son of the elocution master, satirised this call for the education of women, particularly in relation to language, in the figure of Mrs Malaprop in *The Rivals* (1775). In a speech between Malaprop and Sir Anthony Absolute – and the class relations between these two characters are worthy of note – Malaprop at one and the same time makes an appeal for the education of women and embodies the reason for its necessity. She outlines her plan for the education of young women:

> Observe me, Sir Anthony. – I would by no means wish a daughter of mine to be a progeny of learning . . .. But, Sir Anthony, I would send her, at nine years old, to a boarding-school, in order to learn a little ingenuity and artifice. – Then, Sir, she should have a supercilious knowledge in accounts; – and as she grew up, I would have her instructed in geometry, that she should know something of the contagious countries; – but above all, Sir Anthony, she should be Mistress of orthodoxy, that she might not mis-spell, and mis-pronounce words so shamefully as girls usually do; and likewise reprehend the true meaning of what she is saying.
>
> (Sheridan 1975: 21)

If Buchanan's appeal sounds like Mary Wollstonecraft's appeal for the educational rights of women *avant la lettre*, then perhaps it should be a question as to precisely why there were so many appeals for the education of women in the English language. And why so many of them were made by men. Buchanan's call is in fact asserting the right of 'young ladies of rank' to an education in pronunciation and grammar, along with geography and natural history. He outlines the foundation of his assertion:

> By pursuing such a Plan, the advantages which would accrue to so many young ladies and consequently to the interest and future happiness of society, are to every thinking and generous-hearted person, too obvious to require enumeration.
>
> (Buchanan 1762: xxxi)

The 'happiness of society' might better be re-written as the 'happiness of male bourgeois society', if we read closely those texts which argue for the instruction of women in the language. Greenwood, for example, writes that one of the aims of his *Essay Towards a Practical English Grammar* (1711), is 'to oblige the Fair Sex whose *Education* perhaps is too much neglected in this Particular' (Greenwood 1711: i). Quoting from his own letter to the *Tatler*, he indicates how this aim is in itself subservient to another:

> by the Improvement of the Female Sex, you will of course add to the Happiness, Pleasure and Advantages of the Male. And I have often with concern reflected on the Negligence, not to say Ingratitude of our Sex, who seem so generally careless in Cultivating and Adorning the Minds of those Beautiful Bodies that are the Delight and Ornament of Mankind.
>
> (ibid.)

Women were to be trained in language in order to provide company for the male constituents of the public sphere. Without such an accomplishment Buchanan rather brusquely observes, a woman cannot be 'company even to herself' since it is 'a qualification which must more particularly distinguish her from the illiterate vulgar' (Buchanan 1769: xxxii). Women had to swallow their master's tongue in order to qualify for entrance into polite society.

This notion was not an uncommon one and was usually accompanied by an appeal that women's language also needed to be disciplined in order to fulfil its rightful role in the domestic sphere. Lane justifies his *Key to the Art of Letters* (1700) on the grounds that its methods are simpler than those employed by others. This leads him to hope that 'young gentle-women' will

> attain to a perfect knowledge of the art of *Grammar* in the method here proposed, by which they may become as learned as those excellent Greek and Roman matrons recorded in History; which will contribute much more to the good of their children and families afterwards, than all those inferior Attainments which take up so much of their best time.
>
> (Lane 1700: xvi)

Women were to be linguistically educated then for two purposes: to fulfil the role of the mother, passing on pure language to the child (a constant source of anxiety in the century, as we shall see in the case of the treatment of servants), and to act as companion to the male in the public sphere. Wilson gives an accurate summary of the position when he calls for women themselves to take an interest in the language:

> for many a pretty lady by the silliness of her words, hath lost the Admiration which her face had gained. And as the Mind hath more lovely and more lasting charms than the body, if they would capture Men of Sense, they must not neglect those best kind of beauties . . . and as in these Talents Nature hath doubtless been as bountiful to that sex as to our own, those Improprieties in Words, Spelling and Writing, for which they are usually laughed at are not owing to any Defect of their Minds, but the carelessness, if not Injustice to them in their Education.
>
> (Wilson 1724: 37)

If such linguistic and intellectual improvement were not undertaken by women, then the nation itself would suffer:

> And as the forming of the Tongue, Ears and Pronunciation of Children are Works of Mothers while their Understanding and Senses are young, we shall never improve our Nation to any great purpose, till we make our language easy and understood by them, so as we may have their help with us.
>
> (ibid.)

What is more, it is not simply women who need to be taught how to use the language properly, since men too need to be told not to imitate the bad habits of women. If men, Bayly argues,

> think affectation necessary in conversing with them, they would do well to consine (*sic*) the prim mouth and soft voice to those occasions only, and when they speak in public assemblies to assume the voice of a man; that we may not have a female senate, nor women to speak at the Bar, or in the Church.
>
> (Bayly 1758: 172–3)

The media by which women were to be instructed in the language reveal the estimation of female intelligence, and indeed literacy, at the time. Evolving as they did from glossaries (from the Latin *glossa*, meaning an obsolete or foreign word needing explanation), the first English dictionaries were attempts to make the 'language easy and understood' and were often directed at women. The task had been undertaken in the previous century, and the first dictionary proper is usually taken to be Cawdry's *Table Alphabeticall* (1604), which was aimed at 'Ladies, Gentlewomen, or any other unskillfull persons'. The dictionaries which followed often had a similar audience in mind. Bullokar's *English Expositor* (1616) was dedicated to 'the greatest Ladies and Studious Gentlewomen'; Cockeram's *English Dictionarie: or, An Interpreter of Hard English Words* (1623) sought to help 'as well Ladies and Gentlewomen, young Schollers, Clarkes, Merchants, as also Strangers of any Nation'; and Blount's *Glossographia* (1656) was 'chiefly intended for the more knowing women and the less-knowing men; or indeed for all such of the unlearned'.

Language texts in the eighteenth century did not greatly differ from this mode of address. Brightland's *Grammar of the English Tongue* (1711) was proposed for 'Children, Women, or the ignorant of both sexes'. And Loughton (1739) produced his *Practical Grammar of the English Tongue* 'for the use of Schools' and 'calculated chiefly for the use of the FAIR SEX'. Various attempts were made to adapt to this female audience: Buchanan's *Spelling Dictionary of the English Language* (1757b) was 'proposed, especially for the accommodation of the ladies' and designed in order that it 'should take up but small room in the pocket'. And Ussher's *Elements of English Grammar* (1785), written specifically for 'Ladies Boarding Schools', wrote down to its audience:

> As a grammatical knowledge of English is become essentially necessary in the education of Ladies, it is certainly a desirable object to render that study as easy and as useful to them as possible. For this reason, in a treatise of grammar intended for their use, all abstract terms that could be dispensed with, should be rejected.
>
> (Ussher 1785: vi–vii)

Farro's somewhat grandiosely titled *Royal Universal British Grammar*
(1754), published in the form of a dialogue, advertised itself as contain-
ing 'a method so easy that every *Female Teacher* in the British dominions
may open an *English Grammar School*, and render themselves more useful
to the public'. It then begins its address to 'all the worthy Teachers of the
English Language Throughout the British Dominions' with the words
'Worthy Gentlemen'. The rage for dictionaries, those textbooks of
codification and guidance, even spread to non-linguistic areas. Bailey's
Dictionarium domesticum (1736), for example, was a household dictionary
which set out the procedures for the bourgeois home. It aimed to
encapsulate the rules for the 'sustenance, preservation, or recovery of
the health of families, and especially of that part which is most peculiarly
the provenance of the mistress of it' (Bailey 1736: Preface). It was
composed in this way in order to mirror the structure which 'nature,
or at least custom of the most civilised and polite nations' had distributed. Entries range from 'Abcess' ('a disease to which poultry are
incident'), to 'Yeast'.

All of the measures outlined here were attempts to police the language
of women, part of that often subtle, sometimes abrupt, process of
defending the borders of the male bourgeois linguistic sphere. Women
of a certain status could be allowed in, but only, if the pun can be
excused, on certain terms. They could enter this world, but only con-
ditionally, only in so far as they agreed to mind their language. Of course
whether in fact this is what happened is open to dispute. Simply being
told to act in certain ways does not ensure that those addressed will
comply, and there is evidence that many of the rules of what was
constructed as polite discourse were broken. But what we are discovering
here is part of an enormous discursive web around language which
intends to delimit and determine how it is enacted. The fact of heteroglossia cannot be denied, it will always rupture and break through, but
the attempts to silence, or to laugh at, or to allow only on certain
conditions, the language of women is but one part of the defence of
the monoglossia of the male bourgeois linguistic sphere.

Restrictions and prejudices with regard to the language were particularly exacerbated in the case of the heteroglossia rendered by social class.
Even the constrictions placed upon the linguistic performance of women
pale by comparison. And it is here in the eighteenth-century attitudes
towards class and language, the most resolute and determined means of
defence of the monoglossia of the bourgeois linguistic sphere, that we
can see the emergent patterns of social division that are still locatable
today and that we shall trace later. Heteroglot divisions, at the level of
class and regionality, caused particular anxiety and needed to be banished forever in an attempt to solidify bourgeois hegemony. It was a
pattern which was to recur.

Servants constituted one specific source of concern. Locke warned against intercourse between children and servants:

> They are wholly, if possible, to be kept from such conversation: for the contagion of these ill precedents, both in civility and virtue, horribly affects children, as often as they come within reach of it. They frequently learn, from such unbred or debauched servants, such language, untowardly tricks and vices, as otherwise they possibly would be ignorant of all their lives.
>
> (Locke 1823: 53)

This was a warning which echoed across the century as the bourgeois parenthood was advised against the possible pollution of their children's language. Sheridan, writing in the mid-century, claimed that children in Britain are committed 'to the care of some of the most ignorant and lowest of mankind' in regard to language (Sheridan 1756: 195). And Withers, at the century's conclusion, judged an utterance such as 'There's your shoes, Here's your Boots' in this way: 'Such Vulgarisms may be expected from Domestics, and from the Lower Orders of Society; but they are a reproach to people of education' (Withers 1789: 44). Fielding was able to raid this code of representation to depict, by means of mistakes in language, a female servant who represented precisely the 'most ignorant and lowest of mankind'. In *Joseph Andrews*, there is an exchange between Joseph, at this point a servant though later discovered to be of parentage of 'much greater circumstances than those he had hitherto mistaken', and Mrs Slipslop, a maid to Lady Booby. Slipslop has the intention of seducing the young Andrews, and her language reveals the inferiority of her gender, class and morality. She denounces Joseph for his rejection, as she sees it, of her overtures:

> 'If we like a man, the lightest hint *sophisticates*. Whereas a boy *proposes* upon us to break through all the *regulations* of modesty, before we can make any *oppression* upon him.' Joseph, who did not understand a word she said, answered, '*Yes, Madam*; – ' 'Yes Madam!' reply'd Mrs Slipslop with some warmth, 'Do you intend to *result* my passion? Is it not enough, ungrateful as you are, to make no return to all the favours I have done you: but you must treat me with *ironing*? Barbarous monster! How have I deserved that my passion should be *resulted* and treated with *ironing*? 'Madam,' answered Joseph, 'I don't understand your hard words: but I am certain you have no occasion to call me ungrateful . . .'
>
> (Fielding 1977: 52)

Slipslop's lack of virtue and social status are given away in her misuse of words; these qualities in Andrews, however, are vindicated in the fact that he does not understand her 'hard words' (*glossae*). Walker, making specific reference to Fielding's work, says that the illiterate 'fall into the errors we call slops; which is a mispronunciation of hard or uncommon words' (Walker 1783: 4). As with 'malapropism', the gendered social distinctions embodied in this character were significant enough to merit the entry of the term 'slipslop' into the language as both noun and verb denoting a blunder in the use of words.

As a natural consequence of the fears concerning the language of servants, it followed, as Wilson pointed out a little later, that grammar should be taught to all sections of society: 'The children both of the Great and the Learned take their speech from their Servants and Companions; and in this Matter, the Instructions in the lowest schools are of great Influence' (Wilson 1724: 74). The fear of infection which underpinned this remark was relative to the enormous concern over the 'viciousness' of working-class speech. Ignorance amongst the illiterate, Buchanan argued, causes that 'vicious, drawling, uncouth pronunciation among the generality of the people' (Buchanan 1757: vii). There were, argued Sheridan, a number of heteroglot forms of the language: the Scots, Irish and Welsh each have their 'peculiar dialect', as does 'almost every county in England', along with the 'two different modes of pronunciation' in the metropolis (the 'cockney' and the 'polite'). Distinguishing between them, Sheridan selects the central form and says of the others: 'All other dialects, are sure marks, either of a provincial, rustic, pedantic, or mechanic education; and therefore have some degree of disgrace attached to them' (Sheridan 1762: 30). If this was a logical *non sequitur*, then in historical context it made perfect sense. The degree of disgrace attached to the language of the 'mechanic' section of the population was the greatest of all. Johnson excludes it from his *Dictionary* on these grounds:

> Nor are all words which are not found in the vocabulary, to be lamented as omissions. Of the laborious and mercantile part of the people, the diction is in a great measure casual and mutable; many of their terms are formed for some temporary or local convenience, and though current at certain times and places, are in others utterly unknown. This fugitive cant, which is always in a state of increase or decay, cannot be regarded as any part of the durable materials of a language, and therefore must be suffered to perish with other things unworthy of preservation.
>
> (Johnson 1806: II, 59)

Workers are thus taken to use language in a manner which is tied to immediate local needs. It is a characteristic which is shared by savages:

> In countries where people have but few ideas, they will of course have but few words . . .. Amongst savages therefore the language belonging

to the operations of the understanding, or fancy, is scarcely known. Their ideas extend but little beyond the necessaries of life, and their words are circumscribed by their ideas . . .. As the natives of such countries, are little more than mere animals, so have they scarcely the use of any other but their animal faculties.

(Sheridan 1762: 155–6)

Rising just above savages, workers at least had a language which was expansive rather than wholly limited by brute animal existence (a characteristic which Marx was later to see as vital in distinguishing humanity). However, even if expansive, the language was still casual, mutable and tied to immediate convenience. It had none of the surplus value which was the mark of the language of education and leisure.

Such prejudices along the lines of social class produced extraordinary forms of illogicality. Walker, for example, argued that the vulgar make mistakes in language, but that 'by a vernacular instinct as it may be called, may frequently glide into the easiest and most suitable sound' (he has in mind the metathesis ask>ax, which had been the literary form until around 1600). However, he points out, 'it would be high treason in language to follow them'; for 'as it will ever be more reputable to err with the learned, than to be right with the vulgar' (Walker 1774: 11), then the 'correct' pronunciation must be discarded in favour of the form belonging to the prestige group. This particular form of monoglossia was not founded upon reason or truth, but on perceptions of truth underpinned by power.

If the working classes and their language were ridiculed and excluded, then the pronunciation and vocabulary of 'provincials' fared little better. Drawing a contrast with France, Spain and Italy, Sheridan noted that the linguistic situation in Britain was such that the British were considered to be barbarians by dint of the fact that they neglected their speech. 'Barbarian' in Greek, as noted earlier, was originally used to refer to those who did not speak a pure form of the language, but uttered instead rough animalesque sounds such as 'bar-bar'. Applying this model to contemporary Britain, Sheridan specifies 'provincials' as latter-day barbarians:

By Provincials is here meant all British Subjects, whether inhabitants of Scotland, Ireland, Wales, the several counties of England, or the city of London, who speak a corrupt dialect of the English tongue.

(Sheridan 1762: 2)

The 'language properly so called' had been defined by Campbell as that used by the 'upper and middle ranks, over the whole British Empire' (Campbell 1776: I, 353). In fact it was usually taken to be the language of the members of those classes resident in the capital. Bayly simply took it as axiomatic that the metropolis was to offer the model of the best language: 'a language is looked upon to be spoken the purest in and near the capital, as London, Rome, Athens, Jerusalem' (Bayly 1772: 6). This assertion was generally accepted, as was the claim that the further away from London, the greater the possibility that speech would be subject to what Sheridan calls 'a provincial or vicious pronunciation' (Sheridan 1762: 30). Interestingly, this was not a danger which was restricted solely to the working classes. Even the gentry were subject to the danger:

> there are few gentlemen of England who have received their education at country schools, that are not infected with a false pronunciation of certain words, peculiar to each county. . . .. And surely every gentleman will think it worth while, to take some pains, to get rid of such evident marks of rusticity.
>
> (ibid.: 33)

Characteristic errors of provincial speech, listed by almost all the elocution masters, are such as these: swopping *v* for *w* and *w* for *v* (later used by Dickens in his figuration of Cockney speech). Changing *o* in final position to *er*, Sheridan cites the cockney pronunciation of 'fellow, bellow, hollow, follow and window' as 'feller, beller, holler, foller, and winder'. And finally, and ubiquitously, the omission of the aspirate. On this point Sheridan asked:

> If any one were to pronounce the following sentence, Hail ye high ministers of Heaven! how happy are we in hearing these your heavenly tydings! without an aspirate thus – Ail ye igh ministers of eaven! ow appy are we in earing these your eavenly tydings! who does not see that the whole expression of triumph and exultation would be lost?
>
> (ibid.: 35)

Significantly, all these examples are cited as mistakes in working-class speech, since although the gentry were susceptible to error, Sheridan argues that, unlike working-class speech, the gentry's mistakes are not structural. Amongst the gentry he writes, 'there does not seem to be any general error of this sort; their deviations being for the most part, only in certain words' (ibid.: 34). Provincialisms, though a danger to everyone not educated and socialised amongst the upper and middle ranks of the metropolis, were somehow more likely to affect the working class.

Buchanan reinforces this crossing of provinciality with class when writing of the differences between north and south Britain. He argues:

> The manner of accenting, 'tis true, is pretty uniform amongst the learned and polite part of the nation; but the pronunciation of a great

many, and especially of the illiterate, is in most parts woefully grating and discordant.

(Buchanan 1757: xii)

His work is interesting in that it prefigures debates in English education which were to become sharply significant in the late nineteenth and early twentieth centuries, and whose importance continues. His position is that English children should be taught the *vera pronunciatio* of the English language:

> It ought to be indispensably, the care of every teacher of English, not to suffer to pronounce according to the dialect of that place of the country where they were born or reside, if it happens to be vicious. For if they be suffered to proceed in, and be habituated to an uncouth pronunciation in their youth, it will most likely remain with them all their days.

(ibid.: xii)

This is almost word-for-word identical to assertions made in the enormously influential Newbolt report on the teaching of English some 160 years later. The patterns of social and linguistic relations set down in the eighteenth century were to prove very durable; this monoglossia put up an important and active resistance to various forms of heteroglot attack.

Buchanan's work even produces an example which foreshadows *Pygmalion*, Shaw's play which centres upon the relations between language and class in late nineteenth-century England; a play which in a sense can only be written as a result of the war of competing forces within discourse which began in the eighteenth century. Buchanan's child is Eliza Doolittle's great grandmother:

> I had a child lately under my care, of about nine years of age, whose speech from the beginning was unintelligible to all, but those who were acquainted with the manner of her expression. After I had taught her the sounds of the consonants, and the proper motions that were formed by these consonants both in her own, and by looking at my mouth, I brought her by a few lessons to pronounce any word whatsoever. And by a short practice, she spoke with perfect elocution.

(ibid.: xii)

CONCLUSION

In our first case study then we have demonstrated the varying roles of language in the history of Britain in the eighteenth century. The English language became not only the vehicle of the nation's history at this time, it also became the guarantor of the nation's identity. Both were figured variously as heroic or crisis-ridden, depending upon the political viewpoint taken. Yet the language was to have other significant roles. For it became the crucial site of the construction of both gender and class identities. Thus what we can see in this history is the emergence of patterns of linguistic hierarchy with which there are still difficulties. The banishment of heteroglossia depicted in these pages, with the correlative production of a rigid form of monoglossia, was a process which was to have long and continuing effects.

Chapter 4

Forging the nation

Language and cultural nationalism in nineteenth-century Ireland

'CULTURE. *See* LANGUAGE.'
(*Bunreacht Na hÉireann (Constitution of Ireland)* 1937: Treoir/Index)

GATHERING THE THREADS OF THE WEB

If eighteenth-century Britain was fascinated by language, then nine-teenth-century Ireland was similarly concerned with languages: the English and the Irish. The fascination was a complex one, replete with irony and contradiction. The leader of the largest mass political nationalist movement of nineteenth-century Ireland, O'Connell, a Gaelic-speaking Catholic, was not particularly perturbed by the pro-spect of the death of the Irish language. The two major figures in the language- revival movement, Davis and Hyde, on the other hand, were English-speaking Protestants. Likewise, in the early part of the century, the Irish language was taught by Protestant societies set up for the dissemination of the Scriptures. The Catholic hierarchy, at least until the influence of McHale in the mid-century, actively discouraged the learning of Irish. Their flock, the overwhelming majority of the Irish population, voted with their feet and learned English. At the beginning of the century then the rush was to learn English; at the end Irish was the order of the day. The best-selling work popularising the learning of the language, O'Growney's *Simple Lessons in Irish* (1910), was praised for teaching it 'in homeopathic doses'.

Irish was described as 'Adam's language', the pre-Babel language spoken in Eden, the purest of all languages. One writer claimed that the *Iliad* (translated into Irish in 1844), had originally been written in Irish and then translated into Greek. Another asserted that Buddhism was native to Ireland, from whence it had been exported to Asia before finding its way home again. English was taken to be the language of material commerce, Irish the language of the heart; or, English was the language of civilisation, Irish the language of barbarous 'superstition' (Catholicism). The first modern play in the Irish language, *Casadh an tSugáin* (*The Twisting of the Rope*) (1901), was written by Hyde at the end of the period. And Yeats argued for a Gaelic Ireland (though he left the trouble of learning the language to others). Pearse, not particularly impressed with this gesture, described Yeats as 'a mere English poet of the third or fourth rank, and as such he is harmless' (*An Claidheamh Soluis* 1899–1901: I, 157). Hyde's Gaelic poetry, on the other hand, was compared favourably by Pearse with that of Horace. Thousands, including Joyce, attended Gaelic classes; though few seem to have learned much. And the revival was also responsible for some awful poetry, such as that of the following acrostic:

> *Plea for the Mother Tongue*
> Do justice to Irish, and give it a chance
> On its own native soil, as the French has in France;
> No honey so sweet as it drops from the leaf
> Or so thrilling a sound for the bard and the chief.
> The gift of our fathers from sire to son
> Despite the proud Saxon, his steel and his gun.
> Erin's St Patrick through it spread the good news,
> Securing salvation for men if they choose.
> Proud Brian in Gaelic charged his brave men,
> And smote the barbarian on Chran Tairb fen.
> Ireland shall weep if this tongue you don't cherish
> Repeal the disgrace which is yours if it perish.
>
> (Nolan 1877: i)

The complex historical relations between these two languages, and the cultures for which they stood as ciphers in this period, will form the focus of this chapter. In Britain, as we have seen, there had emerged a monoglossic form of the English language, which was strictly constructed and patrolled in terms of both gender and class. In Ireland, on the other hand, the situation can be thought of as polyglossic. Though in fact even this is a simplification, since there was, within both of the main languages, a great deal of regional and class-based difference. The principal feature of the linguistic situation which all commentators note, however, was the competition between the English and Irish languages, a conflict which had arisen out of a long history of colonial struggle. From the Anglo-Norman invasion of 1169 onwards, the Gaelic language of the indigenous inhabitants of Ireland was at odds with the language of the invaders. It had been an enduring, violent and bitter struggle between differing forms of social organisation, cultures, economies and of course languages. For if England in this period had achieved the status of becoming the first nation-state, then Ireland's fate was to be its first colony. And as the English language gradually became a major vernacular language in its own right, in which there was constructed an important literary tradition, the Irish language and its speakers were subject to restriction, punishment and proscription. The language had to suffer not only external attacks launched by the invading culture but the even worse fate of coming to be resented by its native speakers. In order to examine the complexities of the polyglot situation of the nineteenth century then, along with their cultural and political consequences, we need first to give a brief sketch of the fortunes of the language after the first Anglo-Norman invasion.

With the expansion of the conquest throughout the island, there came in time the establishment of Norman French, and later English, as the language of law and government. The nature of the conquest, however, was such that the invaders, known as the 'old English', were assimilated to the native culture. The process of assimilation, which took place primarily at the level of culture and language, though gradual, clearly came to represent a threat to colonial rule. And indeed, outside the area of 'the pale', the area of English writ and jurisdiction which encircled Dublin, Gaelic culture in general followed its traditional patterns. Hence the phrase 'beyond the pale', indicating that which is beyond acceptability or decent constraint. This threat, constituted by 'the wyld Irish', as Boorde later described them in 1547, was met with the measures known as the Statutes of Kilkenny (1366). Assimilation, it was held, put at risk the whole political and cultural legacy of the colonial settlement:

> the said land, and the liege people thereof, the English language, the alliegance due to our lord the king, and the English laws there, are put in subjection and decayed, and the Irish enemies exalted and raised up, contrary to reason.
>
> (Irish Archaeological Society 1842: 6–7)

The threat was countered by harsh measures:

> it is ordained to be established, that every Englishman do use the English language, and be named by an English name, leaving off entirely the manner of naming used by the Irish; and that every Englishman use the English custom, fashion, mode of riding and apparel, according to his estate; and if any English, or Irish living amongst the English, use the Irish language amongst themselves, contrary to this ordinance, and thereof be attainted, his lands and tenements, if he have any, shall be seized into the hands of his immediate lord, until he come to one of the places of our lord the King, and find sufficient surety to adopt and use the English language, then he shall have restitution of his said lands, by writ issued out of said places.
>
> (ibid.: 11–13)

In a sense the statutes offer a blueprint, and one which was to be realised many times, of cultural colonialism. By the time of Tudor rule in Ireland it had become so familiar as to sound, in Spenser's words, almost commonsensical: 'It hath ever been the use of the conquerors to despise the language of the conquered, and to force him by all means to use his' (Spenser 1949: 118–19). 'The speech being Irish', he warned, 'the heart must needs be Irish.'

The eradication of Irish sentiments by way of the destruction of the Irish language was a policy actively pursued by the Tudors and their descendants. A peace treaty between the MacGilpatrick's and Henry VIII, for example, stipulated the following as one of its conditions:

> Item, the said MacGilpatrick, his heirs and assigns, and every other the inhabiters of such lands as it shall please the king's majesty to give unto him, shall use the English habits and manner, and to their knowledge, the English language, and they, and every of them, shall, to their power, bring up their children after the English manner and the use of the English tongue.
>
> (Jackson 1973: 22)

This was so effective that the 'flight of the earls', the fleeing of the Gaelic chieftains after their disastrous defeat at the battle of Kinsale in 1601, is often taken by nationalist historians as signalling the end of Gaelic Ireland. In fact, however, this did not mark the end either of Irish resistance to colonial rule or of the use of the Irish language by the indigenous population. Both of these processes were hastened, though, by the onset of the Ulster plantation.

The plantation of the 'new English', resisted by native revolt in both the Cromwellian and Williamite periods, was consolidated by the victory of William of Orange over James II at the battle of the Boyne in 1690. This date, a crucial one in all the differing forms of Irish historical consciousness, marked the real beginning of the end for Gaelic Ireland, the gradual historical process which was to produce what one writer has called 'the great silence' (De Fréine 1965). Again, as with the Statutes of Kilkenny, the process took legal form. The Penal Code, a set of laws upon which Protestant ascendancy rested, were enacted between 1695 and 1728, and ranged from restrictions on the rights of Catholics to bear arms, to own property, to marry, and to seek education abroad, up to the deprivation of the franchise in parliamentary elections. In short it was a systematic attempt to deprive Catholics of the rights enjoyed by their Protestant neighbours. It did not directly prescribe measures against the Irish language, but then it did not need to, for what it set in place, a Protestant ascendancy in which cultural, political and economic life was conducted in the English language, was sufficient to guarantee that Irish became seen as the language of the excluded, the powerless, those 'beyond the pale'. The practice by which the English language became the only 'linguistic capital' worth having, to use Bourdieu's phrase, was a gradual but nonetheless insistent one. It culminated in Irish-speaking parents teaching their children to be ashamed of their language, and seeking education for them in English. Thus it was that Irish became the language of backwardness and poverty, English the language of progress and modernity.

The prevailing Anglo-Irish attitudes to the Irish language in the eighteenth century were summed up by Swift:

> I am deceived if anything has more contributed to prevent the Irish from being tamed than the encouragement of their language, which might easily be abolished and become a dead one, with little expense and trouble.
>
> (Swift 1957: 280)

The abolition of the language, for Swift, would bring about the rupture of what was later to be called by Joyce the nets of the Irish language, Irish nationality, and the Catholic religion, the existence of which Swift abhorred in the native population: 'This would in large measure civilise the most barbarous among them, reconcile them to our customs, and reduce great numbers to the national religion' (Swift 1971: 89). Yet not all of the literary intellectuals of eighteenth-century Britain felt this way. Johnson, for example, wrote sympathetically of the decay of the language:

> I am not very willing that any language should be totally extinguished. The similitude and derivation of languages afford the most indubitable proof of the traduction of nations and the genealogy of mankind. They often add physical certainty to historical evidence; and often supply the only evidence of ancient emigrations, and of the revolutions of ages, which left no written documents behind them.
>
> (Johnson 1806: XV, 162–7)

In fact, despite the Anglo-Irish contempt for the language, and its growing disuse in the eighteenth century, or perhaps even because of these factors, some of the earliest examples of the modern study of the language began to appear in this period. They were, as Molloy notes in *De prosodia Hibernica* (1677), the first attempts at 'gathering up the threads of that web which was so violently, so savagely torn apart in the seventeenth century' (Molloy 1908: vii). Such works, which pre-date the great Celtic revival of the latter part of the eighteenth century, were important in that they laid down patterns and lines of argument which were to re-appear constantly in the discourses of language and nation in Ireland.

Begly and Mac Curtin, in their *English–Irish Dictionary* (1732), note Irish complaints

> in regard to the injury done to their language, which, without being understood, has been hitherto cryed down and ridiculed by the English in general, and even by some Gentlemen in particular, whose fine sense and good manners in other respects deserved Praise and Imitation.
>
> (Begly and Mac Curtin 1732: i)

Begly's response to attacks such as that made by Swift was an ingenious one and takes the form of a claim that the Irish language was originally excellent, has remained so despite its troubles and could be even better. Asserting that no language is 'more copious and elegant in the Expression, nor is any more harmonious and musical in the Pronunciation than the IRISH', he points out nevertheless that the language, along with the country's fortunes, has been in a state of decline for the past five hundred years. He contrasts this with the fortunes of the modern vernaculars which, he writes, 'have been polishing and refining all that long series of time'. His conclusion draws advantage from adversity:

> This is a Circumstance in favour of the IRISH which no other national language can pretend to; and shews that a Language which was so polite, when the ENGLISH Arms first put a stop to the Progress of it, would have been much more so than at present, had it the like Opportunities of Improvement that the others have met with. Nevertheless, as it is, it will be found inferior to none.
>
> (ibid.)

The confidence of Begly's defence of Irish, though rare at the time, was to become a commonplace later as a major element not only in strategies of defence but in ploys of attack too. It foreshadows many of the later comparisons made between the English and Irish languages.

Many of the early works were, perforce, composed outside Ireland, usually at Irish colleges based in centres of learning in Catholic Europe. There were twenty such institutions established in the period between 1590 and 1690; Molloy's text was published in Rome, that of Begly and Mac Curtin in Paris. The influence of these colleges in the preservation of an Irish culture which was seriously threatened was significant. And although there was other antiquarian work undertaken at the time (Lhuyd's *Archaeologica Britannica* of 1707 for example, in which an Irish–English dictionary was included), the work of the exiled priests was of particular importance.

The significance of the early texts was that they voiced concerns and pointed to areas of interest which later writers took as axiomatic. Molloy posits the historically accurate existence of a 'web' of language and culture which had been systematically attacked in the seventeenth century. Other writers indicated the historical necessity of the study of Irish for the Irish nation. Mac Curtin, for example, jailed for a year in Newgate for his defence of the antiquity of Irish civilisation, appealed to the gentry and nobility for their interest. He writes in *The Elements of the Irish Language*:

> It is certain, most of our Nobility and gentry have abandoned it, and disdain'd to Learn our Speech the same these two hundred years past. And I could heartily wish, such persons would look back and reflect on this matter; that they might see through the glass of their own reason, how strange it seems to the world, that any people should scorn the Language, wherein the whole treasure of their own Antiquity and profound Sciences lie in obscurity, so highly Esteemed by al [*sic*] Lovers of Knowledge in former Ages.
>
> (Mac Curtin 1728: Preface)

The most interesting point of his appeal for the study of Irish here is its basis. For he takes it as axiomatic that the language is the key to the history. This crucial point, which is evidence of the growing awareness of the significance of the historicity of language in the period, is repeated by Donlevy in his Irish catechism:

> there is still extant a great Number of old valuable Irish manuscripts both in public and private hands, which would, if translated and published, give great insight into the Antiquities of the Country, and furnish some able Pen with materials enough, to write a compleat History of the *Kingdom*: what a Discredit then must it be to the whole *Nation*, to let such a Language go to wrack.
>
> (Donlevy 1742: 507)

John Free, an anti-Catholic propagandist, asserts the same point in his *Essay Towards an History of the English Tongue*. Writing on 'the SCOTS from *Ireland*; and the *Extent* of the *Erst* Language', he claims: 'I think much may be gathered concerning the *original Antiquities* of a *People*, where their HISTORY is *dark* and *obscure*, by considering the *Nature* of their *LANGUAGE*' (Free 1749: 71).

Broadening the point, Archbishop O'Brien argued in his *Irish–English Dictionary* (1768), that the Irish language could help to clarify British history since

> the Guidhelians or old *Irish*, had been the primitive inhabitants of Great *Britain* before the ancestors of the *Welsh* arrived in that island, and that the Celtic Dialect of those Guidhelians, was then the universal language of the whole British isle.
>
> (O'Brien 1768: i)

The works of both O'Brien and Free take us to the edge of the Celtic revival, but before we pass on to that we can note another point of focus marked out by one of these early scholars of Irish. For along with the stress on the language being the key to the history, there are other points which will recur in later debates. Two such are made by Donlevy as he writes of the English language in Ireland. He asserts that it has 'suffered vast Alterations and Corruptions; and be now on the Brink of utter Decay, as it really is, to the great Dishonour and Shame of the *Natives*, who shall pass everywhere for *Irish-men*'. He then adds as a rejoinder: 'Although *Irishmen* without *Irish* is an Incongruity, and a great Bull. Besides, the *Irish Language* is undeniably a very Ancient *Mother Language*, and one of the smoothest in Europe' (Donlevy 1742: 506). The assertion that an '*Irishman* without *Irish* is an incongruity' is one which could perfectly fit into the nationalist pamphlets of the Gaelic League, some 150 years later. And the claim that Irish is a '*Mother Language*', that is, not compounded and therefore pure, is one which was to bear a great deal of weight in the debates which occurred in the period of the Gaelic revival.

In this section we have traced briefly the historical emergence of a polyglot situation in Ireland in which Irish was positioned as an inferior and subjugated language. This process occurred as a result of the practices of political and cultural colonialism. We have also noted, however, the appearance of a formal interest in the language which was set against the prevailing tide of history. That interest spawned important topics of concern which were to appear later during the period in which the task of 'gathering the threads of the web' which had been rent, became that of sewing together the cords of the nets of language, nationality and religion. It is to the beginning of that task that we now turn.

A LANGUAGE NEAR AS OLD AS THE DELUGE

The Celtic revival was both a local and a European phenomenon. Stimulated by earlier antiquarian work and the Ossian forgeries of the 1760s, it was aided in no small part by the wide-ranging vision of Romanticism allied to the particular importance afforded to all languages by the new science of comparative philology. No longer did the classical languages dominate at the expense of all others; for what both comparative philology and Romantic philosophy argued was the specificity and consequent value of all languages and cultures, no matter how regional or local. Moving from the turn to the East and the discovery of the significance of Sanskrit, to the turn to the North marked by Bishop Percy's *Northern Antiquities*, this new intellectual interest was characterised by a search for linguistic or cultural authenticity, which was usually realised in the discovery of antiquity. In Ireland, the revival's beginning is marked by Conor's *Dissertations on the Ancient History of Ireland* (1753), O'Brien's *Irish–English Dictionary* (1768), the various works of Vallancey, and the publication of Charlotte Brooke's *Reliques of Irish Poetry* (1789).

One of the most striking and durable characteristics of the early revival is precisely this search for the old. For there, in antiquity, was to be found the essence of identity, whether of nation, people, culture or language. The most antique: the most authentic; this was an equation which was to have deep effects in fields as apparently diverse as theology and archaeology, geology and politics. By a curious paradox at the heart of this logic, it was proof of antiquity that was to engender revolution, the old that was to justify the new. For the test of age was to upset all sorts of chronologies and the hierarchies which accompanied them. If a language could be shown to be older than another, then the logic of this pattern was that the primary language in some sense must be purer, or more authentic. It was of course a theory of origins which was based on the scarcely veiled Christian principle that there was an original language which was disrupted.

The early Celtic revival in Ireland was marked by precisely this search for antiquity, and the results were hugely significant. Vallancey, a correspondent of Burke and William Jones, was the leader in a field which was to produce a number of extraordinary claims. Sweeping away the familiar chronology of Western European history, Vallancey asserted in 1786 that 'the very ancient language of Ireland . . . [was a] language replete and full, before the Greeks and Romans had a name' (Vallancey 1786: 170). It was this belief that led a later commentator to argue that the *Iliad* had been composed in Irish and later translated into Greek (MacHale 1844: 4). Following on from this, Vallancey later posited the affinity of Irish with 'Sanscrit, Hindoostannee, and Egyptian' [*sic*] (Vallancey 1804: xxiii); and on various occasions he classified Irish with the 'Punic language of the Carthaginians' (Vallancey 1772: vii). Such beliefs had important historical and cultural implications, particularly if it were true that the ancient Irish 'must have been a colony from Asia, because nine words in ten are pure Chaldic and Arabic' (Vallancey 1802: 14); or that '*druidism* was not the established religion of the pagan Irish, but *Budhism* [*sic*]' (Vallancey 1812: 56).

What is important about these assertions, however, is not their truth-status, but the motivation which lay behind them. For what we see here is an attempt to validate a language, and by corollary a culture, by way of an appeal to history. To be able to show that Irish pre-dated the great imperial languages of Greece and Rome, and that it was related to the ancient religious languages of Sanskrit, Hindi and Hebrew, was to accord it a tremendous importance. Antiquity signified credibility; let other languages match it. Such validity and significance were of course crucial to a culture and nation struggling to promote both its internal unity and its external difference from its larger and more powerful neighbour. The British Empire might have precedence in terms of brute economic and military power, but Ireland could at least claim priority in terms of its culture and history.

The moment of cultural origins is crucial for any national movement, since its citation is always an act of self-validation. Within the specific limits of a Christian account then, and pushing at the borders of that narrative, the language which can position itself as closest to the original language, that of Eden, is in the strongest position. History and all its misfortunes may have occurred subsequently, but that moment of historical origination, attested by the language, must attract respect, if not outright approval. It is no surprise therefore that this rhetorical move is deployed. O'Conor is one of the first to make this claim, arguing that Irish is a language 'near as old as the deluge' (O'Conor 1753: xi). Vallancey, picking up the theme deduces that 'from its affinity with almost every language of the known world, we might conclude with Boullet, that it was the primeval language' (Vallancey 1782: 5). More specifically, he claims that

> the language of Japhet and his descendants was the universal tongue; it is most wonderfully preserved in the Irish, and with the assistance of this language, the historian will be enabled to unfold the origin of people, and the settlement of colonies in the various parts of the old world.
>
> (Vallancey 1786: 166)

This was a theme, perhaps the ultimate appeal for legitimation available in this model, which was taken into early forms of Irish nationalist discourse. For what greater status could there be than that attached to a culture whose very language was that given to humanity by the deity? Shaw, a Scot whose work shows that the revival was not at first restricted to Ireland, claims that 'Galic' 'is the language of Japhet, spoken before the deluge, and probably the speech of paradise' (Shaw 1780: ii). The Gaelic Society (1808) reiterated his assertion word for word in support of the Irish language. And it rapidly became too important a point to be left open to dispute. Scurry described Irish as possessing 'all the marks of a primordial tongue' (Scurry 1827: 4). The language is also later described as 'Adam's language' (*An Fíor Éirionnach* 1862: 17), and Bourke notes that 'some go as far as to say *it* was the language of Adam and Eve in Paradise' (Bourke 1856: 304). Perhaps the boldest claim for Irish was made in *The Nation*:

> Its importance need not be questioned, even if we begin with the Garden of Eden – and in doing so I do not for a moment think we assume too high a position. We find the meaning of the first word that

necessarily had been spoken by the Creator to his creature pure Irish – Adam, that is *Ead, am – As yet fresh*, which was very appropriately addressed by the object he had just created in his own likeness, and hence was our first father called Adam . . .. I believe that most, if not all the names in Scripture will be found to be pure Irish, or, at least, a more satisfactory radix than any other language we know affords them, will be found in the Irish language.

(*The Nation*, 1842–5: I, 31, 491)

What we find in these protestations is an odd claim for the status of Irish as a monoglossic language. For what could be more self-assured, more self-contained, more self-identical than the original language? The language in which God and Adam had conversed. Yet this *is* a curious claim, since we have already noted that the situation in eighteenth- and nineteenth-century Ireland was not monoglossic but polyglossic; a polyglossia in which Irish was very clearly the subdued element, for as the antiquarians rushed to record and order the Irish language, the majority of those whose native language it was rushed to gain access to the English language. The answer to the puzzle posed by this strange practice was in fact very simple: material survival. The relaxation of the Penal laws in the latter half of the eighteenth century, allied to industrialisation and the growth of the towns, meant that those who were once wholly 'beyond the pale' were now allowed restricted access. The barbarians were not any longer at the gates, but at work within the walls of the citadel, and they were speaking English.

One commentator describes a rich farmer in Connemara:

Notwithstanding his large means and the comfortable position he has always occupied, this shrewd and clever old gentleman does not speak English, and rather prides himself on his ignorance of the language of the Sassenach.

(Coulter 1862: 126)

This was, however, the exception that proves the rule, as many writers testify. English was promoted through hard cash, as Young notes in his *Tour in Ireland*: 'Lord Shannon's bounties come to more than 50*l* a year. He gives them by way of encouragement; but only to such as can speak English, and do something more than fill a cart' (Young 1780: II, 51). Other writers put the matter a little more delicately. In a way which was to foreshadow what the dialectologists in England would later say of the relationship between the dialects and the standard, Anderson describes the relations which hold between the Irish and the English languages. Irish, for native speakers, he writes, 'is to them the language of social intercourse, of family communion; every feeling closely connected with moral duty is closely interwoven with that language'. English, on the other hand, is 'the language of barter, of worldly occupations; taken up solely at the market, laid aside when he returns home, a very confined vocabulary' (Anderson 1818: 54). Or, as Coneys put it more succinctly, English 'is the language of his commerce – the Irish, of his heart' (*The Nation* 1842–5: I, 5, 73).

Be that as it may, there is no doubt that English was also the language of survival and social advancement. Dewar comments of Irish parents:

> if they wish to improve their condition, or to have their sons advanced in the service of their country, they will find it necessary to have some English *book-learning* themselves, and to be at some pains to impart it to their children.
>
> (Dewar 1812: 97)

This was to become the biggest factor in the decay of the language in the nineteenth century. Orpen summarises the situation neatly in replying to the assertion that 'the Irish are more anxious to have their children educated in English' than Irish:

> Certainly they are, very anxious, that their children should know En [*sic*]: and wisely, because by it alone is profit or preferment to be acquired; and they themselves would be glad that they themselves had also learned it, for it is, in almost all cities and towns, the language of shops, markets, fairs; it is the universal language of banknotes, books, and courts of law.
>
> (Orpen 1821: 30)

The difference represented by polyglossia and heteroglossia may well be theoretically more satisfying and radical than monoglossia, but in practice the choice may be more difficult. The Irish may well have been attached to their language, but they were rather more attached to their children.

The polyglossic situation did of course produce difficulties:

> The Magistrate cannot address his subjects, the pastor his flock but by the imperfect medium of an interpreter. Lawyers, Divines, Physicians, Merchants, Manufacturers, and Farmers, all feel more or less this inconvenience when they have to do with those, with whom they have no common language.
>
> (Connellan 1814: iii)

But English was the language of power and the powerful, and it was the Irish who would have to alter. They were after all a colonised people despite, after 1801, belonging to the Union. This was a judgment of the relationship between language and power which even the major Irish politician of the century recognised. O'Connell, commonly called 'the liberator', though Duffy later claims that his nickname was 'the counsellor' (Duffy 1896: 26), conducted two political meetings in Irish, his native tongue, in 1828. Daunt recollects that 'the reporters from a London journal were ludicrously puzzled at an harangue he delivered in the ancient tongue of Erin' (Daunt 1848: 15). His reception seems to have been enough to convince him that he should elect English before Irish:

> Someone asked him whether the use of the Irish language was diminishing among our peasantry. 'Yes', he answered, 'and I am sufficiently utilitarian not to regret its gradual abandonment. A diversity of tongues is no benefit; it was first imposed on mankind as a curse, at the building of Babel. It would be of vast advantage to mankind if all the inhabitants of the earth spoke the same language. Therefore, although the Irish language is connected with many recollections that twine around the hearts of Irishmen, yet the superior utility of the English tongue, as the medium of modern communication, is so great, that I can witness without a sigh the gradual disuse of the Irish.
>
> (ibid.: 14–15)

There is no celebration of difference here in O'Connell's position, nor even any desire to hark back to the monoglossic Irish of the pre-Babelic scene. This was a lesson in the difficult questions of practice and power which many Irish people had to learn in the nineteenth century; 'you don't know the want of education till you come to travel', wrote a recent emigré to California ruefully (Coulter 1862: 327).

All these factors led to a situation in which the Irish language was treated with, at best, indifference amongst the general population. Of course there may well have been more of a sentiment for the language amongst emigrés, and there is evidence for this, particularly with regard to the United States. The New York Society for the Preservation of the Irish Language (SPIL) was set up in 1879, for example. But of Ireland in the mid-century period, the Dublin headquarters of the same society commented: 'it is well known that more Irish can be heard spoken at present in New York, London, Liverpool, or Glasgow, than in Dublin' (SPIL 1882: 16). At best then there was apathy, at worst the language became the symbol of degradation:

> The greatest danger which threatens the language, and one from which it is certain to suffer, is the prejudice entertained against it by the illiterate Irish-speaking peasant, whose phraseology it is. They fancy it is the synonym of poverty and misery, and that many of the evils from which they suffer are traceable to its continued use; that if they could dispense with it altogether, they would elevate them-

selves socially, and be so much more the respectable members of society.

(ibid.: 13–14)

The language had become for many a badge of shame. To the charge that the Irish language brought no material advantage to its speakers, SPIL put the question: 'Are the culture, the language, and the sacred traditions and usages of a people to be weighed by such materialistic and unworthy considerations as these?' (SPIL 1884: 15). For the majority of the Irish people in the nineteenth century the answer was resoundingly in the affirmative. The result, Hyde noted, was that 'what the battleaxe of the Dane, the sword of the Norman, the wile of the Saxon were unable to perform, we have accomplished ourselves' (Hyde 1986: 157).

THE MOTHER TONGUE: PURELY SUPERIOR

The majority of the Irish population then, faced with harsh political realities, turned to English as the language of modernity and progress. In opposition to this shift, however, were the defenders of the language, whose claims became ever more desperate and strident. At one and the same time the language was being abandoned by its native speakers and eulogised by its admirers. In essence these were two sides of the same coin: as it declined in practice, so the need to call for its restoration increased. In this section we will see the nature of the defence of the language, and the way in which the early calls pre-empt the later attempts to make it the national language again.

As demonstrated in the previous section, part of the early defence was to point to the antiquity of the language. Both Brooke and O'Reilly call it 'the mother tongue of all the languages of the West' (Gaelic Society of Dublin 1808: iv). However, the case for the defence did not rest solely on the historical pedigree of the language; rather, it was constructed in terms of the intrinsic qualities which it was held to possess. This in a sense was a case which was difficult to prove empirically, but for the very same reason one which was almost impossible to disprove. It was also a means of defence which was designed to appeal to its audience by dint of the fact that the language was taken to reflect the national character, a linkage which we have noted in English debates and one which also reappears later. Writing in the early nineteenth century, Haliday cites both Lhuyd and Leibniz in support of his assertion:

> The language of a people, it has been universally admitted by all literary men, is the true criterion of their limitation or advancement in civility. If harsh, grating, irregular, barren and incongruous, it is pronounced the dialectic medium of a rude and barbarous people; if harmonious, elegant, flexible, copious and expressive, it is admitted

to be the sentimental communication of a people highly cultivated in mental improvement, and consequently far advanced in civilisation. The latter character has been impressed upon the Gaelic language.

(Haliday 1808: iv)

The connection between the characteristics of a people and those of their language is a central feature of cultural nationalism. In this formulation, the language is taken to reflect directly, even to embody, the mind or, as it had been called in eighteenth-century England the 'genius', of the nation. Vallancey comments:

The Irish language is free from the anomalies, sterilities and heteroclite redundancies, which mark the dialects of barbarous nations; it is rich and melodious; it is precise and copious and affords elegant conversions which no other than a thinking and lettered people can require.

(Vallancey 1782: 3)

Later in the nineteenth century, at the beginning of the last of the revival movements, the professor of Sanskrit at Cornell takes such eulogising of the language to new heights in a letter published by the New York SPIL. The Irish, he wrote, should preserve their language since it is

so superior to the greatest number of languages spoken all around them on European soil, for its antiquity, its originality, its unmixed purity, its remarkably pleasing euphony and easy, harmonious flow, its poetical adaptation, musical nature and picturesque expressiveness; its vigorous vitality, freshness, energy and inherent power; its logical, systematic, regular and methodically constituted grammar; its philosophic structure and wonderful literary susceptibility.

(Roehrig 1884: 4)

Such praise of the language often included elements which were to become part and parcel of the national stereotype, propounded on both sides of the Irish Sea by figures as apparently diverse as Douglas Hyde and Matthew Arnold. Dewar described the 'beautifully simple' language in these terms:

It has already been remarked, that it is altogether idiomatic in its construction, or, to speak more correctly, its idioms are different from those of all the languages of Europe. It is extremely copious, especially on any subject connected with the passions; though it can scarcely be considered a good vehicle for philosophy. No tongue can better suit the purpose of the orator, whose object is to make an impression on a popular assembly, and who, regardless of precision, seeks only to accomplish his end. Hence also, it is admirably adapted to poetry.

(Dewar 1812: 87)

The idea that the language was in some way inherently characterised by a predisposition towards particular functions was a common one. Brooke held that 'the Irish language, perhaps beyond all others, is particularly suited to every subject of Elegy'. She clarified the point by arguing that 'it is scarcely possible that any language can be more adapted to lyric poetry than the Irish' (Brooke 1789: 189), adding later that there never was 'any language fitter to express the feelings of the heart' (Brooke 1795: iv). Orpen, commenting on the purity of the language, agreed on its poeticity: 'must not every language possessing all its roots in itself, as Irish does, be figurative and poetical'? (Orpen 1821: 21). Not all writers characterised the language in the same way, however, since for some the intrinsic nature of the language, and by corollary the culture, was distinguished by different features. A critical notice of Bourke's hugely successful *College Irish Grammar* (1856) described the language thus:

> It is another peculiarity of the Irish tongue that the imperative mood is invariably the root of all the ramifications of its verb. From this a philosophic mind would inevitably infer that the people who spoke this language were not intended by nature to be slaves. On the contrary, command is the foremost characteristic of the Irish. Their imperative mood is well, clearly and prominently defined. It is the first thing you learn in studying the verbs. You learn to command when learning Irish. Now this peculiarity, like the former, must originate in some cause, and this cause is assuredly in the Irish character; it can be no other, for, as a necessay consequence from the nature of the language, it harmonises to, and blends with, the nature of the people who speak it.
>
> (Bourke 1856: 402)

To speak Irish by this definition is an act of rebellion in itself, and acts as an antidote to the servility of speaking English; for, as the much-quoted Tacitus had observed, 'the language of the conqueror in the mouth of the conquered is ever the language of the slave'. Irish could answer the imperial with the imperative.

Some saw the language as poetic and emotional, passionate and rhetorical, others as independent and commanding. There was a view too, rather idiosyncratic, which saw it as a language peculiarly suited to philosophy: 'the Irish is an original tongue, and therefore better suited to convey abstract truths to the mind of the unlearn'd, than any compounded language' (Mason 1829: 14). Whatever the characteristics, it is clear from such claims that what are being asserted here are not propositions about the language alone. They are assertions which are concerned with the cultural and political identity of the Irish in an historical context in which those forms of identity were fiercely contested.

One postulated characteristic which clearly relates linguistic and national identity is that of purity. An early commentator in this respect is O'Conor, who argues that 'the nation was never thoroughly undone nor vanquished by *itself*' (O'Conor 1753: xi) and extrapolates this to the language in order to conclude that Irish is 'the *most original* and UNMIXT Language yet remaining in any Part of *Europe*' (ibid.: 37). O'Reilly describes Irish as 'by far the best preserved from the changes and corruptions incident to other languages' (O'Reilly 1808: iii); and Thomas explicitly compares it in this respect to English:

> What, shall a language confessedly derived from one of the first tongues which subsisted among polished nations, be abolished, merely to make room for another compounded of all the barbarous dialects which imperfectly communicated the thoughts of savages to each other?
>
> (Thomas 1787: 23)

The concept of the purity of the language is evidently related to claims for its antiquity. But the significance of this concept is only comprehensible when viewed in the context of the cultural nationalism beginning to be engendered by the works of the post-Kantian German Romantics. Such works had a direct effect on the thought of the Young Ireland movement of the 1840s, as demonstrated by O'Neill (1976), and we will consider this later in the chapter. However, it is the concept of linguistic purity and its significance that concerns us here.

It is axiomatic for one of the central thinkers in this field, Fichte, that a language influences the history of its speakers:

> What an immeasurable influence on the whole human development of a people the character of its language may have – its language, which accompanies the individual into the most secret depths of his mind in thought and will and either hinders him or gives him wings, which unites within its whole domain the whole mass of men who speak it into one single and common understanding, which is the true point for meaning and mingling for the world of the senses and the world of spirits.
>
> (Fichte 1968: 59)

The importance of Fichte for the Irish debates, however, is his specific stress on the purity of 'original' languages as guarantors of the essence of nationality. His example demonstrates the significance of the concept in his distinction between 'the Germans and the other peoples of Teutonic descent'. The former, he writes,

> remained in the original dwelling places of the ancestral stock; whereas the latter emigrated to other places; the former retained

and developed the original language of the ancestral stock, whereas the latter adopted a foreign language and gradually reshaped it in a way of their own.

(ibid.: 47)

The continuation of the speaking of the 'original' language becomes the touchstone of purity and authenticity, for 'men are formed by language far more than language is formed by men'. And once the 'original' language has been replaced by a foreign language the change is fundamental and irreversible. This identification of a necessary interrelation of language, land and home was to have great significance, as we shall see later.

The desperation of the calls for the acknowledgment of the superiority of the Irish language, allied to the stridency of the appeals for recognition of its antiquity and unmixed purity are understandable within a specific historical context: that is, the conjunction of the emergence of cultural nationalist thought with the drift to the English language of the majority of Irish speakers. We have noted the coupling of language and nation earlier, but its full philosophical exposition, and consequent political effects, are not felt in Europe until the early to mid-nineteenth century. We shall return to these effects later in the chapter.

REVELATION OR REVOLUTION?

The Irish language then, praised by some, increasingly abandoned by most, was situated in a precarious position. The drift to English was rapidly becoming a rush as the language came more and more to signify poverty. In this context, however, there was one body of opinion, at first sight the least likely, which argued forcefully for the teaching of literacy in Irish. The activities of that group, and their reasons for undertaking them, form the focus of this section.

In 1571, Sir Henry Sidney, one of Elizabeth's most successful colonial servants, wrote to the sovereign in relation to the health of the Church of Ireland. Noting that many parishes had fallen into a state of neglect, Sidney proposes that the queen appoint ministers to fill the vacant posts. He continues:

it is most necessary that such be chosen as can speak Irish, for which search would be made first, and speedily, in your own universities; and any found there well affected in religion, and well conditioned beside, they would be sent hither animated by your majesty; yea, though it were somewhat to your highness' charge; and on peril of my life, you shall find it returned with gain, before three years be expired . . . and though for a while your majesty were at some charge, it were well bestowed, for, in short time, thousands would be gained to Christ, that now are lost, or left at the worst.

(Dewar 1812: 132–3)

Elizabeth responded by sending a printing-press, the political potential of which was enormous, as Anderson (1983) has demonstrated. And the first consequences were encouraging: a catechism and primer were printed with the type, and William Daniel began work on a translation of the New Testament. It appeared in 1602, and his version of the Book of Common Prayer was published in 1608. Following this, Bedell, the provost of Trinity College Dublin, attempted a translation of the entire Bible, though he was opposed in this scheme by the more powerful Ussher, archbishop of Armagh. Bedell's Bible was eventually published by Robert Boyle, the Irish scientist, in 1686, and later again by the British and Foreign Bible Society in 1817. Despite these promising beginnings, and occasional flourishes of interest during the eighteenth century, however, the project did not fulfil its potential. Indeed the distinct lack of interest which is characteristic of attitudes towards the Irish language in general in this period is also specifically true of attitudes to the teaching of the language for religious purposes. In the early nineteenth century this situation was altered dramatically by the appearance of proselytising evangelicals, particularly Baptists and Presbyterians. The relationship between print, the vernacular, and the Protestant religion, of which we have noted the importance in English national self-fashioning, had been placed on the agenda in Ireland.

Dedicating his New Testament to King James I, Daniel notes a link between religion and politics: 'the quietness and peace of kingdoms (most gracious sovereign) consisteth chiefly in the planting of true religion, as both examples of the Word and World do prove abundantly' (Daniel 1602: i). The security of the state was held to be bound up with the spread of Protestantism, and it was held that rulers who ignored this maxim were endangering their authority. Yet for the most part in the seventeenth and eighteenth centuries this was precisely what happened. The rulers of Ireland, consolidating their authority by other means, neglected the task of converting their subjects by preaching to them in Irish and translating the Bible. If they had undertaken this task, Dewar later notes, it might have happened that 'the majority of the people would, at this day, have been virtuous, industrious, and enlightened protestants' (Dewar 1812: 112). As it was, the majority of the Irish people were Irish-speaking and suffered from, as one evangelical put it, 'the disease of popery' (Foley 1849: 7).

If the task had been neglected for almost two centuries, it was taken up in the late eighteenth and early nineteenth centuries with enormous zeal. Proselytising societies sprang up numerously, including the Hibernian

Bible Society, the London Hibernian Society, the Baptist Society and, most important of all, in 1808, the Irish Society. What was the reason for the appearance of these societies, and why did the transmission of the true Protestant word become so urgent? Stokes, writing in 1799, gives one answer:

> For the diffusion of religious knowledge it is necessary, that it should be conveyed in the language the people understand . . . . One of the fundamental principles of the reformation was, that every person should address his Maker, and read His word, in his native tongue; yet this was neglected in Ireland, with a view of making the English language universal; but it is easier to alter the religion of a people than their language.
>
> (Stokes 1799: 45)

The central Protestant tenet was that individuals should be able to read the Bible for themselves, and this had as its logical corollary the argument that the Bible should be translated. It is this that Stokes cites in support of teaching literacy in the vernacular to the Irish. And of course it was for this very reason too that the Catholic hierarchy opposed the teaching of Irish in the early nineteenth century. Catholic priests urged their flocks to learn English on the basic assumption that they needed it to survive in Ireland, Britain or America. But the hierarchy was opposed to the teaching of the Irish language for the purposes of biblical study on the grounds that it fitted uneasily into a model of Protestant individualism. Catholic clerical appeals for the translation of the Bible did not appear in any serious way until the appearance in the mid-century of the work of John MacHale, archbishop of Tuam, and important revivalist. The attitude of the hierarchy is signalled by the work of the Catholic Book Society for the Diffusion of Useful Knowledge Throughout Ireland, as specified in its first report. The society published 43,000 catechisms, and 10,000 copies of 'The Grounds of Catholic Doctrine'; all were in English, and the language question was not mentioned.

The spreading of Protestantism then was evidently the priority, and this entailed the recruitment of Irish-speaking ministers. By the end of the eighteenth century it was already clear that this was causing problems. Thomas cites a writer who

> considers as great impediments to the further advancement of the established religion, first, the immoderate extent of the parishes, secondly, the want of churches, fourthly [sic] the ignorance of the language under which the clergyman generally labours.
>
> (Thomas 1787: 22)

The Reverend W. Neilson, in a book dedicated to the earl of Hardwick, the Lord Lieutenant General and General Governor of Ireland, asserted that it is 'particularly, from the *absolute necessity* of understanding this language, in order to converse with the natives of a great part of Ireland, that the study of it is indispensable' (Neilson 1808: ix). The call was out: Irish-speaking ministers in Protestant churches in order to convert the peasantry.

There were other reasons, however, for the urgency of the appeals for the teaching of Protestantism in the vernacular language, as Daniel had noted in the early seventeenth century. Thomas's text in favour of preaching in Irish was also partly concerned with 'the Grievances Under which the Peasantry of Ireland Labours', and was set in the immediate context of 'the late insurrection of Munster' (Thomas 1787: title). Stokes's appeal 'for the diffusion of religious knowledge' in Irish, was composed just after the rising of 1798, the 'civil war' as he describes it, and was entitled *Projects for re-Establishing The Internal Peace and Tranquility of Ireland*. What lay behind these calls for proselytising in the vernacular then was not simply the desire to convert and save souls but the wish to construct a social order. And the key to the project was education. The British people, wrote Taylor (meaning the British ruling class), had discovered the importance of teaching in Irish. In a text entitled *Reasons for Giving Moral Instruction to the Native Irish Through the Medium of Their Language*, he asserts,

> they now perceive it is a *mental* authority which must mould the heart of Ireland in conformation to Irish sentiment, and the interests of a united empire; and they have discovered that the great instrument of this must be EDUCATION.
>
> (Taylor 1817: 8)

Noting that in former times the Irish had been treated 'as connected with an inferior order of beings; viewed merely in the same light as W. Indian slaves' (Dewar 1812: 107), and comparing the fate of Ireland to that of Africa as suffering in a state of 'perpetual war' (ibid.: 120–1), Dewar noted that it was understandable that the Irish should be barbarous and resentful. There was, however, education, the means by which they could be brought to the level of humanity, a way in which it would be possible 'to make the Irish people become the best of all subjects' (ibid.: 63). Education, and specifically a national system of education, 'since it is necessarily subservient to the advancement of order, virtue, and happiness' (ibid.: 73), was the order of the day. For, as Connellan put it, by means of education, the Irish peasantry would avail itself of invaluable social benefits: 'obedience to the laws, good order, mildness, sobriety, industry, cleanliness, mechanical improvements, wealth and happiness' (Connellan 1824: vi).

Education, and in particular literacy in Irish, were the means by which the 'wyld Irish' could be civilised and thus brought in from beyond the pale. Literacy, however, had to be handled carefully, since its revolutionary potential was historically evident. It had of course been one of the prerequisites of the Protestant revolution. And this was a problem which the proselytisers could not answer, except in ways which effectively ducked the question. Anderson argued:

> The great object, it should be recollected, of teaching the reading of Irish &c, is not to make those who are to be the subjects of that instruction a learned, or what may be called a reading people, or to convey to them, through the medium of that language any general knowledge; but almost exclusively to bring them acquainted with the great principles of morality, founded upon the important truths and doctrines of Christianity; and for this purpose the Bible itself, with some few elementary books will amply suffice.
>
> (Anderson 1818: 59)

Orpen explicitly cites the objection which opponents of the education of Irish speakers used to support their case:

> Teaching Irish will excite disaffection to the King, and disincline to English connection; it will impede the amalgamation of the two classes in this country, those who speak Irish, and those who speak English.
>
> (Orpen 1821: 45)

He answers: 'it is not for teaching of Irish that I plead, but for instructing those who know it, to read the Bible in Irish' (ibid.).

Arguing the same line, Dewar asserted confidently: 'the truth is, reading is the chief security of the poor against moral, political and religious error' (Dewar 1812: 71). The problem was that this was a belief which could not be guaranteed to be correct. The difficulty is summarised by this conundrum: how can people be given literacy, without at the same time being taught to read? Or, to put it another way, how is literacy to be promoted, whilst at the same time control is exerted over what is read? Small wonder that English radicals in the early nineteenth century argued against state education on the grounds that it would be education for the purposes of the state.

The answer to this difficulty, it was thought, was to teach literacy and religion simultaneously and thus to make them indistinguishable. 'Education and religion combined', Dewar notes, 'are not only the best, but seem to be the only adequate, means for rendering permanent the blessings of a free government, and the comforts and endearments of civilised life' (ibid.: 112). By religion of course was meant Protestantism, and the aim of such an education was made clear by Taylor when he asserted that it would make the Irish peasant sensible of the odious deformity of that gothic superstructure whose gloomy and fantastic battlements have so long thrown their shadow over his country, chilling its moral bloom, and causing its virtues to perish untimely.

(Taylor 1817: 14)

Access to literacy and the Bible would give the 'degraded Irish' 'the weapons of Christian warfare, which shall prove a deliverance and defence and safeguard against the fetters and assaults of ignorance and superstition' (Connellan 1824: iv); which is to say that the object of such an educational programme was the extirpation of Catholicism.

As noted earlier, however, the aims of this mode of education were not solely religious but often overtly political. Dewar, for example, defends the teaching of Irish at a time 'when the whole of Europe is prostrate at the foot of the tyrant'. He does so by arguing that, precisely because of the Napoleonic threat, it would be self-defeating

not to embrace every measure of uniting the people, of removing every cause of suspicion in the government, every cause of even seeming grievance in the subject, of enlightening, improving, and civilising every part of the population.

(Dewar 1812: 126)

The teaching of Irish would comprise such a measure, since it would pacify that part of the population 'which some consider dangerous to the security of the British Empire'. This would also have the happy consequence of directly saving 'money to the government by rendering the presence of an extensive military establishment unnecessary' (ibid.: 136–7).

One difficulty which was often cited was the belief that an education in Irish would encourage affection for the language and thus for an independent nation. The answer to it was ingenious. For, rather than leading to a love of Irish, it was asserted somewhat counter-intuitively that it would stimulate a desire to learn English. That is, the encouragement of polyglossia would eventually lead to a state of monoglossia, linguistically, culturally and politically. It became a commonplace to propose that 'the most likely way to promote the knowledge, and ultimately the use, of the English language, is to teach the people first their own' (Anderson 1818: iv). This apparent contradiction was explained by Connellan's argument that

with respect to the extension of the English language, it appears likely to be promoted at present by the cultivation of the Irish. This is what will open to the native student, an easy path to the first rudiments of knowledge; when those are obtained, emulation and interest will soon stimulate him to the acquisition of the English language, on which his hopes depend.

(Connellan 1814: iv)

As the same writer notes, however, the learning of English was not simply a linguistic question, for it had important social implications too:

A grammatical knowledge of Irish, as numerous examples prove, is sure to present to the Irish native a more ready and certain path to an acquaintance with the English language and the stores of English literature; and consequently, tends to promote a closer unity between the subjects of both countries, and to insure a similarity and disposition of sentiment, both as Christians and fellow citizens.

(Connellan 1824: iv)

If exposure to literacy would incline the Irish towards the English language, exposure to the Bible and Protestant teaching would complete the ideological feat and lead to ideal subjecthood, and a state of 'quietness and peace' in the kingdom.

We noted earlier how many of the texts in favour of teaching the language for the purposes of proselytising were written with direct reference to the conflictual social history in which they were set. Denying that an education in Irish was likely to encourage 'recollections of past transactions which it were better were forgotten', Anderson argued that it was intended to be eirenic rather than inflammatory:

to enable the native to read the Scriptures in his own tongue is the sole object. You thus afford him that knowledge which is most calculated to heal every irritable feeling, and to allay every animosity which such recollections may unhappily still cherish. If the only language they know has carried the poison of disaffection and disunion through every part of the system which it has visited in its circulation, let it now convey, through ramifications not less extensive, the antidote for that poison.

(Anderson 1818: 77–8)

Irish was to be made the language of 'loyalty and peace', rather than a badge signalling radical difference.

The direct, individual reading of the Bible was thought by many to offer the prospect of almost miraculous social effects. Indeed its previous absence, Orpen claimed, was responsible for Ireland's bitter history. Disunity

has arisen, not from difference of language, but from political and religious feuds, from traditionary practices and hereditary recollections; but above all from the want of a Scriptuary education of the Poor.

(Orpen 1821: 47)

Thus there was a concerted campaign to combine the teaching of Irish
with scriptural education in order to produce a conservative hegemony.
Anderson specifies examples of biblical teachings which could be used:

> Render unto Caesar the things which are Caesar's; let every soul be
> subject to the higher powers; for there is no power but of God: the
> powers that be are ordained by God. Whoever, therefore, resisteth the
> power, resisteth the ordinance of God . . .. Honour the King.
>
> (Anderson 1818: 82)

He comments that these 'truths', in Irish or English, would 'infuse the
most exalted and firmly grounded sentiments of loyalty to the ruling
powers' (ibid.). Whatever the actual effect of biblical teaching, its effi-
ciency was proclaimed generally. Dewar, in an assertion which probably
bears more optimism than truth, claims that an Irishman

> when he read for the first time in his life, a New Testament, which a
> benevolent gentleman put into his hands, exclaimed, 'If I should
> believe this, it is impossible for me to remain a rebel'. Behold the
> means which beneficent providence has appointed to make good men
> and good citizens!
>
> (Dewar 1812: 139)

Commenting that there were 'two inveterate prejudices in the Irish
peasant's mind, that against the Saxon language, and that against the
creed of the Protestant', Mason, secretary of the Irish Society, found a
simple solution: 'by employing the Scriptures in the much loved native
tongue, you neutralise the second prejudice with the first' (Mason 1829:
5). This process was facilitated by the fact that for the peasant 'nothing
could persuade him that heresy can be uttered in his native tongue'
(ibid.: 15). McQuige summed up this whole question when he asserted: 'I
have never known a truly learned Irishman, who was also a believer in
revelation, and yet an enemy to the state' (McQuige 1818: 9). This set of
beliefs, assertions, prescriptions and efforts to cajole amount to an almost
Gramscian attempt to form an hegemony in order to produce a goodly,
ordered, civil and Protestant society. Revelation rather than revolution
was to offer an answer to the problems posed by the bitter history of
Ireland. It was an idea which would later catch on with a significant part
of the late-century revivalist movement, as we shall see.

GAN TEANGA, GAN TÍR: NO LANGUAGE, NO NATION

The first of the language revivals, beginning in the late eighteenth
century and petering out in the early decades of the nineteenth, was
principally stimulated by antiquarians interested in tracing Ireland's
past. It took place against the background of an ever-increasing move

by the population at large to the use of English. The second revival
movement, dating from the 1830s to the late 1840s, was again led
initially by scholarly interest. The works of Petrie, the Irish Archaeological Society (1840) and the Irish Ordnance Survey were all major
examples of such scholarship. The third revival, initiated in the 1880s
and consolidated principally by the Gaelic League, gathered pace until
the gaining of the Saorstát in 1921. Like the first, the second and third
revivals were situated in contexts of historical division, culminating in the
risings of 1798, 1848 and 1916 respectively. Unlike the first, however, the
latter two were distinct in that they came to be used as weapons in the
nationalist cause. Related to, but distinct from, political nationalism,
cultural nationalism became a crucial site of debate concerning the
future state of the nation. We will consider this process in this section.

Cultural nationalism was a European phenomenon with a philosophical basis, and was grounded in the belief that language was the key to
human history. Philosophers, as well as students of language, looked to
language as the most accurate means of understanding the past. This was
particularly true in Germany amongst those of the post-Kantian tradition. Herder had argued that language was the historical repository of
human genius: 'what else, after all, is the entire structure of language but
a.manner of growth of his spirit, a history of his discoveries' (Herder
1966: 132). He continues:

> every stem word, with its family – rightly placed and soundly evolved
> – would be a chart of the progress of the human spirit, a history of its
> development, and a complete dictionary of that kind would be a most
> remarkable sample of the inventive skill of the human soul.
>
> (ibid.)

Schlegel, writing in the same vein, described 'language in general'

> as being the storehouse of tradition where it lives on from nation to
> nation, and as being the clue of material and spiritual connexion which
> joins century to century – the common memory of the human race.
>
> (Schlegel 1847: 407)

If this was true of language in general, would it not also be true of
languages in particular? If language was the living record of human
history, would it not then also follow that languages would be the
histories of their users? This was the step, of which we have noted the
origins earlier, that was to be decisive in engendering the philosophical
and political movement of cultural nationalism. And it was to have
enormous effects in terms of both revolution and reaction. Cultural
nationalists in the nineteenth century, in Germany, Poland, Czechoslo-
vakia, Italy, Switzerland and Ireland, to name but a few, appeared with

dictionaries or language tracts in one hand, and rifles or declarations of independence in the other.

Fichte's *Addresses to the German Nation* (1808) is a paradigm of the cultural nationalist case, not least in the optimistic invocation contained in his address to a nation which did not as yet exist politically. For Fichte and others in this tradition, the key to nationality was above all the speaking of a common language: 'we give the name of people to men whose organs of speech are influenced by the same external conditions, who live together, and who develop their language in continuous communication with each other' (Fichte 1968: 49). What this logically entailed was the irreducible nature of the link between the use of a distinct language and the independence of a specific nation: 'it is beyond doubt that, wherever a separate language is found, there a separate nation exists, which has the right to take charge of its independent affairs and to govern itself' (ibid.: 184). Such a view was enormously influential in nineteenth-century Europe, and beyond, principally as a means of justification for national liberation movements in their struggles against imperial occupation. Humboldt, writing later, specified the definition of nation as 'that of a body of men who form language in a particular way', a belief shared by the Italian nationalist Mazzini (Humboldt 1988: 153). This led to the belief, which we have noted earlier in our examination of eighteenth- and nineteenth-century Britain and Ireland, that language was not simply a guarantor of nationality but the repository of national identity. 'From every language', argues Humboldt, 'we can infer backwards to the national character' (ibid.: 154). What this constitutes is in effect the modern, and often still current, definition of the nation:

> But the individualities to be found in the same nation fall within the *national uniformity*, which again distinguishes each particular turn of thought from those that resemble it in another people. From this uniformity, and that of the special stimulus peculiar to every language, the *character* of that language arises. Every language receives a specific individuality through that of the nation, and has on the latter a uniformly determining reverse effect. The *national character* is indeed sustained, strengthened, and even to some extent engendered by community of habitat and action; but in fact it rests on a likeness of *natural disposition*, which is normally explained by community of *descent*.
>
> (ibid.: 152)

The shift from the etymological origins of the word 'nation' (from the Latin *nasci*, to be born), relating to birth, to the modern sense of 'a distinct race or people, characterised by common descent, language or history, usually organised as a separate political state and occupying a definite territory' (*OED*), was complete.

It is a moot question to what extent the cultural nationalist movements in Ireland had links with their European counterparts, and the matter is controversial. It is certain that major European nationalists such as Mazzini, Cavour and Kossuth snubbed the Irish nationalist cause, for varying reasons. Yet it is also true that the Young Ireland grouping of the 1840s (a title coined as an insult), saw itself precisely as a nationalist movement in line with its European peers. *The Nation*, the principal vehicle of the Young Irelanders, declared as much:

> Were the slave nations of the earth banded together, they would scatter their gaolers as the avalanche breaks the bulwarks on which its snows, if disunited, would have stormed in vain . . . let not us only rejoice, but let all who, like us, are provincials fighting for nationality – let not only Ireland, but Poland, Italy and Hungary, be glad at the progress which the foreign policy of Ireland is making . . .. We are battling for Ireland; if we conquer, 'twill be for mankind.
>
> (*The Nation* 1842–5: I, 377)

Throughout the century in fact there were tensions between the political and cultural wings of nationalism. More often than not, the cultural nationalists saw their project as more important for the achievement of true nationhood. Duffy, for example, reflecting on Young Ireland, noted that Davis, its leading figure, wanted to add 'the subtler teaching of the dramatic poet and the painter of the past in fiction' to the bare 'teaching of facts and principles' (Duffy 1896: 131). Whatever the method, it was clear that for this group of thinkers and writers, cultural emancipation took precedence over political independence. Writing of *Ireland's Battle for her Language*, in a Gaelic League pamphlet, Martyn argued:

> Home Rule, no doubt, is of vital importance to Ireland, but whether it comes in this generation or succeeding generations, although important, is not of vital importance. It is possible for it to wait. *The cause of the Irish language cannot wait.*
>
> (Martyn undated: 4)

In another Gaelic League publication, O'Farrell attacks 'the reign of humbug' administered by the nationalist politicians, on the following grounds:

> why are they not national – not in any party spirit, but in the broadest and most far-reaching sense of the word, teaching their countrymen that green flags and such exteriors are only the symbols, and not in themselves the essentials of nationality – that there is the reality behind, and that reality is the soul of the people; that there dwells the 'form' we are vainly groping for in our ignorance.
>
> (O'Farrell undated: 9)

Rather than direct links with political nationalists elsewhere in Europe, what is of interest here is the way in which cultural nationalism in Ireland was influenced by the philosophical movement which had under-pinned its European counterparts. The questions are: how far indeed did Irish cultural nationalism reflect and embody the beliefs which had been so influential in Europe? And how did it adapt and extend them?

In fact what we find in the discourse of Irish cultural nationalism is many extremely close links between it and its European forebear. For example, the crucial notion that specific languages were naturally fitted to particular peoples (part of Fichte's definition of a people is 'men whose organs of speech are influenced by the same external conditions'), was articulated by Davis thus:

> The language, which grows up with a people, is conformed to their organs, descriptive of their climate, constitution and manners, mingled inseparably with their history and their soil, fitted beyond any other language to express their prevalent thoughts in the most natural and efficient way.
>
> (Davis 1914: 97)

This was to become a common, and eventually dangerous, refrain amongst the leading figures of the nationalist movement. The nation, by dint of its language, had to be designated as being radically unique, a monoglot entity which could not be mixed with any other. In one sense this idea can be read as a reflex against imperialism, in that it denies legitimacy to the principle of assimilation by which the empire justifies and validates itself: that is, to the discursive and practical process by which, under the operation of *pax Britannica*, inferior peoples could be brought into the sphere of British civilisation. The nationalist stance denies this possibility by insisting upon the ineradicable, and thus mono-logic, nature of national identity; such identity being validated, as noted earlier, by reference to the antiquity of the cultural nation. This principle is expressed concisely by Moran in his survey of Irish history: 'the Irish all this time, as they are at the present day, were absolutely different from the English. The genius of each nation was distinct' (Gregory 1901: 27).

It followed from this principle of course that if the state of pristine monoglossia were disturbed, if a new language were to be imposed upon a nation, displacing the original, then great dangers would follow. For what happens when a people shifts to another language is nothing less than the destruction of the national essence, and subsequent linguistic degradation. For the descendants of those who changed, the conse-quences are enormous, as Fichte notes:

> they receive the flat and dead history of a foreign culture, but not in any way a culture of their own. They get symbols which for them are

neither immediately clear nor able to stimulate life, but which must
seem to them entirely as arbitrary as the sensuous part of the
language. For them this advent of history, and nothing but history,
as expositor, makes the language dead and closed in respect of its
whole sphere of imagery and its continuous onward flow is broken off.

(Fichte 1968: 54)

Once again Davis echoes Fichte's formulation closely:

To impose another language on such a people is to send their history
adrift among the accidents of translation – 'tis to tear their identity
from all places – 'tis to substitute arbitrary signs for picturesque and
suggestive names – 'tis to cut off the entail of feelings and separate the
people from their forefathers by a deep gulf.

(Davis 1914: 97–8)

Precisely this principle was taken up and became central to the claim for
cultural and national independence, in which of course the revival of
Gaelic was to be all-important. Following from this belief, Davis asks
rhetorically, was it right for

the fiery, delicate-organed Celt to abandon his beautiful tongue,
docile and spirited as an Arab, 'sweet as music, strong as the wave'
– is it befitting for him to abandon this wild liquid speech for the
mongrel of a hundred breeds called English, which, powerful though
it be, creaks and bangs about the Celt who tries to use it?

(ibid.: 98)

The stress on purity, revealed here in the fear of the miscegenated
mongrel of English, and the national and indeed racial stereotyping
which we find here will be examined later in the chapter. But, however
formulated, the answer to Davis's question was clearly *no*, and it was
repeated endlessly in nationalist works. The Irish had their own language, which reflected their national genius, and any other would distort
it: 'hence the difficulty of worthily clothing the products of the Gaelic
mind in Anglo-Saxon garb' (O'Hickey undated: 5).

The logic of this assertion was followed rigorously. For just as the Irish
had their national language, so the English had their own too. And their
happy position gave great advantages:

English writers are truly national because, for the most part, unconsciously they are the national voice of the English mind and are part
of one unbroken and continuous nationality. They have their own
national language.

(*An Claidheamh Soluis* 1899–1901: I, 16, 248)

So central was this belief to the discourse of Irish cultural nationalism that it became a commonplace of the late nineteenth century in such circles to argue that if the language were not saved and revived, then the nation itself would gradually disappear by succumbing to 'the English mind'. Or, as the slogan had it: *gan teanga, gan tír*, 'no language, no nation'.

Given the importance of this doctrine, it was logical that the imposition of the English language should be viewed as a crude attempt to destroy Irish cultural and political identity. And indeed it was at various times precisely that. In the view of *The Nation*, the colonial powers

> plainly saw that while so powerful, copious and feelingly expressive a language continued to be in use among the people, their nationality sooner or later would grasp the rights of which it was unjustly deprived.
>
> (*The Nation* 1842–5: I, 35, 491)

Thus the English 'put the gibbet and the axe between the Irish people and education, that [they] might totally eradicate the Irish language' (ibid.: 555).

O'Reilly commented later that an understanding of the potential of Gaelic led the colonisers to 'make war on the Gaelic' (O'Reilly 1902: 10). Perhaps the best account of such policy, however, came from the imperialists themselves. In a manner which echoes that of Edmund Spenser in the sixteenth century, the *Daily Mail*, a popular British daily, is quoted thus:

> France, Russia and Germany realise far more fully than we in England ever seem to do the vast importance of the extension of their language among all the races that have fallen under their rule . . .. It is not by arms alone that the influence of Great Britain can be maintained, nor even by the 'divine right of good government' that it can protect itself against the intrigues of rival nations. It needs the magical influence of a common tongue to link all the members of the Empire together; a fundamental policy with all Imperial races except our own.
>
> (*Fáinne An Lae* 1898–1900: II, 44)

What was the answer to this act of cultural and political warfare by the imperial power? The logic of cultural nationalism dictated that it could only be the revival of Gaelic at the expense of English: that is, a reversal of the historical processes which Ireland had suffered, to varying degrees, for several hundred years: a possible resurrection of a long-lost monoglossia. It was thus that the speaking of Irish became the touchstone of fidelity to the patria: 'If you be a patriot you should know Irish and speak it' was a sentence set for translation in the anonymous *Exercises in Irish Composition* (Anonymous 1892: 29). Speaking Irish also became, as

Donlevy had asserted in 1742, the criterion for what might be called 'proper Irishness'. Thus *The Nation* addressed its audience with the question: 'Will they be Irishmen again?' (*The Nation* 1842–5: I, 35, 555). If so, it argued, they must learn the language, since this was the only effective way of resisting cultural imperialism. A poem, one of a number, was composed to articulate how it might be achieved:

How To Learn Irish, And Be Irish
One letter, then another,
And the alphabet is gained;
One word, then another,
And the language is attained;
One speak it, then another,
And 'tis spoken as before;
One man, then another,
And we're Irish as of yore.

(Nolan 1877: 9)

In fact, however, despite the rhetoric, and with the exception of only the most extreme elements of the movement, one of the interesting features of cultural nationalism is that it did not envisage in the near future a state of monoglossia in which Irish would once again be the sole language of Ireland. It aimed instead to achieve a situation of polyglossia in which Irish had superior status, rather than that which currently held in which English retained that position. Davis was clear on this point:

If an attempt were made to introduce Irish, either through the national schools or the courts of law, into the eastern side of the island, it would certainly fail, and the reaction might extinguish it altogether. But no one contemplates this save as a dream of what may happen a hundred years hence.

(Davis 1914: 105)

And Hyde, the other great leader of the revival, took the same position. He considered that 'bilingual races are doubly men, and are double in sharpness and mental capacity' (Hyde 1986: 151). Moreover, in a pragmatic tone he asserted: 'we look upon the English language as a commercial necessity, and if I had a friend in Ireland who did not know the English language, I would be the first to teach it to him' (ibid.: 194).

The position of Davis and Hyde on this point stems from the complexity of the linguistic and historical situation which faced Irish cultural nationalists in the nineteenth century. For clear historical reasons, there was not, despite all the rhetoric which claimed otherwise, a simple choice, though there were contradictory possibilities. These can be summed up in the following way: a monoglot Ireland, with Gaelic as its language, did not seem possible, though this did not prevent its frequent invocation. A polyglot Ireland in which English held sway existed as an historical fact, though this might possibly be altered in favour of Gaelic. And there was also the possibility of a heteroglot Ireland; but this, for reasons of purity and antiquity, was dangerous to the cultural nationalist articulation of identity and was thus viewed only as an unfortunate potential disaster. Thus as the historical situation developed towards the end of the century, all sorts of contradictory positions were taken up. And with the crises of political nationalism, and the ever-increasing influence of English popular culture in particular, the cultural nationalist movement faced its own crisis. In that crisis, the choices on offer, and the strident claims made for them, became starker and more pressing. And so it was that many of the features articulated in the debates around the language and nation for the past century and a half seemed to coalesce in the 1890s and the early twentieth century. Antiquity, purity – whether linguistic, racial or religious – uniqueness, 'proper Irishness', national stereotyping: all were to appear in the battle against the forces of heteroglossia and cultural difference which was waged at the end of the nineteenth century in Ireland.

ANSWERS TO THE QUESTION: 'WHO AND WHAT ARE WE?'

Reflecting upon the years 1840–5, in which Young Ireland had flourished, Duffy described them as constituting the period, 'to which may be traced, as to their fountain-head, many of the opinions now universally current among the Irish people' (Duffy 1896: v). In a general sense he was right, but his comment is most accurate when considering some of the answers which were produced in the late nineteenth century to Moran's significant question 'Who and what are we?' (Moran 1905: 79). For it is in the work of Davis that we find articulated a concept which was to become heavily loaded towards the end of the century in a dangerous manner: that is, the purity of linguistic and racial identity. Davis, as was noted earlier, had stressed the belief that a people's language 'is conformed to their organs' and 'fitted beyond any other language, to express their prevalent thoughts in the most natural and efficient way' (Davis 1914: 97). In the case of Irish, he argued, how could it thus be right for 'the fiery, delicate-organed Celt' to renounce the language 'for the mongrel of a hundred breeds called English' (ibid.: 98). These beliefs, that languages are somehow *naturally* attached to specific groups, and that 'purer' languages are superior, was, as we have seen, in many ways the logical extension of cultural nationalism. Yet they led to a set of opinions which were later to become hardened and much more exclusive by involvement in the discourse of racism.

Hyde, speaking in America in 1906, articulated the developed position
of the Gaelic League in this way:

> The philosophy of the Gaelic League is based principally on this, that
> there is a fundamental distinction between different races of mankind,
> and between no two races, perhaps, does there run a broader line of
> radical distinction than that between the English and the Irish race.
>
> (Hyde 1986: 193)

Thus the aim of the League, as expressed in the pamphlet *Ireland's Ideal*,
was 'the formation of a national character on a sound racial basis'
(Farquharson undated: 12). Such declarations can of course be read in
ways in which the term 'race' is not understood as anything but a cipher
for 'nation' or 'people'. Yet, as Williams has shown, it is precisely at the
end of the nineteenth century that, by dint of various shifts in scientific
and social thought, the term 'race' becomes politically volatile and
dangerous (Williams 1983: 248–50). For at this time 'race' begins to
mean a people radically set off from all others biologically, as well as
geographically, socially or linguistically; genetic nationalism starts to take
the place of its cultural forerunner. And the consequences of that shift
extend far beyond Ireland in the twentieth century.

That such racist doctrines were current in Ireland is beyond doubt,
and they are frequently expressed in the works of the Gaelic League.
Kavanagh described the English to the Irish as 'a people with whom they
have nothing in common but a common humanity. A people between
whom and them nature itself has drawn a broad line of separation'
(Kavanagh undated: 10). Such 'natural' boundaries of course could be
identified and studied scientifically. Thus writing of *The Irish Language
Movement: Its Philosophy*, Forde addresses the reader in this way:

> The science of Ethnology, as you know, inquires into the laws that
> govern the origin and growth of racial diversities, how the many races
> of men who now inhabit this globe differ, and came to differ, from one
> another. For it is noticed that each nation has a character and a
> language of its own, has its own particular and characteristic gifts of
> body and soul, of mind and heart.
>
> (Forde undated: 2)

He continues:

> One of the most valuable means of studying national character is the
> national language; scientists find a real intrinsic connection between
> the two. To appreciate the significance of this last point you should
> bear in mind that science deals with the fixed laws of nature, not with
> accidental or random conventions.
>
> (ibid.)

Science then, deployed here by a Catholic priest, was to be the vehicle by which Irish nationalists could prove their case. The Irish were a different race from the English, as testified by their language, and thus merited a nation of their own. For that, in this sense, would only be returning nature to its proper state.

Perhaps the most forthright of the proponents of this racial view of Irish identity was Dermot Trench, with whom Joyce once spent an uncomfortable night in the Martello Tower, the consequence of which is that Trench is depicted in the character of the language revivalist Haines in *Ulysses*. Trench echoes both Fichte and Davis in his tracing of the organic relationship between language and racial identity. He refuses to believe, he says, that 'the Irish brain has ceased to be convoluted in accordance with the subtle architecture of the Gaelic sentence, or that the Irish larynx has ceased to be the counterpart of Gaelic phonetics' (Trench 1912: 27). For Trench the language is the key to identity in a way which reflects very closely that proposed by Humboldt and which was later developed in the Sapir–Whorf hypothesis (Whorf 1956). Thus he declares:

> That idiom is the counterpart of racial idiosyncrasy, long believed as a matter of intuition, is now being elucidated with scientific certainty. The most rudimentary idioms of speech are found to indicate the psychological angle from which the racial mind confronts the universe . . .. Irish idiom is the logic of Irish psychology, while an Irish sentence, apart from its explicit meaning, commits the speaker, by its grammar and order, to an Irish theory of life.
>
> (ibid.: 26)

The Irish language, he argues, 'is the storehouse of our racial identity' and thus must be preserved. And this in turn leads to Trench's question, which is an extension of that of Moran, posed to his Irish readership:

> Are you or are you not predominantly Irish, and do you not wish to live in an Ireland which reflects your racial type? If so, you will support the language which expresses the Irish nature and which will keep the nation true to itself.
>
> (ibid.: 32)

The rhetorically constructed questions of Moran and of Trench scarcely admitted of a negative answer. And the typical response was articulated by Forde in answer to his own version of this demand. 'Are we', he says, 'mere planters and marchmen of the Pale, or are we Celts, Gaels, Irish?' 'Oh, thank God', he proclaims, 'we know what we are' (Forde undated: 8). The elision here between Celt, Gael and the Irish is significant; but of more import is the note of triumphalism. For out of a desperate situation, the revivalist movement snatched not only hope but racist arrogance. In certain areas, the Irish nationalists mimicked their colonial masters only too well.

Such triumphalism is clearly evident in assertions as to the purity and antiquity of the Irish language made at the end of the century, which clearly echo those of an earlier age. In a sense this was a doctrine which was but the logical outcome of Schlegel's differentiation and ranking of the inflectional and the agglutinative languages (Schlegel 1849: 448–9). In the weekly newspaper *Fáinne An Lae*, for example, it is stressed that 'supremacy of language carries with it supremacy of race', the two languages and races here of course being the Irish and the English. It was such a position that led to further racist description, this time applied to the prospect of the spread of the English language and thus consequent loss of national identity. Should that fate occur, wrote O'Hickey in the first Gaelic League pamphlet, 'it were better, in my opinion, to be something that could be clearly defined and classed; for anything at all would seem preferable to a mongrel, colourless, nondescript racial monstrosity' (O'Hickey undated: 4). Such a process, wrote Moran, would have as its issue, nothing but 'an English-speaking, an English-imitating mongrel' (Moran 1905: 35). Anglicisation meant miscegenation, to use the discourse of racism. Linguistic, national and racial purity would be polluted, the Irish language reduced to the state of the English, that 'mongrel of a hundred breeds' as Davis had called it.

Ireland in this discursive scheme, which was at once both defensive and aggressive, was constructed as Gaelic and, as we shall see later, Catholic. Real Ireland was Gaelic Ireland; or, as one commentator put it in a phrase which reveals the developing notion of 'proper Irishness', 'the best part of Ireland's history – the really Irish part – cannot be read at all without a knowledge of Gaelic' (O'Reilly undated: 12). And thus the Gaelic League had as its aim, as O'Donovan claimed, 'the creation of an Irish Ireland' (O'Donovan undated: 2), the slogan 'Irish Ireland' being popularised by D. P. Moran. Yet this view of Ireland was a stereotype, which like all stereotypes disserves both its object and those making the observation; though it reveals something of the relationship between the two. For Irish Ireland did not exist, and had to be invented in order to serve the ideological requirements of the Gaelic Leaguers.

The fiction created by the League was mostly regressive, as is indicated by an editorial in one of the leading nationalist journals: 'no people can look forward to prosperity who cannot often look back to their ancestors' (*Fáinne An Lae* 1898–1900: 30, 28). In this sense the Irish case is similar to those of the other nationalist movements in the nineteenth century in aspiring to a revolution whose aim was to make everything old (see the triple use of the word in the extract from O'Reilly below). Or, as a Gaelic League pamphlet put it, the purpose for Ireland was 'to restore it to its pristine vigour and ensure its perpetuation' (O'Hickey undated: 15).

This desire for a return to a state of absolute monoglossia commonly took the form, as we have noted earlier, of a return to a lost past, the moment of cultural origination and validation. In Ireland this produced a poetic vision of the history of the Irish language which

> was wrapped and woofed into the same web with things which cannot die. It was bound up with old memories of hearth and home; with fond, old faces, loved old haunts, and happy days – May-time sunsets long ago, when Heaven's voice was in the cuckoo's song and everything was true.
>
> (O'Reilly 1902: 16)

The point at which 'everything was true' is presumably the prelapsarian period, when Adam and Eve were greeting each other in Gaelic. In any case the dream of a return to the organic community (a trope which we shall see in twentieth-century Britain too), was inspired by another part of the revival's invention of 'Irish Ireland'. That is, the mythified representations of the peasantry, the last inhabitants of 'real Ireland'. Aesthetic representations of the peasant were common enough in the literary revival, and were produced by most of the leading writers. But the figure of the peasant also played a crucial role in the linguistic revival. Indeed Gwynn, in a work entitled *Today and Tomorrow in Ireland* – though it might more accurately have been called 'Yesterday and the Day Before' – claims that 'the political movement of the last twenty years has been a movement of the peasants' (Gwynn 1903: 97). This might have been news to the rural populace. Be that as it may, for the Gaelic League the peasant played the same role to the Irish as the Celts themselves did to the English in Arnold's thought: that is, they embodied the crucial values which were missing from Irish life and thus became a mythical touchstone of authenticity. One Gaelic League propagandist noted that 'it is with relief that one turns to the peasantry, by far the most attractive section of the community, by far the least vulgarised and anglicised' (Butler undated: 6). Trench claimed that no one could meet the peasantry without 'being struck by the vigour of mind, the refinement of mind, the genuine literary culture which place them far above the inhabitants of the anglicised districts' (Trench 1912: 10). And Moran saw the peasants as embodying the last remnants of Gaelic Ireland, and thus the last opportunity for the building, or reconstruction, of 'Irish Ireland':

> The ignorant peasants are the most interesting portion of the population. In them are yet to be seen, undeveloped and clouded perhaps, the marks of the Gaelic race. They still possess the unspoiled raw material for the making of a vigorous and real Irish character.
>
> (Moran 1905: 4)

In fact of course what the invention of 'the peasant' did was to distort the real differences (social, economic, gendered and geographical) which existed between various groupings of the impoverished rural populace, and to place them all under one, mainly cultural, category. 'The peasant' as represented both aesthetically and in the writings of the linguistic revival did not exist; it had to be invented in order to provide inhabitants for the equally mythical 'Irish Ireland'.

Racial stereotyping was also common enough. Hyde, for example, compares the Irish and Teutonic races:

> the characteristics of the Irish race of ours are lightness, brightness, wit, fluency and an artistic temperament. The characteristics of the Teutonic race are an intense business faculty, perseverance and steadiness in details.
>
> (Hyde 1986: 180)

This is an apparently neutral, perhaps even half-admiring, account; others were not so restrained. The Reverend J. M. O'Reilly, addressing an audience at Maynooth, described the English mind in this manner:

> The character of the English mind ought to be fairly understood in Ireland . . .. It is a fleshy spirit, bent towards earth; a mind unmannerly, vulgar, insolent, bigoted; a mind whose belly is its God, yet which cannot endure the word belly; a mind to which pride, and lust, and mammon are the matter-of-course aims of life, the only objects conceivably worthy of pursuit; a mind to which real Christian virtue is incredible.
>
> (O'Reilly undated: 4)

Moran continued in much the same manner, constructing the racial other as corrupt and malevolent:

> The English mind is essentially one which justifies the means by the end, though it may be too dull to see it and too self-righteous to suspect it. It is narrow and bigoted by nature, and it is bloated by the fat traditions of success. All people can, to a degree, deceive themselves when it is in their interest to do so; but this dull, prosperous people have a malign genius for it.
>
> (Moran 1905: 45)

Indeed Moran went even further than this, offering a justification for racial hatred:

> Racial hatred is a bad passion at the best, and one which, it appears to me, is absolutely unjustifiable on moral grounds, unless in so far as it is impersonal and complementary to a real desire to keep intact

the distinctive character, traditions and civilization of one's own country.

(ibid.: 67)

The rider 'unless' has significance here, for the language revivalists considered themselves to be in precisely such a position. Racial hatred may well have been viewed as a bad passion, but in times of war it might also have been seen as a necessary evil.

In fact such attacks as those outlined above were broadsides fired in what one Gaelic Leaguer called 'the language war', which was 'a war to the death between Irish ideals and British sordid soullessness' (Butler undated: 2). One of her contemporaries, Dinneen, painted a picture of a battle in which a good deal more than language was at stake: 'The struggle between the languages is a deeper, a more far-reaching struggle that [sic] appears on the surface, it is a struggle between the civilizations which these languages represent' (Dinneen 1904: 28). Or, to put it another way, what was at issue was precisely the answer to the questions 'Who and what are the Irish, and who or what are they to be?'

If the question of who the Irish were was one which remained to be settled, the identity of the English was already recognised. Following from the mental degradation depicted above, by the logic of the nationalist argument the English language, which of course reflected the English mind, would likewise be corrupted. George Moore articulates precisely this point:

> From universal use and journalism, the English language in fifty years will be as corrupt as the Latin of the eighth century, as unfit for literary usage, and will become, in my opinion, a sort of volapuk, strictly limited to commercial letters and journalism.
>
> (Gregory 1901: 49)

The English language was polluted 'with the very names of monstrosities of sin' (O'Reilly undated: 2), and thus a 'poisonous channel' of 'evil power' (O'Farrelly 1904: 168); and anglicisation was described as 'a stalking cancer' (O'Reilly undated: 13). If this process was not halted, the Irish would be reduced by the English mind and language and thus become 'servile copyists' (Kavanagh undated: 3) and a 'tribe of drivellers' (Dinneen 1904: 40).

The English language, however, was but one part of a threat offered by English culture in general. English literature was also denounced: 'the soul of Ireland is being corrupted and poisoned by the stuff that is called literature in England today' (Forde undated: 19). Morris described it simply and damningly as 'Protestant, infidel, immoral' (*Fáinne An Lae* 1898–1900: 13, 8). And the threat was taken so seriously that the Catholic Truth Society launched a 'Crusade against Imported

Literature'. Its aim was the diffusion of cheap texts of 'sound Catholic literature in popular form'. The need for it was clear:

> It is well known that various printing presses in great Britain daily pour out a flood of infidel and immoral publications, some of which overflow to this country. We have a hope that the society's publications will remove the temptation of having recourse to such filthy garbage, will create a taste for a pure and wholesome literature, and will also serve as an antidote against the poison of dangerous and immoral writings.
>
> (*Fáinne An Lae* 1898–1900: 101, 182)

English literature got off lightly, for the most ferocious attacks were made against English popular culture. The Gaelic League denounced 'the penny dreadful, or the shilling shocker, imported from London, and low music-hall ditty' as 'an outrage on the Irish character, and in all cases an outrage on decency and common sense' (O'Hickey undated: 3). Music hall 'ditties' were considered particularly offensive, and were condemned on the grounds that they 'tend to demoralise and denationalise our people, placing them in the position of a wretched English colony' (*Fáinne An Lae* 1898–1900: 53, 2); a 'Songs Column' was started in the newspaper as an antidote. The spread of this material, however, was viewed with alarm by many. A.E. commented on the readers of such work:

> We see everywhere a moral leprosy, a vulgarity of mind creeping over them. The Police Gazettes, the penny novels, the hideous comic journals, replace the once familiar poems and the beautiful and moving memoirs of classic Ireland. The music that breathed Tír-nan-óg and overcame men's hearts with all gentle and soft emotions is heard more faintly, and the songs of London music halls may be heard in places where the music of the fairy enchanted the elder generations.
>
> (Gregory 1901: 19–20)

It was a scenario of course which dismayed the Gaelic Leaguers on two counts; for it represented both a moral threat, by the nature of its corruption, and an attack on traditional Irish culture by its popularity:

> Think of it, and all it portends – the purity of the Celtic mind coming in contact with London's exhalations! The philosophic spirit of the thinking Irishman being nourished on the third-rate literature of England! . . . Soon our power of distinguishing good from ill will have passed in 'cosmopolitan' vapours, and weakness of soul will be ours – the last sign that we are not to be redeemed.
>
> (O'Farrell undated: 6–7)

O'Farrell mentions here the one word which the Gaelic revivalists inflected as an insult above all others: 'cosmopolitanism'. Gwynn sees the revival itself as a 'vehement reaction against cosmopolitanism, a protest against the confounding of differences' (Gwynn 1903: 2). In this sense 'cosmopolitanism' refers to the forces which were spreading the values and commodities of industrial modernity and its technological changes: that is, those of international capitalism, particularly that branch of it based in England. The railway system was one example of this process, upon which there was much comment. Just as in England, where the dialectologists were blaming the railways for the disappearance of the rural dialects, their Irish contemporaries were also noting their effect. 'I may here remark', notes one of them, that the railway

> seems to have trailed a something [sic] of English taste right through the county [Wexford], and the influence is felt on both sides of the line to a breadth of some miles . . .. There is nothing necessarily English about a railway of course, but 'tis a mark of progress, and so is English thought to be unfortunately.
>
> (An Claidheamh Soluis 1899–1901: 29, 454)

Against such forces, Gwynn, like the revival movement in general, pits 'tradition', which

> aims at maintaining the living symbol of nationality, at encouraging love of race and pride of race in a world whose ideals seem to tend towards the creation of cosmopolitan financiers and whose drift is to denationalise.
>
> (Gwynn 1903: 91)

A.E.'s comment articulated the economic side of this argument precisely: 'Ireland Limited is being run by English syndicates' (Gregory 1901: 20).

Against such potentially overwhelming forces, there was of course only one possible defence. And that, as Davis had asserted, was the Irish language:

> A people without a language of its own is only half a nation. A nation should guard its language more than its territories – 'tis a sure barrier, and more important frontier, than fortress or river.
>
> (Davis 1914: 99)

This was a motif which appeared repeatedly in the discourse of late century nationalism; Ireland's Defence – Her Language was the title of one Gaelic League pamphlet. The language in this account became the only sure weapon against 'the curse of Anglicisation', as Hyde put it, by dint of being 'the one invincible barrier against national disintegration' (O'Hickey undated: 2). It was, however, not only a general defence, but one which guarded against specific elements of the threatening culture. In the programme for 'Language Sunday' (18 September 1910), the language was described as 'the most perfect shield and safeguard we can oppose to the encroachment and influence of foreign peoples'. Specifically, the language was viewed as a moral defence:

> the use of the Irish language is the only human device by which our people will be saved from sinking to the same level of immorality as prevails in England at the present time. The universal use of our own pure tongue by ourselves is the one means by which we may escape our final and complete debasement by the filthiest Press in Europe – the Press of England.
>
> (Gaelic League 1910: 10)

For Yeats too the language could act as 'a barrier to the vulgarity and coarseness which is today the plague of Ireland' (Yeats 1975: 239).

The recourse to the Irish language as the guardian of Irish morality was one which had important repercussions for the shaping of Irish national identity. For despite Hyde's repeated assertions that 'the Irish language, thank God, is neither Protestant nor Catholic' (Hyde 1986: 191), the Irish nationalists were to adopt and adapt Kant's dictum in *Perpetual Peace* that nature 'employs two means to separate peoples and to prevent them from mixing: differences of language and religion' (Kant 1957: 31). And in this case the language was Irish and the religion Catholicism. In fact, as we have seen, the Catholic clergy in the early part of the nineteenth century actively worked against the promotion of Irish, as a number of commentators recalled. Towards the end of the century, however, with the closer involvement of the hierarchy in nation-alist politics, there was a campaign to place the weight of the Catholic church behind the revival. *The First Irish Book* (1877), a popular primer published by the Society for the Preservation of the Irish Language, appointed the Catholic clergy as 'the guardians of what remains of our mother tongue' (SPIL 1877: 9). And this role was one which was eventually officially recognised by the church itself in Cardinal Logue's blessing of the 1899 Oireachtas, and the adoption, in 1900, of the League's policies by the hierarchy.

The influence of the church in the nationalist movement in general was acknowledged by O'Reilly when he commented that 'if England could destroy that loyalty of the irish people to their pastors, there would be no further trouble about Home Rule' (O'Reilly undated: 2): a statement which supports the Unionist argument that Home Rule would mean Rome Rule. The role of the Catholic clergy in the language revival, however, was also clearly recognised. For, as *Fáinne An Lae* thundered in response to an attack on the clergy in *An Claidheam Soluis*, 'take the priest out of the Language movement and it is doomed' (*Fáinne An Lae* 1898–1900: 93, 10). A more sophisticated argument claimed that such an idea was actually ineffable in the Irish language: "No priests in politics". That phrase could not be rendered into Irish idiom. The genius of the Gaelic tongue could no more assimilate it, than the human system could assimilate a dagger in the stomach' (O'Reilly undated: 5). By the end of the century, Kant's proposition that nature had marked out nations by determining differences of language and religion had been modified. And in the new formulation it was the deity that had ordained the existence of autonomous nations. This point was made severally in Gaelic League pamphlets, particularly by Forde:

> each nation has been sent by God to do a special and particular work, for which the whole circle of its characteristic endowments is but the qualifying equipment, while its actual history is merely the fulfilment of that work. Therefore each nation has its own country and its own soul, its own language and its own liberty given to it by God, as the means by which the Divine plan is to be wrought out.
>
> (Forde undated: 2)

However, not only had the deity been provident enough to create independent nations with their own languages; in the Irish case God had been particularly diligent in providing the Irish with a language which was religious.

For some writers the language was religious in the sense that it had 'a vocabulary incredibly copious and capable for religious expression' (O'Reilly undated: 2): that is, that the language had been adopted and made the vehicle of religious worship. For other writers the language was considered religious by dint of the fact that until recently it had been the language in which Irish Catholics had worshipped. Thus Morris appeals to that constituency to give the language

> the veneration that is due to it by reason of its close and inseparable connection with their holy Faith . . .. This is why it behoves Irish Catholics of today to pause and consider is it their duty, is there any moral obligation on them to preserve the Irish language merely and solely *for the sake of their religion?*
>
> (*Fáinne An Lae* 1898–1900: 13, 8)

This identification of the language with Catholicism was an important development in the revival movement and one which had marked effects. On the one hand the revival gained enormously since it had the weight of the Catholic church behind it; on the other hand, however, it also had the consequence of alienating potential Protestant support. This shift can be traced in the discourse of the Gaelic League itself. The *Gaelic League Catechism* (1900), for example, mimicked the format and style of the Catholic catechism, as well as claiming that the revival would lead to 'increased religious faith and fervour'. And in the programme for the

'Language Sunday' procession the League told its workers to preach the 'gospel' of the revival, and to constitute themselves as 'missionaries' in order 'to preach the faith': 'Let every good Gael consider himself an evangeliser – let him study the gospel of the League in the various pamphlets issued – let him go and spread the light in dark places' (Gaelic League 1910: 14–16). Despite the inevitably alienating effects, the link between the language and Catholicism was increasingly articulated as fact:

> The mind of this nation is still to a great extent the Irish language mind. But, sixty years ago the Irish language was the engine and factory of the people's thought, as well as the organ of its conveyance; and those people and the men who came immediately after were Irish and Catholic in a way that we are undoubtedly not.
>
> (O'Reilly undated: 3–4)

'Real Ireland' was Gaelic, Catholic and in the past. But since Irish was the language of Irish Catholic morality, it followed of course that its opponent in the 'language war' would be considered as the language not merely of moral decadence, as we have already noted, but of that deadly foe the Protestant faith:

> English is the language of revolt, of proud, successful rebellion, against all effective sanction in religious authority. It is the tongue of private judgment. It is the vehicle, the traditional vehicle, of mockery and scorn, of some of the most sacred practices, and most august functions of religion.
>
> (O'Reilly 1902: 17)

For other writers, the language was not religious by dint of its use as the language of Catholicism; precisely the opposite in fact. For Irish was the language of Catholicism because it was intrinsically religious. This was a fact not about the use of the language but about its nature. McNulty, writing on the theme 'Irish for the Irish', comments that 'our Gaelic race is pre-eminently a religious race, and our Gaelic tongue, to my mind, is beyond all others a religious tongue'. And he adds that there is no language superior to the Gaelic

> in supplying the very tones that seem to deepen and sweeten, to enrich and to dignify the outpourings of the heart towards God. So resonant and so full, so soft and so liquid, the very sound of the syllables helps to stir the heart.
>
> (*Fáinne An Lae* 1989–1900: 114, 5)

For O'Reilly, the language, by its very nature, instilled the Catholic faith in children:

the Irish language itself was instinct with religious life; that no one might speak it from infancy without finding himself so constituted and framed that, to him, acting, living faith was the very breath of his being; while the development of an infidel mind was not only impossible in himself, but inconceivable and incredible to him in others.

(O'Reilly 1902: 14–15)

Or, as he put it more concisely, 'we learned our religion by learning to talk' (ibid.: 16). What this formation, in which the language and Catholic faith are tied to 'proper Irish' identity, effects is precisely the nets of nationality, language and religion from which Stephen Dedalus is so keen to escape in Joyce's *Portrait of the Artist as a Young Man*. The ideological force of that net in the late nineteenth and early twentieth centuries in Ireland is difficult to overestimate.

Who were to be the guardians of this educational structure? Who were to cast the net? The answer was Irish women. In fact women had been importantly involved in Irish language movements from the late eighteenth century. Charlotte Brooke's work was of particular significance; Maria Edgeworth's aptly titled *Forgive and Forget* was translated into Irish for the Ulster Gaelic Society in 1833; and the Ladies' Gaelic Society published *An Irish Primer* in 1838. Barron, in a typically patronising manner, tried to persuade women that because they 'have been the subjects of the greater part of the poetry in the Irish language . . . it would, therefore, now appear to be a duty incumbent, *in a particular degree upon them*, to promote its revival by every means in their power' (Barron 1835: 15). And an article in *The Nation* entitled 'The Mission of Women', advised women to become involved in politics; 'Speranza', Oscar Wilde's mother, took the advice and contributed poems to the paper.

Yet it was not until the language revival had taken off in the late century that the clearest address to women was made. In a letter to SPIL in 1900, John Nylan asserted:

I am of the opinion that, in order to have the movement crowned with success, the womanhood and girlhood of Ireland must enter the ranks; by doing so they will prove of infinitely greater service to Mother Ireland than their Limerick sisters of the historic past.

(SPIL 1877–1914: 23, 16)

'Mother Ireland' had by that time become one of the standard motifs of the nationalist cause. Ireland as a sorrowful mother mourning her lost children was one version of this trope. Another was that proposed by A.E.: 'the national spirit, like a beautiful woman, cannot or will not reveal itself wholly while a coarse presence is near, an unwelcome stranger in possession of the home' (Gregory 1901: 22). And this gendered version of both nation and home was that which became dominant in the language revival and indeed Irish cultural nationalism in general. It produced a view of women which was eventually to be enshrined in the constitution:

> 41.1   In particular, the state recognises that by her life within the home, woman gives to the state a support without which the common good cannot be achieved.

> 41.2   The state shall, therefore, endeavour to ensure that mothers shall not be obliged by economic necessity to engage in labour to the neglect of their duties in the home.
>
> *(Bunreacht Na hÉireann* 1937: 136–8)

The indexes of constitutions can often be revealing as to the social values which govern a country; the entry in the Irish constitution for 'women' reads: '*See* FAMILY, SEX'.

The Gaelic League saw women as ideologically crucial in the 'language war', not least because 'what is she doing at home all day long? Many things; but one thing incessantly. Let it be written in capital letters – TALKING'. It followed therefore that 'a language movement is of all movements one in which woman is fitted to take part' (Butler undated: 2). Moreover, in the view of the League, Irishwomen were particularly suited to the role allotted to them by dint of their docility. A woman Irish Leaguer describes her sisters thus:

> Women of the old school, and in Ireland we are all of the old school – the new woman has not made her appearance amongst us – are given to thinking in grooves and to taking their opinions unquestioningly from those who went before them.
>
> (ibid.: 4)

Whether Lady Gregory, Countess Markievicz, or Maud Gonne would have concurred is a different matter. Nonetheless women were given the important role of imbuing children, Ireland's future, with the Irish language:

> the work they can best do is work to be done at home. Their mission is to make the homes of Ireland Irish. If the homes are Irish the whole country will be Irish. The spark struck on the hearth-stone will fire the soul of the nation.
>
> (ibid.: 2)

The 'language war' was to take place primarily in the *domus*, and the role of women was clearly specified:

it is warfare of an especial kind, warfare which can best be waged not by shrieking viragoes or aggressive amazons, but by gentle, low-voiced women who teach little children their first prayers, and, seated at the hearth side, make those around them realise the difference between a home and a dwelling. To most Irish people it is extremely distasteful to see a woman mount a platform and hold forth in public. We are the most conservative people in the world . . .. Let it then be thoroughly understood that when Irishwomen are invited to take part in the language movement, they are not required to plunge into the vortex of public life.

(ibid.)

The ideological and political struggle was gendered: politics for the men, culture for the women; independence to be gained by male endeavour, but the nation to be built by women:

When they have nationalised the home circle – it is here that their work must start – they may then nationalise the social sphere, and convert the atmosphere of an imitative, petty, provincial town, into that of a proud capital, living its own life, originating its own ideas and customs, speaking its native speech . . .. While the men are striving for the establishment of a native seat of government, the women might so mould the tone of life in the metropolis, that when the day of political independence arrives, it may be found that the Parliament is situated in a genuine capital, the home of a true nation.

(ibid.: 6)

CONCLUSION

In our second case study we have traced again many of the features which appeared in our earlier period. The discourse which links language and nation has been significant in both examples. In the last chapter we saw scattered remarks and empirical observations on this link. In the present chapter, however, we have considered the fuller philosophical version of this connection, and its specific effects in a period of Irish history. We have seen how the web which was torn in the seventeenth century came to be replaced in the nineteenth century by a triple net. Yet, as we have also noted, the attempts either to forge a Gaelic monoglossia, or a polyglossia in which Irish had a privileged position, ran into the difficulty that for material reasons the population at large seemed to want neither. This forced the holders of such beliefs into a series of proposals which had clear implications for debates concerning the nation and the categories of race and gender at the end of the nineteenth century. The effects of those arguments, like those engendered by the debates around the language in eighteenth-century Britain, were to have a durable history. We turn again then to Britain in the nineteenth and early twentieth centuries in order to see how the language was studied and categorised there.

Chapter 5

Science and silence

Language, class, and nation in nineteenth- and early twentieth-century Britain

'In modern times the science of language has been called in to settle some of the most perplexing political and social questions. "Nations and languages against dynasties and treaties," this is what has re-modelled, and will remodel still more, the map of Europe.'

(Müller 1862: 12)

SCIENCE OR MORE LINGUISTIC WARFARE?

In Ireland the railways were blamed for the spread of English cultural influence; in England Elizabeth Wright blamed them in part for the disappearance of dialectal speech: 'with the spread of education, and the ever-increasing means of rapid locomotion throughout the length and breadth of the land, the area where pure dialects are spoken is lessening year by year'. This, she added, is not surprising when one sees 'hoardings decorated with garish posters portraying the arid sands and cloudless skies of Blackpool or Morecambe' (Wright 1913: 1). The forces of modernity were clearly imposing monoglossia upon the land; all those working-class, or rural, people gathering together were evidently work-ing out a common and unified language. There were, however, some things upon which one could rely: people were still dropping or adding the aspirate. Described by Alford as 'that worst of all faults', it was 'common throughout England to persons of low breeding and inferior education, particularly to those among the inhabitants of towns' (Alford 1864: 5). Commenting on such attitudes, Shaw noted that 'it is impos-sible for an Englishman to open his mouth without making some other Englishman despise him' (Shaw 1941: 5). On a slightly higher plane, language was the key to understanding the human condition. 'Is man of divine birth and stock?', asked Archbishop Trench. 'We need no more than his language to prove it.' But, he added, 'has man fallen and deeply fallen from the height of his original creation?' The answer of course was: 'We need no more than his language to prove it' (Trench 1851: 26). English was thus to be the 'moral barometer' of the nation; the way in which words had changed their meaning thereby demonstrating the national moral state. One writer, in a manner reminiscent of Swift, linked the state of the language with that of the nation: 'a corrupt and decaying language is an infallible sign of a corrupt and decaying civilisation. It is one of the gates by which barbarism may invade and overpower the traditions of a great race' (Dowling 1986: 87).

Language then embodied both history and morality for there are, Müller claimed, 'chronicles below its surface, there are sermons in every word' (Müller 1862: 2–3). Indeed the language is the only reliable teller of the past, for 'often where history is utterly dumb concerning the past, language speaks' (Mathews 1882: 226). Language might speak, but the working class was considered to be silent, by both sides of the political divide. Masterman, commenting on a queue for a pub in a working-class area one Sunday lunchtime, comments that 'there is no speech nor language, no manifest human discourse' (Masterman 1902: 86). Sunday was of course the only day guaranteed to be away from the noise of industrial work, and Masterman later describes the pub as humming with noise, and thus the claim merits scepticism. Sampson, on the other hand, claims of working-class children in an elementary school that 'in a human sense, our boys and girls are almost inarticulate. They can make noises but they cannot speak' (Sampson 1925: 21). A lot depended on the definition of 'human sense' of course, for the 'best English', a leading linguist of the early twentieth century proclaimed, was 'consistently heard at its best, I think, on the whole . . . among officers of the British Regular Army' (Wyld 1934: 614). Before attempting to consider the ways in which language was closely tied to issues of nation and class, however, let us turn first to another image of the study of language in the nineteenth century, that propagated by some of its practitioners and some of those who have written its history.

The development of the first science of language, comparative philology, and its influence on the study of language in nineteenth-century Britain, have had an effect on how such study is described. For there is a view which argues that what appears to happen is that there is a shift in language study, particularly in relation to the English language. In the eighteenth century, as we have traced above, social issues dominated, to a very large extent, the ways in which the language was categorised and described. In the nineteenth century, however, rather than social prejudice, the objective methods of science are used in order to derive reliable and accurate accounts of the language. In the eighteenth-century context, the need to shape the newly emergent culture of the bourgeoisie at the linguistic level heavily skewed the study of the English language. Social snobbery, class identification and differentiation, national pride: such were the dominant forces which attempted to abolish heteroglossia in favour of a stable, confident and exclusive monoglossia which was tied to the new class. In the nineteenth century, particularly after the victory over the Napoleonic threat, the nation was more at ease with itself, both more mature and more powerful, and the centripetal forces which had dominated language study in the eighteenth century were banished in the name of science, that objective and veridical instrument of progress. The study of language was to be as rigorous and scientific, and therefore as socially neutral, as, say, that of geology, a sister discipline with which it was often compared.

Foucault marks this shift by arguing: 'From the nineteenth century language began to fold in upon itself, to acquire its own particular density, to deploy a history, an objectivity, and laws of its own. It became one object of study among others' (Foucault 1974: 296) In Britain Max Müller makes the same point in his assertion that 'in the science of language, languages are not treated as a means; language itself becomes the sole object of enquiry . . .. We do not want to know languages, we want to know language' (Müller 1862: 23). In many ways what this version of the situation does present accurately is indeed the emergence of the principle of scientificity in the study of language in Britain. There can be no doubt either as to the extent or the quality of the achievement of such study. And yet the account, if allowed to stand in this way, is misleading and in danger of too easy a credence in the self-image of the linguists. For along with the scientific work there was also linguistic warfare of the type which we have followed in the eighteenth century. Prescriptivism did not disappear in the later period; on the contrary, it was often validated by claims to scientificity. The forces of centripetalisation did not so much disappear as re-appear in a different guise. To argue, as one critic has, that 'for the philologists, the study of language became removed from the social and rhetorical concerns of the eighteenth century, and thus became an abstract and objective study' (Stalker 1985: 45), is simply wrong. Linguistic warfare flourished in nineteenth- and early twentieth-century Britain. It was bound to do so for two reasons. First, many of the eighteenth-century debates were not fully resolved; and, second, an already complex social arena was complicated still further by the appearance of the industrial proletariat. Nineteenth-century Britain then was not simply a mature and affluent society which enjoyed the fruits of its power, including those produced by its scientists. Though in many ways it was precisely such a place. It was also a bitterly divided, contradictory, self-doubting and harsh place, where eighteenth-century arguments and prejudices were not dislocated but often renewed. The centripetal and centrifugal forces took new forms for new ends, but the warfare in which they took part persisted throughout.

One example of the study of language in Britain in this period which combines both scientific rigour and social concern is the appearance of 'the history of the language' as a distinct disciplinary field in the mid-century. In making this claim it should be clear that what is being asserted is not that an interest in the history of the English language had not existed before this point. We have already traced such interest in our treatment of eighteenth-century Britain: Swift gave his own version of the linguistic and political history of the nation. Johnson prefaced his *Dictionary* with a 'History of the English Language', and Free's *Essay Towards an History of the English Tongue* (1749), along with Peyton's *History of the English Language* (1771), is further testimony to such interest. However, this does not amount to the appearance of the new academic subject at an earlier time. For the interest was hardly sustained and was often sketchy and limited. In fact it was the developments in the new science of comparative philology that in part prompted the appearance of the new area, since by the rigorous methods used even by the early comparativists, the linguistic researches of such as Swift or Johnson were, to say the least, dubious. As Hensleigh Wedgwood (Charles Darwin's brother-in-law) put it, as far as accurate knowledge of the history of the language went, 'we have little to show beyond the uncertain guesses of Junius or Skinner' (Wedgwood 1844: 2). Kemble, commenting on the ignorance of one specific period of the history of the language, that of the 'comparative anatomy of the Anglo-Saxon', claims:

> In spite of a certain outward activity which has always existed and does yet exist in England with regard to that language, there is reason to suspect that very few persons indeed have penetrated its secret, or possess any beyond the merest superficial acquaintance with its philological character.
>
> (Kemble 1846: 131)

As the term 'comparative anatomy' demonstrates, the real neglect was in the area of comparative philological study of the language. It is a point which De Quincey, whose essay 'The English Language' (1839) was to become influential in the formation of the new discpline, articulated clearly:

> As to the investigation of its history, of its gradual rise and progress, and its relations to neighbouring languages, *that* is a total blank; a title pointing to a duty absolutely in arrears rather than to any performance ever undertaken as yet, even by way of tentative essay.
>
> (De Quincey 1890: 147)

For purely scientific reasons then the new disciplinary area became one of specific interest. There were, however, other reasons. Guest, whose own *History of English Rhythms* was also highly influential, makes the general point about such neglect but gives it a cultural nationalist twist:

The history of our language has suffered equally with that of our poetry, from overlooking the peculiarities of our poetic dialect . . .. A complete history of our rhythms would probably lead to a very satisfactory arrangement of our poetry; and enable us to trace, with more truth and precision than has hitherto been done, at once the progress of our language, and the gradual development of our inventive genius.

(Guest 1882: 301)

Here the interest is in tracing not simply the accurate history of the language, but that too of the poetry in order to plot out the 'inventive genius' of the nation. In fact the concern for the neglected area covering the history of the English language was one which was heightened when the English linguistic scientists looked to their European counterparts:

While Frechmen are sending agents over Europe to scrutinise every MS which may shed light on their early literature, Englishmen are satisfied with knowing that Anglo-Saxon MSS may be found in France, in Holland and in Sweden. The German publishes the most insignificant fragment connected with the antiquities of his language, while *our* MSS lie mouldering in our libraries.

(ibid.: 702–3)

Such circumstances, he continues, 'reflect no less a discredit on our patriotism than on our scholarship'. The 'we' which lies behind this sentiment is of course not merely the community of scientific linguists but the nation itself. What was required to supply the lack was what De Quincey called a 'monument of learning and patriotism':

The most learned work which the circumstances of any known or obvious case will allow, the work which presupposes the amplest accomplishments of judgement and enormous erudition would be a history of the language from its earliest rudiments, through all periods of its growth, to its stationary condition.

(De Quincey 1890: 149)

What this demonstrates is that language study in this period was subject not simply to the exigencies of scientific discipline, but to those of social and political concern. The rise and demise of Anglo-Saxon at either end of the period under consideration in this chapter provides further evidence for this point. Ingram, Rawlinsonian Professor at Oxford, defended Anglo-Saxon in his inaugural lecture, entitled provocatively *The Utility of Anglo-Saxon Literature*, on the grounds that it 'is of the greatest importance to Englishmen, in that it is intimately connected with the original introduction and establishment of their present language and laws, their liberty and religion' (Ingram 1807: 2).

This was of course a time when England was under threat of invasion by Napoleonic France. Sir Arthur Quiller-Couch, on the other hand, writing in 1918, was able to deny any contemporary importance to that which had earlier been declared to be central:

> From Anglo-Saxon prose, from Anglo-Saxon poetry, our living poetry and prose have, save linguistically, no derivation . . . always our literature has obeyed, however unconsciously, the precept *Antiquam exquisite matrem*, 'seek back to the ancient mother'; always it has recreated itself, kept itself pure and strong, by harking back to bathe in those native – yes, native Meditterranean springs.
>
> (Quiller-Couch 1918: 25–6)

English poetry and prose derived from the democratic Greeks, not the Teutonic barbarians.

The 'history of the language' was the product then not merely of scientific recognition of a gap in knowledge but of an emerging set of social concerns too. For what happened in the 1830s and 1840s was the appearance of a force which threatened to tear the nation apart. The state, faced with mass Irish dissension abroad, also confronted organised political opposition at home in the form of Chartism. Chartism, greatly feared by the bourgeoisie, operated effectively not least by dint of the fact that it changed the nature of political discourse, as Stedman Jones among others has shown (Jones 1983), by its positing of the people as the working class (with a consequent redefinition of the nation). The response was dual in its nature. The first response was of course that of force, brute violence of either the physical or the juridical kind. The second was cultural and was more interesting from our point of view in that it shows how the forces of centripetalisation operate both discursively and politically. It is in this context that we can best evaluate the appearance of 'the history of the language' as a new discipline. Not of course as a direct, panic response, but as one which attempts to think through and organise the basis of all sorts of crucial concepts such as the nation, loyalty, allegiance, that which we hold in common and which unites us, and so on. Chartism promised conflict and upheaval; 'the history of the language' belonged to the discourse of cultural nationalism which stressed continuity, that which is known, a sense of history, and gradual evolution. Or, to put it another way, Chartism was centrifugal; 'the history of the language' and discourses like it were centripetal. One stressed class as a way of understanding history, the other the nation; language was central to both.

De Quincey had appealed for a 'monument of learning and patriotism' which was to be dedicated to ascertaining the history of a particular language which had evolved gradually, according to specific laws, until it had achieved its present great state. Following the logic of cultural nationalism, the influence of which is often underestimated in such debates in relation to nineteenth-century Britain, what this learning traced was at one and the same time the English language and the English nation. Craik reversed the usual formulation in his representation of the unity of language and nation:

> Taking a particular language to mean what has always borne the same name, or been spoken by the same nation or race, which is the common or conventional understanding of the matter, the English may claim to be older than the majority of the tongues in use throughout Europe.
>
> (Craik 1861: I, 30)

Though reversed, the pointed relationship between language and national, even racial, identity is preserved here. And a related distinction made by the linguists also maintained the *organic* nature of the relationship; for when the linguists distinguished between the internal history of the language, usually dealing with syntax and grammar, and the external history, usually dealing with word-borrowing, attitudes to usage, and so on, they made an important discursive point.[1] For though the essence of the language (and *mutatis mutandis* the nation) evolved internally, so to speak, the incidental, accidental features changed constantly. To put it another way, Englishness and the English language evolved continuously, despite whatever it was with which the facts of history confronted them. Or, to use Bakhtinian terms, the forces of English centripetalisation would always prevail over those of English heteroglossia. The English language, and thus nation, had a complex but ultimately unified history:

> Of the English language, we have a continuous succession of written remains since the seventh century at least; that is to say, we have an array of specimens of it, from that date, such as that no two of them standing next to one another in the order of time could possibly be pronounced to belong to different languages, but only at most to two successive stages of the same language. They afford us a record of representation of the English language in which there is no gap.
>
> (Craik 1861: 30)

The discipline of 'the history of the language' undoubtedly had its origins in problems prompted by the importation of the new science of comparative philology into England, and the consequent revelation of the lack of rigour of the preceding research. But it was also crucially entwined with political discourses concerned with definitions of the nation, in particular how the national past is represented to the critical present. That double-voicing is one which we shall see repeated in other work on the English language in the nineteenth and early twentieth centuries.

THEOLOGICAL ETYMOLOGY: DIGGING FOR MORALS

If Irish was posited as the language which had been spoken before the deluge, as the speech of paradise, 'Adam's language', then in mid-century Britain English was posited as the language in which the roots of God's language could be traced. In both cases a resort to etymology was propelled by theological and political concerns; or to put it another way, the new science of language was deployed in a discourse of moral and political order. Such a linkage was widespread in nineteenth-century Britain, and it took various forms. Donaldson, for example, saw 'the philosophy of grammar' as being the key to the refutation of those, such as Herder and Rousseau, who posited the human origin of language and of those, such as Horne Tooke, who gave a materialist account of its development. The new science, he claimed, demonstrated

> the impossibility of the hypothesis, maintained by many, of the human invention of language, and a progression from barbarism to metaphysical perfection. In this point the conclusions of our science are identical with the statements of revelation.
>
> (Donaldson 1839: 14)

Philology, he argued, 'is but a branch of theology'. In a similar manner, for Bunsen, as for Kant, language and religion had important roles in the comprehension of human history. For Kant it was in relation to the natural definition of nations. For Bunsen, language and religion marked 'the two poles of our consciousness, mutually presupposing each other' (Burrow 1967: 197). Theology and the study of language then had much in common; they illuminated each other and offered the means of understanding history, or the various histories, of humanity itself.

One way in which etymology was deployed for moral and political ends is demonstrated by the work of R. C. Trench, the archbishop of Dublin who supervised the disestablishment of the Church of Ireland, and who was thus an important religious and political figure in his own right. For Trench, language is, as Emerson had formulated it, 'fossil poetry': that is, the study of language is like the study of geology in that it reveals the past to us in important ways; ways which reveal how the human species has developed morally, socially and politically. In Trench's view, history is not simply conveyed through discursive narratives, oral or written, since 'often also in words connected [singly] there are boundless stores of moral and historical truth' (Trench 1851: 1). Language was not, however, simply to be examined in terms of how a particular social group had evolved, which was the central tenet of cultural nationalism; since it was also the key to understanding the *moral* history of the group, be that racial, national or that of humanity itself. For Trench, language was not merely an objective structure to be studied abstractly by scientists; it was an active and powerful agent. Words, Trench argued,

> do not hold themselves neutral in the great conflict between good and evil, light and darkness, which is dividing the world . . . they receive from us the impressions of our good and evil, which again they are active further to propagate amongst us.
>
> (ibid.: 55)

Language was thus, to use Humboldt's term, *energia*, an active and ongoing process in which the present is in dialogue with both the past and the future. It was the carrier and maker of values, the medium by which both interpretation and judgment were embodied and transmitted. Language became the repository of any specific group's set of values, be they historical, political or, importantly, moral; though in Trench's view, unlike that of Humboldt or Bakthin, such values were not dialogically open but fixed, closed and eternal. For Trench, language spoke of divine creation *and* of human transgression:

> Is man of divine birth and stock? Coming from God, and when he fulfils the law and intention of his creation, returning to him again? We need no more than his language to prove it . . . .. But has man fallen and deeply fallen from the height of his original creation? We need no more than his language to prove it.
>
> (ibid.: 26)

Thus language became the means by which morality could be judged, a group's language offering material evidence as to the state of its moral standing. It was the 'moral barometer' which measured the weight or pressure active in relation to moral issues. Words embodied 'facts of history or convictions of the moral sense'; and in this sense they were utterly reliable, since 'so far as that moral sense may be perverted, they will bear witness and keep a record of that perversion' (ibid.: 5). However, as well as being reliable in terms of representing the morality of a community, language was also dangerous. For it not only recorded deviations from good moral order, it also acted to promote or halt them. And for that very reason it was important to police words, to subject them to strict supervision, to make them serve the ends of a particular monologic order.

Such a theoretical account of the English language, in which dialogism was to be resisted by monologism, was closely linked to a view of language itself as being originally monoglot. For it presupposed that there was some original state of language in which a given order of morality was embodied, and from which later states had deviated. Unlike Irish, English was not proclaimed to be the language spoken in Eden, but it did offer access to the proper moral order, since it bore the material evidence of that order and the consequent deviations from it. God, in creating perhaps the absolute form of monoglossia and monologism, had 'impressed such a seal of truth on language that men are continually uttering deeper truths than they know' (ibid.: 8). That is, in a neat, pre-emptive reversal of Freud's interpretation of slips of the tongue as revelations of the dark repressed aspect of humanity, Trench reads the human use of language as revealing moral truth in spite of any conscious intention. Such an account does, as noted earlier, depend upon a belief in an absolute form of monoglossia and monologism, in which words have original, true meanings (which can be traced) and subsequent perverse meanings (which provide us with a history of fallen human thought). Trench makes the point clearly: 'we can always reduce the meanings which a word has to some point from which they all immediately or mediately, proceed, [as] no word has more than one meaning' (ibid.: 9). Such a belief informed the search (to use Trench's own method) for the *etumos logos*, the real, authentic, true, original meaning of a word, by tracing it back to its root etymon. It is posited upon the complete denial of the significance of historical difference, or heteroglossia, except as evidence of perversity, in the quest for monoglot and monologic truth. It takes the form of an inquiry into 'the witnesses to God's truth, the falling in of our words with his unchangeable word: for these are the true uses of the word while the others are only its abuses' (ibid.: 38–9). Here we find typical claims by which monological forces justify themselves: this particular interpretation posits an eternal truth, from which all else is perverse abuse. It is an account which denies that language is historically changing according to the needs of its users in the social circumstances in which they find themselves, but, rather, argues that it is constantly falling from the original standard which God has imposed. There were then for Trench

> words which bear the slime on them of the serpent's trail; and the uses of words, which imply moral evil – I say not upon their parts who now employ them in the senses which they have acquired, but on theirs from whom little by little they received their deflection and were warped from their original rectitude.
>
> (ibid.: 41–2)

Small wonder that Vološinov was later to assert:

> The first philologists and linguists were always and everywhere *priests*. History knows no nation whose sacred writings or oral traditions were not to some degree in a language foreign and incomprehensible to the profane. To decipher the mystery of sacred words was the task meant to be carried out by the priest-philologists.
>
> (Vološinov 1973: 74)

For such priests and philologists the aim was to seek to recover the original transparency of language, the point at which word and world coincided absolutely for the purposes of reference. Language referred to the world in a simple way, and the world itself was divinely ordered. It was only the Fall and the subsequent development of human history (of abuse and perversion) that had distorted language. And it was this original state of monoglossia and monologism that could be traced etymologically. For any word could be shown to demonstrate, if analysed closely enough, the original bonding between language and morality. 'Pain', for example, a word significant in many important discourses in the period, was interpreted by Trench:

> [It] is the correlative of sin, [in] that it is *punishment*; and to this the word 'pain' which there can be no reasonable doubt is derived from 'poena' bears continual witness. Pain *is* punishment, so does the word itself declare no less than the conscience of everyone that is suffering it.
>
> (Trench 1851: 36)

'Punishment', 'pain' and *poena* are all linked in an etymological web which bespeaks the moral order ordained by God.

What Trench's writings exemplify then is that the study of language in the nineteenth century was not less rhetorical and socially motivated than that of the eighteenth, but perhaps even more so. There is in Trench's works a concern for the methods of etymology, but not for 'neutral' scientific ends. Rather, the status bestowed upon the science of language is deployed on behalf of a specific social project. In this case it is the forging of a monologic discourse of moral order. Elsewhere in the century it is dedicated to other, no less political, ends.

STANDARDS FOR ENGLISH

We noted earlier how the study of 'the history of the language' was double-voiced, in that it was motivated both scientifically and politically. This was true also of the project to which it gave rise, and which was to prove its most lasting achievement: that is, the study of the English language which was gathered around the construction of the *New/Oxford English Dictionary* (*OED*). For the *OED* was itself to produce a term and concept for which many had appealed in the past, and which has caused so much confusion since: 'standard English'. In this section then we will consider how this term and concept emerged through the dictionary project, and how it developed through its use in quite distinct discourses.

One problem above all others faced the lexicographers engaged in the *OED*. And it was one which was so central that it had to be resolved *before* work could begin. The problem was that of determining what it was precisely that they were aiming to record. The simple answer, of course, was 'the English language'. But the problem was more complex than that. For to what exactly did the phrase 'the English language' refer? Did it mean all the words of the language? But then there was the problem of whether it meant speech or writing. And how could all spoken words possibly be recorded, since there was no way of knowing which had appeared and disappeared without trace? If it was written words that were to be recorded, did it mean that all writing was to be examined – including obscure scientific treatises, abstruse philosophical tracts, daily newspapers, the secret codes of the underworld? There were other problems too. When did 'the English language' begin? When, for example, did it stop being Anglo-Saxon? And to what point could the dictionary reasonably extend? The present, 1800, 1755? There was also the problem of the relationship between 'the language' and the dialects. What constitutes dialectal usage? On this point one linguist offered a rather unhelpful observation:

> if the question is asked, what is a dialect? No scientific or adequate definition can be given. For all practical purposes this will suffice. A language is a big dialect, and a dialect is a little language.
>
> (Meiklejohn 1891: 7)

For the lexicographers then there was a whole set of *theoretical* problems to be solved before they could undertake their appointed task. It is to their solutions that we now turn.

The *OED* project began as a rather limited project to collect words not published in the dictionaries of Johnson or Richardson. In 1857, at the instigation of Archbishop Trench, the Philological Society set up the 'Unregistered Words Committee' for this purpose. It rapidly became evident, however, that such an aim could not be achieved successfully by means of a supplement to existing dictionaries and so it was declared that 'a New Dictionary of the English language should be prepared under the authority of the Philological Society' (*Proposal* 1858: 8). The *Proposal* described it as a 'national project', and set out five points which were to guide the lexicographers. These stipulated: (1) that the dictionary should be exhaustive; (2) that it was to 'admit as authorities all English books'; (3) that it was to set the historical limits of the English language; (4) that words were to be treated according to the 'historical principle'; that is, their sense traced and the history of their appearances rendered; (5) that the etymological origins of words should be given. These theoretical delimitations were clearly crucial to the development of the work; lacking them, the lexicographer simply faced a chaotic mass of material: in Johnson's words, 'copious without order and energetic without rules' (Johnson 1806: 32). Furnished with them, the task of ordering and classification could begin.

The first three points are of major interest. Point 3 demands that the 'beginning' of 'the English language' had to be demarcated:

> The limits of quotation in point of time are next to be fixed. We have decided to commence with the commencement of English, or, more strictly speaking, with that definite appearance of an English type language, distinct from the preceding semi-Saxon, which took place about the end of the reign of Henry III.
>
> (ibid.: 4)

This was to prove a particularly difficult limit upon which to fix, and it caused problems for Murray, the *OED* editor, throughout his work. He noted in the 'General Explanations' to volume I of the dictionary, that 'the language presents yet another undefined frontier, when it is viewed in relation to time'. Be that as it may, the limits of the language were indeed set out by the *Proposal* thus:

> The periods into which the language may, for philological purposes, be most conveniently divided, are three: 1. From its rise, cir. 1250, to the Reformation – of which the appearance of the first printed Bible in 1526 may be taken as the beginning. 2. From the Reformation to Milton (1526–1674, the date of Milton's death). 3. From Milton to our day.
>
> (ibid.: 5)

The time limits then were set, but other problems remained, principally that of determining what was to be included in the dictionary. The 'General Explanations' of the *OED* addressed this point by stipulating that the materials to be recorded consisted of 'English words now in use, or known to have been in use since the middle of the twelfth century' (Murray 1888: I, xviii). The problem had merely been displaced, for where were the lexicographers to find such words? The answer of course was in written records, or 'literature' in the eighteenth-century sense of all writing. The *Proposal* clarified the issue:

> We may begin by asserting that, according to our view, the first requirement of every lexicon is that it should contain *every word occurring in the literature of the language it professes to illustrate.*
>
> (ibid.: 2)

What this presupposes, of course, is the existence of a clearly demarcated concept of what 'English literature' was. There was as yet, however, no such clearly constructed canon, and so began the proper work on the writing of English literary history which was indispensable for the lexicographers.

F. J. Furnivall, one of the pioneers in this field, described the project in this way:

> the notion was to strain all English literature through a sieve, as it were, and so to catch the first appearance of every word as it came into the language, and its last appearance before it died out.
>
> (Benzie 1983: 91)

'English literature' as a recognisable, ordered canon was appearing by dint of the requirements of the lexicographers. Numerous societies were engaged in producing accessible editions of previously rare and obscure books. Furnivall himself founded the Early English Text Society (1864), the New Shakespeare Society (1873), the Browning Society (1881), the Wyclif Society (1881) and the Shelley Society (1886). From lexicographical need there arose an historical account of English literature which served later as the basis for the development of English studies as an academic discipline.

The 'General Explanations' make clear the requirement for the most exhaustive account of the literature:

> The vocabulary of the past times is known to us solely from its preservation in written records; [and] the extent of our knowledge of it depends completely upon the completeness of the records, and the completeness of our acquaintance with them.
>
> (Murray 1888: I, xviii)

This was required not simply for the recording of the vocabulary, but for the determination of the meaning by illustrative quotation and the tracing of the word's appearances. The 'Preface' to volume I explained this principle:

> It was resolved to begin at the beginning, and extract anew typical quotations for the use of words, from all the great English writers of all ages, and from all the writers on special subjects whose works might illustrate the history of words employed in special senses, from all writers before the sixteenth century, and from as many as possible of the more important writers of later times.
>
> (ibid.: I, 5)

What we have in these assertions is the gradual clarification of the object which was to be the focus of the lexicographer's study. It was to be called the 'standard language'. Ironically the phrase was not included under the entry for 'standard' in the original *OED*, and appeared only in the 1933 Supplement. The illustrative quotation identified the source of the phrase, which was the *Proposal* itself: 'As soon as a standard language has been formed, which in England was the case after the Reformation, the lexicographer is bound to deal with that alone' (*Proposal* 1858: 3). This is,

however, an inaccurate manner of expressing the case. For the lexicographers did not find the 'standard language' waiting to be recorded;
instead they invented it as a theoretical term in order to satisfy a
methodological difficulty. Bakhtin describes the process in the following
way:

> Unitary language constitutes the theoretical expression of the his-
> torical processes of linguistic unification and centralization, an
> expression of the centripetal forces in language. A unitary lan-
> guage is not something given (dan) but it always in essence posited
> (zadan) and at every moment of its life it is opposed to the realities
> of heteroglossia.
>
> (Bakhtin 1981: 270)

'Standard English' then was a necessary theoretical invention, organised
by the forces of centripetalisation, and one which produced a form of
monoglossia at the level of writing. Elworthy, in his *Dialect of West Somerset*,
notes exactly this process:

> The education Act has forced the knowledge of the three Rs upon the
> population, and thereby an acquaintance in all parts of the country
> with the same literary form of English, which it has been the aim and
> object of all elementary teachers to make their pupils consider to be
> the only correct one. The result is already becoming manifest . . ..
> There is one written language understood by all, while the inhabitants
> of distant parts may be quite unintelligible to each other *viva voce*.
>
> (Elworthy 1876: xliii)

It is important to note at this point that this is an example of an occasion
when the forces of centripetalisation are acting in a radical rather than a
reactionary way. For what is produced here, a form of monoglossia,
clearly fulfils one of the functions which Bakhtin specifies for it:

> it makes its real presence felt as a force for overcoming . . . hetero-
> glossia, imposing specific limits to it, guaranteeing a certain maximum
> of mutual understanding and crystallizing into a real, although still
> relative, unity.
>
> (Bakhtin 1981: 270)

The emergence of the 'standard language' is not merely of importance
for the lexicographers, since it is crucial too to the project of introducing
mass literacy, as Elworthy recognises. The existence of a 'standard
language' in the sense of a common and uniform language of writing
throughout the nation is important. For it should not be forgotten that
Tory pamphleteers in the late eighteenth and early nineteenth centuries
attempted to prevent the spread of literacy by their use of regional uses
of written English in their political pamphlets (Smith 1984: 69). This

then is an example of the way in which the use of Bakhtin's terms has to be historicised in order to give us productive readings of language in history.

The *OED* required and produced the concept of what Wright called 'a standard literary language' (Wright 1924: 1). There was, however, another use of the phrase 'standard English', one which started to appear slightly later than the original, though its roots, as we shall see, lie in an earlier period. This use referred to something quite distinct. And it was linked in fact, very clearly, to the attitudes and practices which we considered in the account of the construction of the bourgeois public sphere in the eighteenth century. B. Smart, writing significantly in a revised version of the eighteenth-century elocutionist Walker's *Pronouncing Dictionaries*, gives us an excellent example of the continuity of nineteenth-century attitudes with those of the eighteenth century. Writing on the 'principles of remedy for Defects of Utterance', he specifies the central form of the spoken language:

> The dialect then, which we have here in view, is not that which belongs exclusively to one place, – not even to London; for the mere Cockney, even though tolerably educated, has his peculiarities as well as the mere Scotchman or Irishman; but the common standard dialect is that in which all marks of a particular place of birth and residence are lost and nothing appears to indicate any other habits of inter-course than with the well-bred and well-informed, wherever they may be found.
>
> (Smart 1836: xl)

The 'standard dialect' here refers to a particular form of speech which evidently has specific social importance. What is more, as a corollary of this, it means that other spoken forms, as they had in the preceding century, invited social difficulty. Foreigners, Smart asserted, could be excused for failing to acquire the 'standard dialect' perfectly, but 'a rustic or cockney dialect meets not the same quarter; or a man display-ing either the one or the other, must have a large portion of natural talent or acquired science who can overcome the prejudice it creates' (ibid.). What we have here is a use of the term 'standard' which is related to but distinct from the one we traced earlier. For in the earlier use the word 'standard' meant that which was uniform and common. In the new sense of the term 'standard', as used here, it cannot refer to something which is uniform or common (for if it did there would be no rustic or Cockney dialects), but rather to a level of excellence which is to be achieved: a *social* target for the speaker. This is demonstrated in Walker's advice to the reader: 'it may be that a person cannot altogether reach this standard; but if he reach it very nearly, all the object of a complete uniformity may be gained' (ibid.). 'Standard' in this sense is quite different from our first use; and it is that distinction, or rather the lack of appreciation of that difference, that has caused so much of the subsequent confusion and controversy.

At the level of speech, what was the difference between a dialect and a language? Garnett offered this observation on the attempt 'to establish a clear and positive distinction between the vaguely employed terms *dialect* and *language*':

> Within the English pale the matter is sufficiently clear; all agree in calling our standard form of speech the English language, and all provincial variations from it – at least all that assume a distinct specific character – dialects.
>
> (Garnett 1859: 42)

This appears to be analogous to the definition of dialect and language at the level of writing. For just as with writing, where there is the central, 'standard' form, so with speech. Within Britain, within the jurisdiction of the English language and law, there is also a demarcated, central, 'standard' form of speech, from which any deviation can be marked as dialectal. This seems to be a valid analogy and presents only one simple problem which needs resolution. That is, if 'standard English' in the sense of the uniform literary language, was to be found in the mass of materials which formed English literature, where was 'standard English' to be found in terms of speech, in relation to a standard of excellence to which speakers should aspire?

In fact the answer to this problem was easily discovered, and it came in a form which was couched in terms which were wholly familiar to eighteenth-century debates. The fact was that definitions of 'standard English' in terms of a particular form of spoken excellence were extremely common and rather uniform in their nature. Various minor writers on the language had definitions such as this:

> It is not easy to fix a standard of pronunciation. At one time the stage, then the bar, and later still the pulpit, have been considered as authorities in this matter. But all these are now rejected, and the conversation of the highest classes in London society is now looked upon as the standard of English pronunciation.
>
> (Graham 1869: 156)

White took it for granted that 'in saying that the standard of pronunciation is and must be mere usage, the usage of those who are of the highest social culture and position, I am merely uttering a truism' (White 1880: 88). These were, however, amateurs in the study of language and in all likelihood reflected the social prejudices of their time and class. What of the professionals, those scientists of language who, at least in part, had helped to create the concept of the standard literary language as a remedy for the lexicographer's difficulty? How did the scientists of language approach the problem of identifying 'standard English' at the level of speech? Henry Sweet, one of the pioneering proponents of the developing field of phonetics, defines 'English' in the title of his *New English Grammar* thus: 'by which we understand the English of the present time as spoken, written and understood by educated people' (Sweet 1891–8: I, 291). Joseph Wright, an eminent dialectician, argued that there had been a shift in the state of the language:

> In the earlier New English period there was no such thing as a standard pronunciation in the precise sense that we now apply that term to the pronunciation of educated and careful speakers of the present day.
>
> (Wright 1924: 3)

Daniel Jones, Reader in Phonetics at London, gave a series of definitions of 'standard English': in 1907 it is 'the pronunciation of the majority of educated Southern English speakers' (Jones 1907: iv); in 1908 it is 'educated people in London and the neighbourhood' (Jones 1908: 1); in 1909 it remained the same; though by 1912 it had broadened to the 'pronunciation used by the educated classes in the South of England' (Jones 1912: iii). But what did 'educated' mean? Jones specified:

> Many suitable standards of English pronunciation might be suggested, e.g. educated Northern English, educated Southern English, the pronunciation used on the stage, etc. It is convenient for present purposes to choose as the standard of English pronunciation the form which appears to be most generally used by Southern English persons who have been educated at the great English public boarding-schools.
>
> (Jones 1972: 4)

Henry Wyld, a prolific and important historian of the language, also indicated the form of the language with which he was dealing in his *Elementary Lessons in English Grammar*:

> Our business is only with one main form of English, that form that is generally called 'Educated English', that is a sort of general average English which has a wide circulation among educated people, and is what is generally referred to by the rather vague name 'correct English', or better, *Standard English*. Unless it is otherwise stated, therefore, 'English' in this book means only this particular type of English.
>
> (Wyld 1909: 2)

Wyld did not, however, leave it at that, since his awareness of the way in which language is heteroglot led him to develop further distinctions. Thus there is 'Received Standard', 'Modified Standard', 'Regional

Standard', as well as a number of 'Social or Class Dialects'. 'Received Standard' was the central form and was defined as

> that form which all would probably agree in considering the best, that form which has the widest currency and is heard with practically no variation among speakers of the better class all over the country. This type might be called Public School English.
>
> (Wyld 1927: 148–9)

Even this definition, however, was not yet specific enough, since the category which includes those at the most exclusive fee-paying schools might appear to some to be a broad category. Thus he asserts:

> If I were asked among what class the 'best' English is most consistently heard at its best, I think on the whole, I should say among officers of the British Regular Army. The utterance of these men is at once clear-cut and precise, yet free from affectation; at once downright and manly, yet in the highest degree refined and urbane.
>
> (Wyld 1934: 614)

Such thinking was not, however, confined to linguists, but had spread across the whole range of the professions. Thus the important educationalist Sampson resisted defining the concept and simply pointed instead to its embodiment:

> There is no need to define standard English speech. We know what it is, and there's an end on't. We know standard English when we hear it just as we know a dog when we see it, without the aid of definition. Or, to put it another way, we know what is *not* standard English, and that is a sufficiently practical guide. If anyone wants a definite example of standard English we can tell him that it is the kind of English spoken by a simple unaffected young Englishman like the Prince of Wales.
>
> (Sampson 1925: 41)

What is clear from these extracts from the leading linguists and educationalists – and this is the reason why they are quoted extensively – is that 'standard English' in this second sense was not at all concerned with anything which was uniform, or common. Instead it was a phrase which referred to the speech of a very narrowly defined social group. And it asserted that there was an intrinsic value in the speech of that group which all others ought to seek to emulate. This is a return then, articulated in the most important works of the leading scientific linguists of the day, to the same privileging of a form of the spoken language as had been made in the eighteenth century. Again we note the double-voicing of the study of language in the nineteenth and early twentieth centuries: it is motivated both scientifically *and* socially. The fact that these utterances were now clothed in the garb of science does not negate the fact that they are clear expressions of the social prejudices of their time.

'Standard English' was defined in the 1933 *OED* Supplement thus:

> applied to a variety of the speech of a country which, by reason of it cultural status and currency, is held to represent the best form of that speech. *Standard English*: that form of the English language which is spoken (with modifications, individual or local), by the generality of the cultured people in great Britain.

The quotation used to illustrate the definition was taken from Sweet's *The Sounds of English*: 'Standard English, like Standard French, is now a class dialect more than a local dialect: it is the language of the educated all over Great Britain' (Sweet 1908: 7). What we have then is the construction of a form of monoglossia at the level of speech which is also thoroughly monologic. Deviations from it are not so much non-standard (for even this might be construed as implying neutrality) as sub-standard. It is, as such, a repetition of the process which we have already identified in the eighteenth century: the hailing of one form of speech as superior, and the relegation of the others as stigmatised, socially disadvantageous, and *intrinsically* inferior forms.

LANGUAGE AND CLASS: THE LINE OF CLEAVAGE

The task of recording the standard literary language in order to present it in the *OED* was a massive one, and it had many ramifications in the study of the language in general. In particular it prompted interest in the study of dialects, and, as a result, the English Dialect Society (EDS) was formed in 1873. The study of dialects, however, was of more than purely linguistic interest, for in it we see again the traces of social attitudes and prejudices which make it more than simply a scientific undertaking. Dialectal study was both popular and respectable. George Eliot, for example, wrote to the secretary of the EDS and asserted:

> It is a just demand that art should keep clear of such specialities as would make it a puzzle for the larger part of its public; still, one is not bound to respect the lazy obtuseness or snobbish ignorance of people who do not care to know more of their native tongue than the vocabulary of the drawing room and the newspaper.
>
> (Eliot 1877: viii)

Such a defence of this area of study has, implicitly, a political edge, since it is directed at a particular social class. This is echoed in Wright's denunciation of the opinion of 'educated people' towards dialects:

Among common errors still prevailing in the minds of educated people, one error which dies very hard is the theory that a dialect is an arbitrary distortion of the mother tongue, a wilful mispronunciation of the sounds, and disregard for the syntax of a standard language.

(Wright 1913: xix)

And Ellis, the instigator of the EDS, argued that 'dialectal speech is of the utmost importance to a proper conception of the historical development of English pronunciation' (Ellis 1869–89: IV, 1089), which was a bold claim for its significance.

Why did the dialects gain this importance at this particular moment? How did what had previously been dismissed as peripheral now attract such attention? And how does this interest reflect social prejudices? The answer to the first two of these questions lies partly in the fact that the study of language in England, under the influence of the comparativists and their successors, did broaden out and become more scientific in its range of reference. The desire to know language rather than languages also covered a desire to know dialects rather than just the standard language. So much is true. But the rise of dialect study has also to be situated in its historical context in order to answer the questions posed earlier. We have an indication of what lies behind the novel interest in Ellis's own description of where to find a dialect. It was, he argued, to be discovered by studying 'the illiterate peasant, speaking a language entirely imitative, unfixed by any theoretic orthography, untramelled by any pedant's fancies' (ibid.: IV, 317). Once considered, this claim is surprising, since it asserts that 'the peasantry' could still be found in nineteenth-century Britain. In fact, however, this is an assertion which demonstrates the social concerns of the early dialectologists. For they, along with many others, turned to the fictive figure of the peasant as a consoling force; their counterparts in Ireland did precisely the same thing. In the midst of all the enormous social changes brought about by industrialistion and urbanisation, the dialect-speaking peasant stood for continuity, purity and an important link to the rural past.

The anxiety which dialect study manifests is testimony to the social concerns of a social group which saw its traditional culture under threat. The forces of centripetalisation, those of industrial capitalism in particular, with its demand for a huge workforce which it tempted from the countryside, were creating a new culture, smashing traditions and inventing new ones apace. To the dialectologists this meant one thing: along with old England, the dialects would disappear. Thus Ellis warned dialectologists to record only genuine dialects:

No pronunciation should be recorded which has not been heard from some speaker who uses it naturally and habitually. The older peasantry and children who have not been at school preserve the dialectic sounds most purely. But the present facilities of communication are rapidly destroying all traces of our older dialectic English. Market women who attend large towns, have generally a mixed style of speech. The daughters of peasants and small farmers, on becoming domestic servants learn a new language, and corrupt the genuine Doric of their parents.

(Ellis 1869–89: III, vi)

Elworthy commented that 'railways, telegraphs, machinery and steam will soon sweep clean out of the land the last trace of Briton, Saxon and Dane' (Elworthy 1875–6: 4). For Peile it is the 'railroad which levels all local peculiarities' (Peile 1877: 15); while Lounsbury blamed 'the whole tremendous machinery of education' (Lounsbury 1894: 494). Old England, the historic England of 'Briton, Saxon and Dane', was being swept away by the new England, modern England. Elizabeth Wright noted that 'the area where pure dialects are spoken is lessening year by year'. This is unsurprising, she observes,

when one looks at the placards announcing in large letters the extraordinarily cheap day trips offered by the Great Western or the Midland Railway, or sees hoardings decorated with garish posters portraying the arid sands and cloudless skies of Blackpool or Morecambe.

(Wright 1913: 1)

Her observation here is important since it gives a clue to the cause for concern which underlies these assertions. For Blackpool and Morecambe were primarily working-class resorts, locations where the working classes met their peers from the different regions. The real fear then, expressed by the dialectologists, was not just that the dialects were disappearing but that new forms of language were taking their place. While the dialectologists flocked to the countryside to record the last words of old England, the people poured into towns looking for work in the new England. And, once there, they created their own, new language.

The effects of this process are marked in the works of the dialectologists and indeed of many other linguists of the day. Alford, for example, criticising the use and misuse of the aspirate, noted that it was a vulgarism 'common throughout England to persons of low breeding and inferior education, particularly to those among the inhabitants of towns' (Alford 1864: 5). Urban space was the location of linguistic degradation, particularly amongst the working class. It is a prejudice echoed by Elworthy in his defence of rural against urban speech. In the country, he claims, 'the people are simple, and although there is a superabundance of rough, coarse, language, yet foul-mouthed obscenity is a growth of the cities' (Elworthy 1875–6: xii). Such views were later elevated to the status of science in the work of Wyld. In his account he notes that there are different dialects and that they are respectable in their place:

> The first thing is to realise that in itself a Provincial or Regional accent is just as respectable, and historically quite as interesting, as Standard English. The next thing is to realise that if you want to speak good Standard English, pronunciations which belong typically to a Provincial Dialect are out of place. It is probably wise and useful to get rid of these Provincialisms since they attract attention, and often ridicule, in polite circles. The best thing to do, if you have a native Provincial Dialect, is to stick to it, and speak it in its proper place, but to learn also Standard English.
>
> (Wyld 1909: 208)

The solution proposed here is a form of bilingualism. Compare this, however, with his definition of a vulgarism:

> a peculiarity which intrudes itself into Standard English, and is of such a nature as to be associated with the speech of vulgar or uneducated speakers. The origin of pure *vulgarisms* is usually that they are importations, not from a regional but from a class dialect – in this case from a dialect which is not that of a province, but of a low or uneducated social class.
>
> (Wyld 1927: 55)

Thus, he concludes, a vulgarism 'is usually a variety of Standard English, but a bad variety'. His examples are the pronunciation of 'tape' as 'type', and 'when people say '*orse* for *horse*'. What we see in general here, in the various claims of the linguists, is a defensive form of traditionalism which envisages 'real England' as existing in the rural space. From the new England of industrialised urbanity they recoiled with fear and anxiety. It was not the case here that they wished to impose a form of monoglossia, unlike the proponents of standard spoken English, for they above all were interested in certain forms of linguistic difference. It was more that they discovered heteroglossia and thought of it in terms of a discursive hierarchy. That hierarchy, as we shall see, was constructed in exactly the same moral, social and political terms as had been used in the previous century.

One linguist of the time noted a marked difference in the way in which centripetal and centrifugal forces were operating in relation to writing and speech. He commented:

> The school teaching sets the model for the written language and home influence for everyday talk. The result is that at the present moment

our people are learning two distinct tongues – distinct in pronunciation, in grammar and in syntax.

(Elworthy 1875–6: xliv)

Here we have an account of monoglossia at the level of writing and, presumably, heteroglossia at the level of speech. For the spoken language depended on the 'home influence', and it was clear that there were many different types of home. As the Newbolt Commission later put it, pupils in private preparatory schools 'have as a rule, much better home opportunities for learning English than elementary school pupils have' (Newbolt 1921: 96). What the Newbolt report meant here of course was that such pupils would have greater opportunity to learn standard spoken English, taken metonymically here to be synonymous with 'English'. What this reveals is the evident awareness of, and sensitivity to, class division:

Between the man of one tradition and another, of one education and another, of one domestic habit and another, of one class feeling and another class feeling – that is where the line of cleavage runs through town and country alike.

(Reynolds and Woolley 1911: xvii)

Such division was extremely clear when it came to cultural differences, particularly those of language. As Galsworthy, president of the English Society, put it, 'there is perhaps no greater divide of society than the differences in viva-voce expression' (Galsworthy 1924: 8). Shaw, making the same point, declared: 'it is impossible for an Englishman to open his mouth without making some other Englishman despise him' (Shaw 1941: 5). And Sweet, building upon such sentiments, argues for universal speech training on the grounds of social unity:

When a firm control of pronunciation has thus been acquired, provincialisms and vulgarisms will at last be entirely eliminated and some of the most important barriers between the different classes of society will thus be abolished.

(Sweet 1877: 196)

This was an argument which was eagerly taken up by the Newbolt report itself, and was again proposed as a way of negating the particularly dangerous class divisions which had appeared by 1921 in Britain. The report asserts:

Two causes, both accidental and conventional rather than national, at present distinguish and divide one class from another in England. The first of these is a marked difference in their modes of speech. If the teaching of the language were properly provided for, the difference between educated and uneducated speech, which at present causes so much prejudice and difficulty of intercourse on both sides, would gradually disappear.

(Newbolt 1921: 22–3)

The notion that there was such a simple bipartite division was a common one; Graham, for example, rather blithely argues that 'there will always be a refined and vulgar mode of speech' (Graham 1869: 159). It was, however, an idea which could not be supported by the weight of the material; for, rather than a single clear division, there were in fact many divisions at the level of speech, which reflected those at the level of social class. There was heteroglossia in the spoken language, but it was a system of difference which was highly ordered according to particular social assumptions. To return to Bourdieu's account of habitus, what we discover in nineteenth-century England is the consequences of the linguistic warfare which began in the eighteenth century. The public sphere had become rigidly stratified and ordered in terms of both social identity and, as part of that process, language.

We have noted earlier how standard spoken English became identified as the prestige dialect, the class language of the educated and powerful. It had become part of the process of self-identification of that class. The rules of the game had, by the late nineteenth century, been set out clearly, as the following extract from Besant demonstrates. It is an account of a meeting in a street:

> She stopped him and offered him her hand. He did not take it, but made as if he would take off his hat. This habit, as has been already remarked, is an indestructible proof of good breeding. Another sign is the handling of the knife and fork. A third is the pronunciation of the English language.

(Besant 1894: 187)

One of the burgeoning group of novelists describing life amongst the London poor makes a similar point when describing the precarious social position of one of his characters: 'And ah, how little separates her in essentials from the smartest and the best bred! – the cockney aspirate, the cockney vowel, a tendency to eat jam with a knife' (Whiteing undated: 247). Language specifically had become a key factor in the logic of this practice: 'all are not gentlemen by birth', Alford claimed, but they can make themselves so by careful attention to their language. 'For it is in this', he argues, 'in manner of speech and style', that we find 'the sure mark of good taste and good breeding' (Alford 1864: 281). 'Taste' and 'breeding' were of course central concepts in the construction of this particular social identity, along with 'culture'; for, as Arnold asserted,

> Culture says: 'Consider these people then, their way of life, their habits, their manners, the very tones of their voice; look at them

attentively; observe the literature they read, the things which give them pleasure, the words which come out of their mouths.

(Arnold 1965: 97)

It was possible then, given the right financial circumstances, to set about fashioning an identity to accompany them; and this is of course the central theme of *Pygmalion*. But it was a dangerous task and one which demanded rigid training. For, as Young pointed out in his account of the Victorian scene,

> The world is very evil. An unguarded look, a word, a gesture, a picture or novel, might plant a seed of corruption in the most innocent heart and the same word or gesture betray a lingering affinity with the class below.
>
> (Young 1936: 2)

The 'self-made men', a significant and revealing phrase, were the Victorian period's version of the character portrayed by Withers in the eighteenth century as Alderman Leatherhead. They 'made' themselves both financially and culturally, but they were often rather more successful at the former rather than the latter. This class, 'the vulgar rich', was indeed often caught out by the unguarded word or gesture. Sweet remarked of the sugar merchants of Liverpool, the core of the mercantile class, that when they

> began to 'speak fine', they eagerly adopted the thin Cockney *a* in *ask*, which many of their descendants keep, I believe, to the present day long after this 'mincing' pronunciation has been discarded in the London dialect.
>
> (Sweet 1890: vii)

The situation was so precarious that Kington-Oliphant proposed that

> many a needy scholar might turn an honest penny by offering himself as an instructor of the vulgar rich in pronunciation of the fatal letter. Our public schools are often railed against as teaching but little; still it is something that they enforce the right use of the *h*.
>
> (Kington-Oliphant 1873: 332–3)

The 'fatal letter' was enough to destroy a carefully constructed identity; the aspirate was the means by which social aspiration could be extinguished:

> The Cockney dialect seems very ugly to an educated Englishman or woman because he – and still more she – lives in perpetual terror of being taken for a Cockney, and a perpetual struggle to preserve that *h*

which has now been lost in most of the local dialects of England, both North and South.

(Sweet 1890: vi–vii)

The division between those who were born to their elevated social position, and those who achieved it through financial success, was clear. It was quite simply a matter of language and history. As one of the leading scientific linguists of early twentieth-century Britain put it when writing of the 'various forms of Modified Standard of Towns',

> First of all it should be noted that the kind of speech referred to is a tissue of affectations. Nothing is natural, everything – vowels, the cadency of the sentence, every tone of the voice – bears evidence of care, and the desire to be 'refined'. The result is always ludicrous, and sometimes vulgar. The whole utterance is pervaded by an atmosphere of unreality, and the hearer not infrequently gets the impression that the speaker is endeavouring with the utmost care, by means of a mincing, finicky, pronunciation, to avoid or cover up, some terrible natural defect. We feel in listening to such speakers, that they are uneasy, unsure of themselves, that they have no traditional social or linguistic background, but have concocted their English upon some theory of what is 'correct' and 'refined' instead of absorbing it, and reproducing it unconsciously, from the converse of well-bred and urbane persons.
>
> (Wyld 1934: 614–15)

The key concepts in forging, and destroying, a particular type of social identity in England at that time are all present here: 'natural', 'refined', 'vulgar', 'natural defect', 'uneasy', 'unsure', 'tradition', 'well-bred', and 'urbane'. This is a significant part of the vocabulary of the class warfare in which the English language itself was used as a weapon. Compare the description of urban modified standard above to that of 'Received Standard' and its speakers:

> It is characteristic of RS that it is easy, unstudied, and natural. The 'best' speakers do not need to take thought for their utterance; they have no theories as to how their native tongue should be pronounced, nor do they reflect upon the sounds they utter. They have perfect confidence in themselves, in their speech, in their manners. For both bearing and utterance spring from a firm and gracious tradition. 'Their fathers told them' – that suffices. Nowhere does the best in English culture find a fairer expression than in RS speech.
>
> (ibid.: 614)

The linguistic warfare, in which social identity and status within the bourgeoisie were at stake, was intense. But what of the language of that other class which appeared and consolidated itself in nineteenth-century Britain? What of the language of the industrial proletariat which had emerged in the large cities of the period? Earlier we saw how the dialectologists largely ignored this group, apparently in the belief that the dialects could only exist in the rural space and that they were thus witnessing their disappearance. And in fact it was not linguists who first made any observations on the language of the urban working class but early sociologists and educationalists. To a great extent they characterised such language as either perverse or, in a curious way, non-existent.

If the bourgeoisie was intensely divided in many ways, it was united in one thing: the fear of, and hostility to, the working class. For many at the end of the nineteenth century, one factor dominated more than any other, and that was the 'struggle growing ever more bitter between the holders of property on one hand, and workers on the other' (Masterman 1901: 2). The 'new city race', a 'weird and uncanny people', represented a threat by dint of their 'turbulent cheerful indifferent' attitude to the 'assumed proprietorship' of the streets by the bourgeoisie (ibid.). Their carnivalesque presence was 'charged with a menace to the future' and thus represented an object of fear for the bourgeoisie:

> They dread the fermenting, in the populous cities, of some new, all-powerful explosive, destined one day to shatter into ruin all their desirable social order. In these massed millions of an obscure life, but dimly understood and ever increasing in magnitude, they behold a danger to security and all pleasant things. Therefore the cry goes up as foretold by Mazzini: 'The Barbarians are at our gates'.
> (Masterman 1904: 61–2)

'Barbarian' is a key word here since, as we noted earlier, its derivation lies with the distinction made by the Greeks between those who spoke Greek (the Hellenes) and those who did not (the *barbaroi*). In this case it is those who do not use the authorised, codified language of power. Instead they invade the public sphere and break the rules:

> As the darkness drew on they relapsed more and more into bizarre and barbaric revelry – where they whispered now they shouted, where they had pushed apologetically, now they shoved and collisioned and charged. They blew trumpets, hit each other with bladders; they tickled passers by with feathers; they embraced ladies in the streets, laughing generally and boisterously. Later the drink got into them, and they reeled and struck, and swore, walking and leaping and blaspheming God.
> (Masterman 1902: 3)

The fear which the working class inspired is difficult to overestimate, for here were new forces, strange, unfamiliar and apparently hugely threatening. Gissing is one author of the period who conveys this sense of threat and hatred. In *Born in Exile*, the young Peak declares:

'I hate low, uneducated people! I hate them worse than the filthiest vermin! . . .. They ought to be swept off the face of the earth! . . .. All the grown-up creatures, who can't speak proper English and don't know how to behave themselves, I'd transport them to the Falkland Islands . . .. The children should be sent to school and purified, if possible; if not, they too should be got rid of.

(Gissing 1978: 40)

The older character later asserts:

the London vulgar I abominate, root and branch. The mere sound of their voices nauseates me; their vilely grotesque accent and pronunciation – bah! I could write a paper to show that they are essentially the basest of English mortals.

(ibid.: 135)

In another of Gissing's novels, *Demos, A Story of English Socialism*, there is a representation of a confrontation between a factory owner and his workers:

I speak of how intercourse with them affects me. They are our enemies, yours as well as mine; they are the enemies of evey man who speaks the pure English tongue and who does not earn a living with his hands. When they face me I understand what revolution means; some of them look at me as though they had muskets in their hands.

(Gissing 1892: 376)

Later in the same novel there is another account of a workers' meeting, during which the workers become violent: 'Demos was roused, was tired of listening to mere articulate speech; it was time for a good wild-beast roar, for a taste of bloodshed' (ibid.: 453). 'Articulate speech' is replaced by an animalistic cry, order by shouting and roaring, civilisation by violence, middle-class values by those of the workers.

In fact this figuration of the working class as unable to engage in articulate speech was a key trope in the period. And it demonstrates how effectively centripetal forces had composed the rules of discourse. Masterman, writing sympathetically of the 'new city race' at the heart of the Empire, noted that they 'never reach the level of ordered articulate utterance; never attain a language that the world beyond can hear' (Masterman 1902: 20). Occasionally Masterman uses this figuration in a way which suggests that he means that the working class is literally silent. Writing of 'The Silence of Us', he comments:

> If the first thing to note is our quantity, the second is our silence – a
> silence that becomes the more weird and uncanny with the increasing
> immensity of our number. That one or a few should pass through life
> dumb is nothing noteworthy; when the same mysterious stillness falls
> upon hundreds of thousands the imagination is perplexed and baffled.
>
> (ibid.: 18)

In fact, however, the silence to which he refers has to be read metaphorically, for, he writes in full; 'always noisy, we rarely speak; always
resonant with the din of many-voiced existence, we never reach the level
of ordered articulate utterance; never attain a language that the world
beyond can hear' (ibid.: 20). What is represented here is the effect of a
certain organisation of discourse, in which the working class engages in
utterance, but utterance which falls outside the boundaries of articulate
speech. Or, to put it another way, they speak, but not in a language
which is socially acceptable, or understood. They are not so much silent
as silenced. The forces of monologism in the social order, which take
standard spoken English, the language of the educated, to be 'proper
English', have the effect of silencing the working class in this particular
historical context.

There were others who also appeared to claim that the working class
was literally silent. Sampson, for example, argued of working-class
schoolchildren, that 'what they lack most of all is language' (Sampson
1925: 23). He asserted that in London elementary schools the observer

> will notice, first of all, that in a human sense, our boys and girls are
> almost inarticulate. They can make noises but they cannot speak.
> Linger in the playground and listen to the talk and shouts of the
> boys; listen to the girls screaming at their play; listen especially to
> them as they 'play at schools'; you can barely recognise your own
> native language.
>
> (ibid.: 21)

Again, however, this is best understood metaphorically. For what Sampson means here is not that the children cannot speak (how else do they
communicate in their play?) but that they do not have the ability to use a
particular form of the language. This defect thus dictated the whole
curriculum around which the education of the schoolchildren was to be
based. The Newbolt report, heavily influenced by Sampson's views,
offered a remedy:

> Plainly, then, the first and chief duty of the Elementary School is to
> give its pupils speech – to make them articulate and civilised beings,
> able to receive the communication of others. It must be remembered
> that children, until they can readily receive such communication, are
> entirely cut off from the life and thought and experience of the race

embodied in human words. Indeed, until they have been given civilised speech it is useless to talk of continuing their education, for in a real sense, their education has not begun.

(Newbolt 1921: 60)

What is to count as 'civilised speech' is of course the central question here. If, as Wyld had argued, it is best represented by the language of the 'officers of the British Army', then it is clear that the vast majority of the population are doomed to belong to the infantry, those who are without speech. What is more, that majority will, like the children, be cut off from the rest of humanity in any meaningful sense.

When it was discussed, working-class speech was usually dismissed in the harshest terms. Sampson, for example, took it as axiomatic that 'the elementary schoolchild begins his education with his language in a state of disease, and it was the business of the teacher to purify and disinfect that language' (Sampson 1924: 28). Teachers, argued the Newbolt report, 'have to fight against the powerful influences of evil habits of speech contracted in home and street' (Newbolt 1921: 59). It was thus, the report continued,

> emphatically the business of the Elementary School to teach all its pupils who either speak a definite dialect or whose speech is disfigured by vulgarisms, to speak standard English, and to speak it clearly and with expression.

(ibid.: 65)

It might be expected that such derision and contempt would discourage working-class children, and indeed adults, and that it would damage their confidence and self-esteem. They were after all being told that they could not speak or communicate. It did indeed produce social difficulties for them: particularly for women, for whom the difficulties were exacerbated by other pressures related to gender. We noted earlier how Sweet described the 'educated' as living in fear of being taken for a Cockney: that is, for a member of the working class. Sweet distinguished, however, between men and women in this regard, since although it worried the educated man, women – 'still more she' – are even more concerned. Such anxiety thus produced special provision in education according to the Newbolt report: 'Time should be found for phonetics in the many schools that do not yet attempt this subject, though in the girls' schools, speech training generally based on a study of phonetics is not now uncommon' (ibid. 108). All women were affected by linguistic prejudice of course, not least since the repository of 'the best English' was taken to be the officers' mess of the British army. Evidence of such general prejudice is given in *Pygmalion*, in which the speech trainer Higgins (often thought to have been modelled on Sweet) asks: 'Can you shew me any English woman who speaks English as it should be spoken? Only foreigners who have been taught to speak it speak it well' (Shaw 1941: 97). The prejudice then was general, but working-class women were particularly affected by such attitudes. In *Pygmalion* Higgins warns Eliza to use her handkerchief rather than her sleeve to wipe her face by saying: 'Don't mistake the one for the other if you wish to become a lady in a shop' (ibid.: 40). This warning about the conventions of social behaviour is a metaphor for the greater transformation of Eliza's identity which takes place primarily at the level of language. A great deal was at stake in such processes: not simply the question of silence and silencing but social existence itself. Higgins addresses Eliza early in the play, before her speech has been 'trained', by saying: 'A woman who utters such depressing and disgusting sounds has no right to be anywhere – no right to live' (ibid.: 26). He then goes on to remind her of her moral and historical obligations to articulate what Sampson had called 'civilised speech':

> Remember that you are a human being with a soul and the divine gift of articulate speech: that your native language is the language of Shakspear [*sic*] and Milton and The Bible; and don't sit there crooning like a bilious pigeon.
>
> (ibid.: 26–7)

The triple net appears again here as the invocation of language, nationality and religion acts as the means by which the forces of centripetalisation engage in conflict with centrifugal forces, represented here by Eliza's class and gender.

The sentiments expressed in the play are clearly exaggerated, but they do indicate the force of the social attitudes towards particular forms of speech. To say that this produced difficulties is to underplay the matter. For a working-class woman, such difficulties were complex. Reynolds cites an example of a young woman who has entered domestic service. When she returns home, she falls between the two codes which she has known: that of her class, and that of her employment:

> In imitating the one code, unsuccessfully, they lose their hold on the other. Their very speech – a mixture of dialect and standard English with false intonations – betrays them. They are like a man living abroad who has lost grip on his native customs, and has acquired ill the customs of his adopted country.
>
> (Reynolds 1909: 217)

Between codes, the young woman is lost, an internal exile, inner emigré, who no longer belongs in either camp.

However, although there is clear evidence as to the difficulties caused for working-class speakers, it is nonetheless important to notice that prejudice and resentment were not simply one-sided. Wyld, writing of standard spoken English, claimed:

> It has largely influenced the local dialects, for the children hear a form of it from the teachers in their schools, servants hear it from their masters, tradesmen from their customers – everyone hears it in the parish church.
>
> (Wyld 1907: 48)

In a sense, Wyld's claim for the influence of standard spoken English is a practical example of Gramsci's theory of hegemony which, as we noted earlier, was in turn a product of the theories of the 'spatial linguists' in Turin. This group had argued that linguistic change (and thus, for Gramsci, by corollary political change) takes place by the effect of a prestige form of the language operating upon other forms; or, in Bakhtin's terms, what we see in Wyld's claim is the operation of mono-glossia upon heteroglossia, the forces of centripetalisation upon centri-fugal forces. As we saw earlier, Gramsci's account is useful in that it draws attention to the need to historicise Bakhtin's theoretical terms. And yet here we can see a flaw in the Gramscian account which can be remedied by Bakhtin's concepts. For the doctrine of change through hegemony presupposes that the prestige forms will be recognised as such and thus desired by the group which does not as yet have them. But what of a situation in which that group does not want them? It is here that Bakhtin's historicised concepts can be of use. For in such a case the forces of centripetalisation are in operation in quite crude and 'symbolically violent' ways (to use Bourdieu's terminology). And such 'symbolic violence' is demonstrated in the attitudes towards the language of the working class which we have noted above.

We can see precisely this struggle between different forces in discourse if we consider Wyld's claim in the light of further evidence. The claim asserts that there is a victory for the forces of centripetalisation at the expense of social and linguistic difference. What is thus produced is a context in which standard spoken English, a form of monoglossia, acts as a monologic force of authority. But this is to allow too easy an history; for perhaps this form of monologism was dialogised, opposed, undermined, not treated with the respect it 'deserved'? Wyld himself argued:

> Most people find it distressing to listen to a discourse uttered with a pronunciation unfamiliar to them. The effect is a continuous series of surprises which startle and distract the attention from the object under consideration, and at last excite amusement or disgust.
>
> (Wyld 1934: 606)

If this were indeed true of 'most people', however, it must also be true of the working class. It may be that Gramsci's theory of hegemony is just too consensual, that in fact there is a conflictual aspect to this process. It may, for example, be the case that working-class speakers reacted with amusement or disgust to standard spoken English. Reynolds's woman servant may well have felt that she had to conform to a different code; but it may well also be true that she resented it. If audiences in general had social expectations about accents and forms of speech, could that not be true of working-class listeners in particular? In Charlotte Brontë's *Shirley* for example, the narrative voice comments on the language of Donne, a curate:

> You must excuse Mr. Donne's pronunciation, reader; it was very choice; he considered it genteel, and prided himself on his southern accent; northern ears received with singular sensations his utterance of certain words.
>
> (Brontë 1979: 322)

William Barnes, the Dorset dialectologist and poet, noted that in his region, '*fine-talking* (as it is called) on the lips of a home-born villager, is generally laughed at by his neighbours as a piece of affectation' (Barnes 1869: v). Apparently not everyone was quite so eager to subscribe to monoglossia, and where it did take place, in particular contexts, it was met with ridicule. In the *Dorset Dialect Grammar* Barnes gives an account of this:

> This will be understood by a case of which I was told in a parish in Dorset, where the lady of the house had taken a little boy into day-service, though he went home to sleep . . . the lady had begun to correct his bad English, as she thought his Dorset was; and, at last, he said to her, weeping, 'There now. If you do meäke me talk so fine as that, they'll laef at me at hwome zoo, that I can't bide there'.
>
> (Barnes 1885: 34–5)

Standard spoken English then was not simply passively accepted as intrinsically superior to their own forms by speakers who did not use it. As in this example, it could be the case that it was the prestige form that was stigmatised. It did not follow either that such speakers would use standard spoken English to better their situation, for, as is shown here too, the price might not be worth paying. The reality of the situation was in fact much more complex. There was no monoglossia at the level of speech, though there was a strictly organised heteroglossia which had monologic effects. That monologism, however, was resisted in many different ways, ranging from outright refusal to the carnivalesque practices of the 'new city class' as described by Masterman. For, as Shaw's comment demonstrates, linguistic antagonism on class grounds was reciprocal. Whenever *any* English person opened their mouth, *someone* would despise them. It was not simply a case of patrician distaste for the lower orders, for the lower orders had their own hatred too. And this was a legacy of the class formation which had emerged from the eighteenth-century settlement and the Industrial Revolution. Society itself was highly stratified and codified along 'the line of cleavage' and this was mirrored in the language. Social difference and linguistic difference were barely under control, although the centripetalising forces which were intended to effect order were formidable. At times it appeared that they had lost.

A NATION AT PEACE WITHIN ITSELF?

It was argued earlier in the chapter that the influence of cultural nationalism in both the linguistic and the political debates of our period has often been underestimated. We have noted already the force of particular strains of cultural nationalism in eighteenth-century Britain and in nineteenth-century Ireland. Why then should it not have significance in our later period in British history? One answer might be that it was not necessary, since the British were not a people whose nationality was determined at this particular conjuncture, unlike so many other nations in nineteenth-century Europe. That task, it might be argued, had been achieved in the eighteenth century. Nor were the British a people whose identity was under threat from a foreign power, at least not since the defeat of Napoleon; there was no independence struggle. Thus, it might be argued, cultural nationalism was simply redundant. And yet when we consider the evidence it is clear that, far from being redundant, cultural nationalism was an important force in the linguistic and political debates of the day. How are we to understand this apparent paradox? The answer lies in the fact that national identity is not something which is fixed for ever, an eternal set of values, but rather something which is often proposed at particular times of crisis as a way of negating difficulties. Which is to say that national identity is not something waiting to be discovered, but something which is forged. It is a weapon in particular types of discursive struggle, and though it is often represented mono-logically, it is in fact the site of great contestation. Thus the fact that national identity had been forged according to particular requirements in the eighteenth century did not mean that it could serve the same purpose in the nineteenth and early twentieth centuries. By dint of the fact that there was no longer an external threat, the representation of national identity which had been made in the earlier period now needed to be altered; because the new danger was internal rather than external. And it is in the light of this new development that we have to understand the new relations between language and national identity which are forged in this period.

A key to this problem is given by Dover Wilson when he writes on the close association between education and politics. He claims that 'it is no great accident that 1832 and 1867, the dates of two great Acts of political enfranchisement, coincide with dates equally important in the history of education' (Wilson 1928: 22–3). If we extend this argument to include 1918 we find a significant pattern: at times of political crisis there is a response at the level of education. There is also, importantly, a response in the form of an assertion of cultural nationalism, which is of course precisely a discursive form which yokes together politics (nationalism) and education (culture). In this section then we will consider how the English language gains particular importance in cultural-nationalist debates which arise out of moments of historical crisis.

Max Müller commented on the political role that the study of language had played in nineteenth-century Europe when he noted that 'in modern times the science of language has been called in to settle some of the most perplexing social and political questions'. In such disputes, Müller asserts, it had acted in favour of 'nations and languages against dynasties and treaties' (Müller 1862: 12). But what if a nation were to be challenged not from without, by another power, but from within, by dissident forces? What role could language then play? The answer was that it could be deployed by the forces of centripetalisation.

It was, as we have already noted, one of the commonplaces of cultural nationalism to see language as reflective of the national character. Thus in 1869, Graham defined language as

> the outward expression of the tendencies, turn of mind, and habits of thought of some one nation, and the best criterion of their intellect and feelings. If this explanation be admitted, it will naturally follow that the connection between a people and their language is so close, that the one may be judged of by the other; and that the language is a lasting monument of the nature and character of the people.
>
> (Graham 1869: ix)

Trench, archbishop of Dublin, but a strong English nationalist, viewed the language in quasi-divine terms as 'the embodiment, the incarnation if I may so speak, of the feelings and thoughts and experiences of a nation' (Trench 1851: 21–2). Thus the English language, at the core of Trench's concerns, was the site of national history and thus doubly instructive:

> We could scarcely have a lesson on the growth of our English tongue, we could scarcely follow upon one of its instructive words, without having unawares a lesson in English history as well, without not merely falling upon some curious fact illustrative of our national life, but learning also how the great heart which is beating at the centre of that life, was gradually being shaped and moulded.
>
> (ibid.: 24)

Teaching the history of the language amounted to teaching the history of the nation, no more no less.

If this familiar trope of cultural nationalism was replayed in the period, however, there were others no less familiar or significant. Both the eighteenth-century English nationalists and the nineteenth-century Irish nationalists had figured their respective languages as superior to all others. We find this again in writings upon English as the language of a major empire in the mid-nineteenth century. Higginson, for example, wrote:

> for all the mixed uses of speech between man and man, and from man in aspiration to the one above him, we sincerely believe that there is not, nor ever was, a language comparable to the English. The strength, sweetness and flexibility of the tongue [recommend it].
>
> (Higginson 1864: 207)

Skeat wrote later that England was 'fit to lead the world, especially in the very matter of language' (Skeat 1895: 415). Of course these opinions contradicted flatly those expressed with equal confidence by the Irish cultural nationalists. What was it then that gave the English language such superiority? It was, of course, as with the Irish language for its supporters, the fact that the language reflected a superior national character, and thus a superior nation. The language, Trench argued, was like the nation in terms of its generosity and liberality. Thus, just as 'it is in the very character of our institutions to repel none, but rather to afford a shelter and refuge to all, from whatever quarter they come', so with the language. For no other language, the same writer argued,

> has thrown open its arms wider, with a greater confidence, a confidence justified by experience, that it could make truly its own, assimilate and subdue to itself, whatever it thought good to receive into its bosom.
>
> (Trench 1855: 43)

Whether appropriation, assimilation and subjugation are quite laudable values when considering such matters is a question that does not appear to have troubled Trench. Rather, English generosity and liberalism at the level of culture and politics are posited:

> The English language, like the English people, is always ready to offer hospitality to all peaceful foreigners – words or human beings – that will land and settle within her coasts. And the tendency at the present time is not only to give a hearty welcome to newcomers from other lands, but to call back old words and phrases that had been allowed to drop out of existence.
>
> (Meiklejohn 1891: 279)

This concatenation of language, people and nation enabled one writer to echo Johnson in his refusal of rational or theoretical approaches to particular discourses. Thus language, nationality and religion were figured in this reassuring manner:

> [the language] is like the English constitution . . . and perhaps also the English Church, full of inconsistencies and anomalies, yet flourishing in defiance of theory. It is like the English nation, the most orderly in the world, but withal the most loyal, orderly, and free.
>
> (Swayne 1862: 368)

Teaching the language thereby entailed (it could not be avoided) teaching the nation's history. And given that both the language and history demonstrated that the nation was both benevolent and beneficent, what else could this lead to but patriotism? Once more then, against those who were threatening to tear the nation apart in the name of sub-national interests (class for example) the language offered national unity and coherence:

> It is evident therefore that unity of speech is essential to the unity of a people. Community of language is a stronger bond than identity of religion or government, and contemporaneous nations of one speech, however formally separated by differences of creed or of political organisation, are essentially one in culture, one in tendency, one in influence.
>
> (Marsh 1860: 221)

There could be no clearer expression of the stitching-together of the triple net. And its importance in both cultural and political terms should not be underestimated. For Trench describes the study of the English language in these terms: 'we cannot employ ourselves better. There is nothing that will more help to form an English heart in ourselves and others' (Trench 1851: 24). Or, as he puts it more succinctly, 'the love of our language, what is it in fact but the love of our country expressing itself in one particular direction?' (Trench 1855: 1).

Thus far we have noted how a particular form of English cultural nationalism, with language as its focal point, appeared at a time of pressing political crisis. That crisis was formed around the war in the Crimea, and the Indian Mutiny. In order to illustrate the validity of our claim that this is an historically typical response to crisis we now turn to that other major conflict in which Britain became enmeshed in the early twentieth century, the First World War. The war was in fact but one factor in a general crisis, for the forces of centripetalisation, usually referred to at the time as 'tradition', were under threat from various centrifugal forces. These were women, in their pursuit of suffrage, the Irish, in their search for national independence, and the working class, in its quest for economic and social justice. We turn then to that fragile, conflictual and difficult period in British history, the first quarter of the twentieth century.

If the war, and the social upheavals of the period were tearing the nation-state apart, then there were other forces which were attempting to unify and centralise. For the hard and important questions which were being set by those opposed to colonialism, gender discrimination and class oppression were met with some very familiar answers. Against division there was pitted unity, against rupture there was continuity, against conflict there was 'tradition', against race, gender or class there was the nation and its cultural heritage. One example of such a process is cited by a contemporary observer when he notes that 'among the minor results of the Great War has been a revival in the interest taken by educationalists and by the general public in the historical study of English literature and of the English language' (McKerrow 1921: 3). The apparent neutrality of this historical fact is an ideological mask; for what the interest in English studies offered was a way of reviving the national spirit at a time of crisis. If this analysis appears a little over-emphatic, let us see how contemporary observers understood the situation. The poet Bridges comments upon the work of Bradley on the *OED* project in this way:

> He recognised the national importance of that work. He understood thoroughly the actual conditions of our time, and the power of the disruptive forces that threaten to break with our literary tradition. He also knew that these conditions differ from any that we have ever encountered before in as much as we are now possessed by the scientific knowledge and social organisation which can to some extent control the adverse forces, and enable us to guide, if not determine, the development of our speech.
>
> (Bradley 1928: 50)

This merits analysis: the nation, under threat from 'disruptive' and 'adverse' forces embodied in scientific and social developments, can only be redeemed by a return to the literary tradition and by the development of the language. Though of course such a return and such a development were to be undertaken only on very precise grounds. Thus the heteroglossia of modernity, one commentator argued, resulted in 'a slackness as opposed to a virility of speech, [which] threatens a degeneracy of speech which will end by corrupting our literature to a more or less extent' (O'Neill 1915: 114). It was to be defeated by resort to the language, but the language figured in a particular way:

> How is the enemy's growing tyranny to be most effectively fought today? . . . It is because I know that the power of the evil is so strong,

and the power of the good as yet so small, that I beg the place of honour in the fight for our own great native force – 'the illustrious, cardinal, courtly and curial' vernacular of England.

(Sampson 1925: 109)

The language, alliteratively stressed as 'cardinal, courtly and curial', was to be the saviour of the day, the bastion of tradition against the evil new forces, the restorer of the appropriate cultural forms of history.

In a sense what we see here is precisely the re-appearance of linguistic nationalism, a fact noted in a contemporary debate 'On the Terms Briton, British, Britisher', published significantly in a pamphlet of the Society for Pure English:

> In both Europe and Asia legislators are at this time anxiously in search of factors that determine nationality, and among the determinants it would seem that language, which prescribes our categories and forms of thought, shapes our ideals, preserves our trade, and carries all our social relations and intercourse, had the most solid claims.

(Bradley 1928: 11)

Language, described here to a certain extent in neo-Kantian terms, was the determining factor of nationality. The nation, defined by Barker in a phrase which steals from both Burke and Marx, is constituted by 'the communism of the quick and the dead in a common citizenship'. What that communism itself consists of is the sharing of a language:

> Just because a nation is a tradition of thought and sentiment, and thought and sentiment have deep congruities with speech, there is the closest of affinities between nation and language. Language is not mere words. Each word is charged with associations that touch feelings and evoke thoughts. You cannot share these feelings and thoughts unless you can unlock their associations by having the key of language. You cannot enter the heart and know the mind of a nation unless you know its speech. Conversely, once you have learned that speech, you find that with it and by it you imbibe a deep and pervasive spiritual force.

(Barker 1927: 13)

Thus the teaching of English language and literature, and more specifically the language, 'would form a new element of national unity, linking together the mental life of all classes ' (Newbolt 1921: 15). Indeed for Sampson it was the only possible means to defuse class antagonism:

> There is no class in the country that does not need a full education in English. Possibly a common basis of education might do much to mitigate the class antagonism that is dangerously keen at the moment and shows no sign of losing its edge . . .. If we want that class

antagonism to be mitigated, we must abandon our system of class education and find some form of education common to the schools of all classes. A common school is, at present, quite impracticable. We are not nearly ready to assimilate such a revolutionary change. But though a common school is impracticable, a common basis of education is not. The one common basis of the common culture is the common tongue.

(Sampson 1925: 39)

This was published a year before the General Strike; it is tantamount to saying that given that the revolutionary concept of the comprehensive school is not possible, then the only answer is to fall back on the language as a force of social unity. Indeed the Newbolt report saw the language, as many had during an earlier moment of social crisis, as the means by which patriotism and national pride could be inculcated. If the language was placed at the centre of the educational curriculum, Newbolt argued,

The English people might learn as a whole to regard their own language, first with respect and then with a genuine feeling of pride and affection. More than any mere symbol it is actually part of England: to maltreat it or deliberately to debase it would be seen to be an outrage; to be sensible of its significance and splendour would be to step upon a higher level . . ... Such a feeling for our own native language would be a bond of union between classes, and would beget the right kind of national pride.

(Newbolt 1921: 22)

The language was both the repository of the national tradition, and the only way of ensuring its continuity. Its finest achievement was of course a set of texts which, as we might expect, were deeply informed by the triple net of language, nationality and religion. The Conservative Prime Minister Baldwin articulated the point:

Fifty years ago all children went to church, and they often went reluctantly, but I am convinced, looking back, that the hearing – sometimes almost unconsciously – of the superb rhythm of the English Prayer Book Sunday after Sunday, and the language of the English Bible leaves its mark upon you for life. Though you may be unable to speak with these tongues, yet they do make you immune from rubbish in a way that nothing else does, and they enable you naturally and automatically to sort out the best from the second best and the third best.

(Baldwin 1928: 295)

Against the fact of heteroglossia (since there were some who could not use the language of the Prayer Book and Bible) a form of monoglossia is pitted. It is the language of authority, tradition, seamless history, and national continuity. Thus there was, Newbolt stressed, a 'direct linguistic descent of modern English from Anglo-Saxon' (Newbolt 1921: 224). And Fowler, in his *Dictionary of Modern English Usage* defines 'Englishman', against 'Briton', in part according to a strict linguistic training:

> How should an Englishman utter the words *Great Britain* with the glow of emotion that for him goes with *England?* He talks the *English* language; he has been taught *English* history as one continuous tale from Alfred to George V; he has known in his youth how many Frenchmen are a match for one *Englishman*.
>
> (Fowler 1926: 139)

Such discursive operations needed to be adopted, for otherwise the dangers were great: 'Deny to working class children any common share in the immaterial, and presently they will grow into the men who demand with menaces a communism of the material' (Sampson 1925: x). If not the forces of centripetalisation, then those of disunity, difference and conflict. If not a form of monoglossia, authoritative and assured, then heteroglossia, divisive and stratified. Language, at once both immaterial and central, had become the key to history.

CONCLUSION

In this third case study we have considered the validity of the claim that in the nineteenth and early twentieth centuries the study of the English language became objective and neutral: that is to say, scientific. Contrary to that claim, we have noted how the language once again became the site upon which various forms of social conflict were fought. The nation, and national identity in particular, were crucial areas of contestation in which language played an important role. Against the heteroglossia embodied primarily in class and gender difference there was pitted a monoglot and monologic representation of the language. It was a representation which was crude in its form and brutal in its exclusivity; and it still has effects in the present. For the question of the use of 'standard English' in education debates has yet to be resolved, even though that failure of resolution has been, and is, unnecessarily damaging. It is a prime example of the significance of language in history. Symmetrically we now turn to Ireland again, to contemporary Ireland, in order to see how language is used to figure possible futures for a number of very different and contradictory sections of the communities who live there.

Chapter 6

Conclusion

Back to the past, or on to the future?
Language in history

'It is not the literal past, the "facts" of history, that shape us, but images of the past embodied in language.'

(Friel 1981: 66)

NORTHERN IRELAND? THE REPUBLIC OF IRELAND? INDEPENDENT ULSTER? ÉIRE NUA?

In the last three chapters we have used our re-reading of central points in the work of Saussure and Bakhtin in order to produce accounts of the significance of language in history at particular historical moments. By doing so we have traced the crucial role of language in the construction of various social and political formations. And we have noted the specific ways in which language has been entangled with racial, class-based and gendered identities. At particular points there appears a stress on language and class, frequently in the form of a desire either for mono-glossia or for a form of rigidly hierarchical heteroglossia. Gender has been notably articulated in terms of a monologic male order at specific points, with women's language being devalued or allowed only upon certain well-defined terms. Racial identity has also often been built upon certain linguistic characteristics in order to supply a way of categorising and demarcating human beings. And this has occurred most strikingly in the case of the articulation of national identities, where language has been used to differentiate, as Kant argued it should, nations and peoples from one another. Language has been at the centre then of an enormous number of highly significant debates and has had crucial effects, some-times positive and sometimes harmful. And in a sense this is hardly surprising, since linguistic debates are very rarely about language alone. Another way of putting the same point is proposed by Williams when he asserts that 'a definition of language is always, implicitly or explicitly, a definition of human beings in the world' (Williams 1977: 21).

But what importance do such debates have today? And what role does language play in them? Are they not debates which have long since been finished, no longer relevant in a world of 'free and democratised language', as Bakhtin put it? Or, by contrast, is it the case that in fact such debates go on? Are there still demands for forms of monoglossia, or are all cultures now heteroglot and happy with it? Has language become free and democratised? Or is there still a need for the politicised versions of Bakhtin's concepts in linguistic and cultural analysis? In order to attempt to answer these questions we can turn to one of the most pressing of contemporary debates, that concerning the future of the peoples living in the Republic of Ireland and those in Northern Ireland. For here too it will be instructive to use Bakhtin's politicised concepts in order to understand how particular views of language are also accounts or representations of the present and of imagined futures.

We examined earlier the close connections between the Gaelic language and the formation of a particular type of national identity in nineteenth-century Ireland. What then of the fate of the Irish language and the English language in the Republic of Ireland after independence had finally been achieved? What too of their fate in Northern Ireland, created at the same time? Is the language question still a significant one? Is it still being used to figure possible nations? Or have such questions been relegated to secondary importance, lost among the more desparate questions posed by a twenty-five-year war? It would be understandable if they had, but what we find in fact is that such debates are never conclusively terminated; nor, according to Bakhtin's model of constant dialogical struggle, should we expect them to be. And their continuation is a key to understanding the forces, and the balances which hold between them, at play in this specific historical context. Again then Ireland, Northern and Southern, is an illustrative example, and we can use it to demonstrate the continuing relevance of the study of language in history.[1]

In the Republic of Ireland, Éire, the linguistic situation is complex: the official language of the state (as ordained by the constitution) is Gaelic, though the massive majority of people use a form of English (Hiberno-English) in their everyday interactions. In Northern Ireland, a separate state still under direct British rule though claimed by the Republic, again under its constitution, the dominant form is Ulster English (also known as Ulster Scots). Here too there is a complexity, in that small but growing numbers of Irish republicans and nationalists, opposed to the existence of Northern Ireland and desirous of unification with the Republic, use Gaelic for their everyday purposes. Many republicans learn the language during long terms of imprisonment; hence the emergence of the term 'jailtacht' to complement the name of the official Irish-speaking areas of the republic, the Gaeltacht. The linguistic complexities of this situation are perhaps mirrored only by its political difficulties, in particular the sustained guerrilla war between republicans and the British state which has provided the context for intricate and seemingly intractable political viewpoints. In the light of this situation it may perhaps be possible to extend Gramsci's claim, noted earlier, that the surfacing of the language question indicates the presence of other political problems. For what the contemporary Irish situation shows is that in particular contexts, when specific political problems occur, such as the contestation of national identity, political independence, sovereignty and so on, then the question of the language not only appears, it becomes crucial.

The validity of this claim can be demonstrated by a brief analysis of a number of texts produced in this highly charged context in the past fifteen years. In each of these texts connections are made between forms of language and types of historical and political identity. In many ways the first two examples are the most clear by dint of the fact that they are the most simple. First we can consider a pamphlet issued by the republican movement entitled *The Role of the Language in Ireland's Cultural Revival.* Already in the title there is a presupposition which for the nationalist is the *sine qua non*: that there needs to be a cultural revival in Ireland. That is, that there has been a fall from a previous position which was happier, a presupposition which we have noted often in our analyses of language debates. In the title essay O'Maolchraoibhe outlines the contemporary cultural nationalist standpoint:

> The Irish language holds the history, the feelings, the thoughts, the culture of our people for the past 2,000 years. It is the continuing – but weakening – influence of that culture which the Irish language represents, that still gives us something of a national personality. But this will not last long should the language be completely lost. We are too close to England, and the Anglo-American language and culture is too all-pervasive for us to preserve a separate identity without the Irish language.
>
> (O'Maolchraoibhe 1984: 3)

There are a number of familiar key features here: the stress on continuity through a large expanse of time, the figuration of language as the repository of culture, and the threat of foreign influence against which the language will act as a barrier. These are all common tropes of nationalism, but perhaps the most frequently invoked is the stress on origination and purity: that is, the idea that if a particular group returns to its origins, it will then be able to rediscover itself properly. In this case Gaelic is the monoglossia which will be sealed off from foreign interference and which will guarantee the nation's purity:

> It is highly unlikely that the British Government will leave in the morning just on the supposition that we would all learn Irish over-

night. But you can be sure that it would help weaken their grip, because it would show them that the people of this nation are returning to their real identity once again.

(ibid.: 19)

The 'real identity' of Irish people, presumably in this case the Gaelic identity, can only be guaranteed by the monoglossic Irish language. Denying any of the discontinuities of history, any sense that there may be Irish people who do not identify with the pure, original Gaelic identity, the nationalist call is at one and the same time ashamed of its past loss but confident of its future gains, stern with its ancestors but demanding of its contemporaries: 'Any spirit of slavery is dead and gone. The people will re-establish the tongue of the Gael of these past 2,000 years. That task is the right and duty of every Irish person' (ibid.: 10).

If the Irish nationalist position appealed to a monoglossic view of the Irish language as a guarantor of its legitimacy, then what of the position of those who are opposed to the nationalists? One example of a way in which language is used to combat the nationalist position is that articulated by Adamson in *The Identity of Ulster: The Land, the Language and the People*. If the republicans and nationalists use the Gaelic language as their mode of acquiring historical legitimacy, Adamson uses much the same tactic but with a different aim. In an interesting re-reading of history, Adamson reaches further back than the nationalists in identifying the earliest inhabitants of Ulster:

> The name 'Ulster' ultimately derives from the ancient tribe of the 'Uluti' who inhabited the North-Eastern part of Ireland in the early centuries of the Christian era. The Uluti are recorded by the geographer Ptolemy in the earliest known map of the British Isles made in the 2nd century A.D. This showed that similar British people such as the 'Brigantes' lived in both Britain *and* Ireland in early times. The two islands were known to the ancient Greeks as the 'Isles of the Pretani'. From 'Pretani' are derived both the words 'Cruthin' and 'Briton' for the inhabitants of these islands. The ancient British Cruthin or 'Cruithne' formed the bulk of the population of both Ulster and North Britain in early Christian times and they are therefore the earliest recorded ancestors not only of the people of Ulster but those of Scotland as well.
>
> (Adamson 1982: 1)

Such claims for origination of course are a familiar enough tactic: origins in a certain sense lend legitimacy to claims for cultural recognition. What is important from our perspective is what Adamson then goes on to claim about linguistic history:

The oldest Celtic language, however, spoken in Ireland as well as Britain, was Brittonic (Old British) and this has survived as Breton, Cornish and Welsh. Gaelic did not arrive in Ireland until *even later*, at a time when the ancient British and Gaels thought of themselves as distinct peoples.

(ibid.)

This is an impressive piece of political outflanking. Far from Gaelic being the language which was stamped out by colonialism, with all that engenders for the nationalist cause, Adamson points out that it is Gaelic itself that was once the instrument of conquest: 'Old British was displaced in Ireland by Gaelic just as English later displaced Gaelic.' What Adamson does here in effect is to take over the nationalist representation of a monoglossic language and culture (Gaelic), and to turn instead to another monoglossic language and culture (the Old British), which he claims can still be found in Ulster. In both representations the monoglossic language is used as the basis of a claim for legitimacy and representation. Just as the nationalists look to the Gaelic past as their guarantor of cultural identity, likewise Adamson appeals to all those united by their Old British inheritance:

So today we must evolve in Ulster a cultural consensus, irrespective of political conviction, religion or ethnic origin, using a broader perspective of our past to create a deeper sense of belonging to the country of our ancestors. For this land of the Cruthin is our Homeland and we are her children. We have a right to her name and her nationality. . . .. Only in the complete expression of our Ulster identity lies the basis of that genuine peace, stamped with the hallmarks of justice, goodness and truth, which will end at last the War in Ireland.

(ibid.: 108)

Another representation of Ireland in terms of its linguistic state is presented in Friel's play *Translations*, set in August 1833 in a hedge school in an Irish-speaking community. The action of the play is concerned with the relations between the Irish population and the British soldiers who have arrived to carry out an ordnance survey of the area. In the course of the survey the Irish names are translated into English and marked upon the map. This process, which is of course symbolic of the great language shift taking place at the time, throws up some crucial accounts of the relationship between language and cultural identity. One character, Maire, cites Daniel O'Connell in support of her demand to be taught English:

I'm talking about the Liberator, Master, as well you know. And what he said was this: 'The old language is a barrier to modern progress.'

He said that last month. And he's right. I don't want Greek. I don't
want Latin. I want English.

(Friel 1981: 25)

Maire's reasons for wanting the English are primarily material: she wants
to emigrate to America in order to improve her condition. Ironically she
falls in love with Lieutenant Yolland, a young Englishman, who wants to
learn Irish. Each romanticises the other's language and culture, finding
them both exotic and attractive at the same time. Yolland feels isolated in
the Irish community:

And I was trying to explain a few minutes ago how remarkable a
community this is . . . .. And your place names – what was the one we
came across this morning? – Termon, from Terminus, the god of
boundaries. It – it – it's really astonishing.

(ibid.: 42)

Maire, on the other hand, after Yolland's mysterious disappearance,
remembers his description of his home:

He drew a map for me on the wet strand and wrote the names on it. I
have it all in my head now: Winfarthing – Barton Bendish – Saxing-
ham Nethergate – Little Walsingham – Norwich – Norfolk. Strange
sounds, aren't they? But nice sounds.

(ibid.: 60)

Such stereotyping, for in essence this is what it is, can also be seen in the
claims made by Hugh, the schoolteacher, for the Irish language:

A rich language. A rich literature. You'll find, sir, that certain cultures
expend on their vocabularies and syntax acquisitive energies and
ostentations entirely lacking in their material lives. I suppose you
could call us a spiritual people . . . .. Yes, it is a rich language, Lieutenant, full of the mythologies of fantasy and hope and self-deception – a
syntax opulent with tomorrows. It is our response to mud cabins and a
diet of potatoes; our only method of replying to . . . inevitabilities.

(ibid.: 42)

What we see in the development of the relationship between the young
Irish woman and the British soldier is the situation in which individuals
are placed when, from a monoglot state, they encounter cultural difference. The individuals may be able to communicate on a private level, as
Yolland and Maire do, but at a public level it is far more difficult.
Yolland, for his part, is quite aware of the fact that a monoglot form
of the English language is an imposition on the Irish community and that
it induces loss: 'something is being eroded', he says. He recognises too
the great difficulty involved in the crossing of the borders set up by the
forces of monoglossia and monologism:

Poteen – poteen – poteen. Even if I did speak Irish I'd always be an outsider here, wouldn't I? I may learn the password but the language of the tribe will always elude me, won't it? The private core will always be . . . hermetic, won't it?

(ibid.: 40)

The answer to that question, upon which the whole play rests, is given by the schoolmaster as he replies: 'you can learn to decode us'. The problem is whether this is possible. And this is of course quite clearly a meditation upon cultural identity and what it means to belong. If two monoglot languages meet, can they be brought into dialogue? Or must one finally vanquish the other? Can there be a recognition of polyglossia or even heteroglossia, or are certain cultures doomed to be isolated and at odds? The play itself is deeply ambivalent about this question, as is signified by the dubious nature of the acts of translation which occur at key points. Hugh, the schoolmaster, seems to sense the inevitability of the loss of the Irish language, and the consequent 'erosion' of something. But he tells the soldier that he can belong too:

To return briefly to that other matter, Lieutenant. I understand your sense of exclusion, of being cut off from a life here; and I trust you will find access to us with my son's help. But remember that words are signals, counters. They are not immortal. And it can happen – to use an image you'll understand – it can happen that a civilisation can be imprisoned in a linguistic contour which no longer matches the landscape of . . . fact.

(ibid.: 43)

The soldier can belong by learning Irish, but it may well be the case that his very presence there means that the monoglot Irish community is already doomed; and with it too a specific form of cultural identity. This is demonstrated when Yolland protests against the proposed re-naming of a crossroads called Tobair Vree. Owen, the native Irish translator in the employ of the British, explains that 'Tobair' means a well, and 'Vree' is a corruption of the Gaelic pronunciation of 'Brian', Brian being an old man who drowned in the well. Owen asks:

I know the story because my grandfather told it to me. But ask Doalty – or Maire – or Bridget – even my father – even Manus – why it's called Tobair Vree; and do you think they'll know? I know they don't know. So the question I put to you, Lieutenant, is this: What do we do with a name like that? Do we scrap Tobair Vree altogether and call it – what? – The Cross? Crossroads? Or do we keep piety with a man long dead, long forgotten, his name 'eroded' beyond recognition, whose trivial little story nobody in the parish remembers?

(ibid.: 44)

It is part of the complexity of the play that it is Yolland, the British soldier, who takes on the part of the cultural nationalist by insisting that it stay. What we see here of course is precisely Saussure's distinction between the diachronic and the synchronic aspects of language. Owen's point is that for the contemporary language-user the history of Brian and his misfortune is irrelevant. Yolland's response is that there is more to language than simply communication, that there are cultural and historical factors to be taken into account too. This is developed later in the play when, after Yolland's disappearance, the Irish community is facing reprisals by the British Army. Hugh comments 'that it is not the literal past, the "facts" of history, that shape us, but images of the past embodied in language'; though, he adds, 'we must never cease renewing those images; because once we do we fossilise' (ibid.: 66). The power of language in history then is stressed here in the statement of its significance in constructing a cultural identity. But the stress is on flexibility and openness to change rather than on the inflexibility of a monoglossic state. The play ends with a warning against the dangers of such monoglot cultural inflexibility, expressed in highly charged language. Jimmy asks:

> Do you know the Greek word *endogamein?* It means to marry within the tribe. And the word *exogamein* means to marry outside the tribe. And you don't cross those borders casually – both sides get very angry.
>
> (ibid.: 68)

As a comment on contemporary froms of cultural identity in Britain and Ireland the warning is stark.

If the three previous examples were concerned with forms of monoglossia, all of which were used to stake important claims for identity and recognition, the poet and critic Tom Paulin offers us a more complex view. For Paulin, language is again significant by dint of the fact that it is deeply entwined with cultural and political conflict: 'The history of a language is often a story of possession and dispossession, territorial struggle and the establishment or imposition of a culture' (Paulin 1984: 178). Nowhere, as we have seen, is this more the case than in Ireland. Paulin is critical of the ethnic purism of 'the old-fashioned nationalist concept of the "pure Gael"'. Yet he is also opposed to Adamson on the grounds that Adamson's vision is too insular and thus refuses 'the all-Ireland context which a federal concept of Irish English would necessarily express' (ibid.: 191). Paulin's vision of the ideal set of linguistic, and therefore cultural, relations in Ireland is one which avowedly advocates an egalitarian form of polyglossia:

> in Ireland there would exist three fully-fledged languages – Irish, Ulster Scots and Irish English. Irish and Ulster Scots would be

preserved and nourished, while Irish English would be a modern form of English which draws on Irish, the Yola and Fingallian dialects, Ulster Scots, Elizabethan English, Hiberno-English, British English and American English. A confident concept of Irish English would substantially increase the vocabulary and this would invigorate the written language. A language that lives lithely upon the tongue ought to be capable of becoming the flexible written instrument of a complete cultural idea.

(ibid.)

Paulin's essentially rational conception of a federal Irish English is based of course upon Webster's call for a federal form of American English. Both are in fact appeals for a political and cultural settlement based upon a model of language. For Webster, as we saw earlier, the call is for a monoglossic language which will shun its historical roots; for Paulin the appeal is on behalf of a resolution by which the three main languages, and their users, can reside in a harmonious, balanced and ultimately civic context. Of course Paulin's vision sounds almost old-fashioned itself in its constitutionalism, and he does admit to the apparent impossibility of achieving his aim 'in the present climate of confused opinions and violent politics' (ibid.: 192). But it is nonetheless the case that his vision of a polyglot Ireland represents a tolerant and rational one.

Our final piece is Seamus Heaney's essay 'The Interesting Case of John Alphonsus Mulrennan', which takes as its subject the imposition of the English language in Ireland and its cultural effects. At times the argument reads like' that of the cultural nationalists of the Gaelic revival:

Whether we wish to locate the breaking point of Gaelic civilisation at the Battle of Kinsale and the Flight of the Earls in the early seventeenth century or whether we hold out hopefully until the Jacobite dream fades out after the flight of the Wild Geese, there is no doubt that the social, cultural and linguistic life of the country is radically altered, and the alteration is felt by the majority of Irish people as a kind of loss, an exile from an original, whole and good place or state.

(Heaney 1978: 35)

The hankering after a lost state of monoglossia, a period when linguistic purity represented most clearly, and indeed guaranteed, cultural purity, was, as we have described, a common reflex of nationalism. In particular the lamenting references to an epic golden age when language and land were tied together in easy unity is a familiar rhetorical trope of this type of thinking. In Heaney's case this form of linguistic nationalism even stretches to his vision of the English language as used in England:

Words like 'ale' and 'manor' and 'sheepfold' and 'pew' and 'soldier' have a charge of fidelity and implication for an English person that is indigenous and uncontested and almost imperturbable. They are to a certain extent exclusive words. All of us whose language is English are familiar with them, but unless we are English by birth and nurture, I suspect that these words and words like them do not possess us and we do not possess them fully. We know the sense of them but we are not intimate with the musk of their meaning.

(ibid.)

This is a vision of English as a monoglossic language which would do credit to English nationalists such as Stanley Baldwin or the Prince of Wales.[2] The denial of difference within English (there is no mention of the various ways in which the language is fractured by class, race, gender or region), the positing of common access to the language by all who 'are English by birth and nurture' (which can be read as having dangerously racist overtones), and the choice of words which mostly have rural associations (founded upon a vision of England which is utterly out-dated), is typical of assertions by English cultural nationalists. Of course Heaney's intent is surely not to offer such an account; rather, he is attempting to illustrate the trauma induced by colonial imposition:

History, which has woven the fabric of English life and landscape and language into a seamless garment, has rent the fabric of Irish life, has effected a breach between its past and present, and an alienation between the speaker and his speech.

(ibid.)

There is of course no doubting the psychic and cultural rupture brought about by linguistic imposition. But the view of the English language which is offered here is misleading; rather than a 'seamless garment', the language in fact resembles an untidy patchwork quilt in which the seams are very evident.

If Heaney's linguistic nationalism leads him to view Gaelic and the English language in England as two hermetically sealed forms of mono-glossia, his view of the English language in Ireland leads him to a more complex position. Noting the difference between national language and mother tongue, Heaney describes how Irish writers have taken the language imposed upon their forebears and created it anew. Joyce of course is identified as the most striking forger of all:

Joyce's great root was in an Irish city with its own demotic English. His work took hold of the European rather than just the Irish heritage, and in the end it made the English language itself lie down in the rag and bone shop of its origins and influences.

(ibid.: 37–8)

Joyce was the writer who quite literally took the language of Lower Drumcondra and made of it 'the best English'. What Heaney describes here of course is the forging of heteroglossia, the process by which this Irish writer does not fall prey either to the blandishments of the monoglossic Gaelic culture with its accompanying nostalgia and reverence for the epic past or to the terrors imposed by cultural domination by the monoglossic English language, the instrument of everyday humiliation. What occurs instead is a revelation of the heteroglot nature (though they are not necessarily best represented in this light) of all languages and consequently all forms of identity. Rather than a secure form of purity, what Heaney ends with is the hailing of the creativity and novelty of a new form of language, inherited from the past but made new in the present. It is a language which scorns the policing of linguistic and cultural borders and even questions their very necessity. In the context of the divisions and static positions taken by all sides at various points in this historic conflict, and the importance of all sorts of physical and mental borders, the diversity, plurality and openness of this account of heteroglossia can be read as a radical vision. It can also be read as an indirect comment on the significance of an understanding of language in history.

Notes

1 FOR AND AGAINST SAUSSURE

1 The Introduction to the *Course* takes up 38 pages; the Appendix on 'The Principles of Physiological Phonetics' 26; 'Part One, General Principles' 34; 'Part Two, Synchronic Linguistics' 40; 'Part Three, Diachronic Linguistics' 50; 'Part Four, Geographical Linguistics' 22; 'Part Five, Questions of Retrospective Linguistics, Conclusion' 19.

2 FOR AND AGAINST BAKHTIN

1 Gramsci's admiration for Bartoli was genuine, as expressed in the notebooks: 'Bartoli's innovation lies precisely in this: that he has transformed linguistics, conceived narrowly as a natural science, into an historical science, the roots of which must be sought in "space and time" and not in the vocal apparatus in the physiological sense' (Gramsci 1985: 174).

2 Gramsci was familiar with the work of Vossler (Gramsci 1985: 178) and repeatedly and explicitly takes issue with Croce's arguments.

3 Gramsci's position on this matter is one which illustrates both his pragmatic realism and his debt to the spatial linguists: 'In reality, one is "always" studying grammar (by imitating the model one admires etc.)' (Gramsci 1985: 187).

3 WARS OF WORDS: THE ROLES OF LANGUAGE IN EIGHTEENTH-CENTURY BRITAIN

1 Seventy years later Sheridan wrote that in the 'Augustan age of England', there was uniformity of pronunciation in all the polite circles; and a gentleman or lady would have been as ashamed of a wrong pronunciation then, as persons of literal education would now be of misspelling words' (Sheridan 1780: iii).

2 Later in the century, Webster cited this principle repeatedly in his *Dissertations on the English Language* (1789), in his attempt to forge a language for the newly independent nation of the United States.

3 Whether the language of the monarch had ever served as the model for 'common use' or 'usuall speach' must be open to doubt. As Anderson points out, the nation, in its various forms, has not been ruled by an 'English' monarch since the early eleventh century: 'since then a motley parade of

Normans (Plantagenets), Welsh (Tudors), Scots (Stuarts), Dutch (House of Orange) and Germans (Hanoverians) have squatted on the imperial throne' (Anderson 1983: 80). Swift's Queen Anne was succeeded by the Hanoverian George, a German with very little English.

5 SCIENCE AND SILENCE: LANGUAGE, CLASS, AND NATION IN NINETEENTH- AND EARLY TWENTIETH-CENTURY BRITAIN

1 In a sense their distinction is taken up later by Saussure in his definition of internal and external linguistics.

6 CONCLUSION: BACK TO THE PAST, OR ON TO THE FUTURE? LANGUAGE IN HISTORY

1 The following analysis is based on that articulated in my article 'Bakhtin and the History of the Language' in Hirschkop and Shepherd 1989. The same materials are discussed in Wills 1993.
2 For an account of how the Prince of Wales has become involved in such debates, see Crowley 1991.

Select bibliography

Aarsleff, H. (1992) *From Locke to Saussure*, London: Athlone Press.

Achebe, C. (1975) 'English and the African Writer', in A. Mazrui, *The Political Sociology of the English Language: An African Perspective*, The Hague: Mouton.

Adamson, I. (1982) *The Identity of Ulster: The Land, the Language and the People*, Belfast: Pretani.

Alford, H. (1864) *A Plea for the Queen's English: Stray Notes on Speaking and Spelling*, London.

Allnutt, G., *et al.* (1988) *The New British Poetry*, London: Paladin.

An Claidheamh Soluis, (1899–1901), vols I–II, Dublin.

Anderson, B. (1983) *Imagined Communities: Reflections on the Origin and Spread of Nationalism*, London: Verso.

Anderson, C. (1818) *A Brief Sketch of Various Attempts Which Have Been Made to Diffuse a Knowledge of the Scriptures through the Medium of the Irish Language*, Dublin.

———— (1828) *Historical Sketches of the Native Irish and their Descendants*, Edinburgh: Oliver and Boyd.

An Fior Éirionnach (1862), Tipperary: D'Alton.

Anonymous [Richard Steele] (1711) *Grammar of the English Tongue*, London.

Anonymous (1716) *Some Rules of Speaking and Action*, London.

Anonymous (1892) *Exercises in Irish Composition*, Dublin.

Arnauld, A., and Lancelot, C. L. (1975) *General and Rational Grammar: The Port Royal Grammar* [1660], ed. J. Rieux *et al.* The Hague: Mouton.

Arnold, M. (1965) 'Culture and Anarchy: An Essay in Political and Social Criticism' [1869], in *Complete Prose Works*, vol. V, Ann Arbor: University of Michigan Press.

Ash, J. (1761) *Grammatical Institutes*, 4th edn, London.

Bacon, F. (1857) *Novum Organum* [1620], *The Works of Francis Bacon*, vol. I, ed. and trans. J. Spedding and R. Ellis, London: Routledge.

———— (1861) *Of the Proficience and Advancement of Learning* [1605] ed. G. W. Kitchen, London: Bell and Daldy.

Bailey, N. (1721) *An Universal Etymological Dictionary*, London.

———— (1730) *Dictionarium Britannicum*, London.

———— (1736) *Dictionarium domesticum*, London.

Baker, R. (1770) *Reflections on the English Language*, London.

Bakhtin, Mikhail (1981) *The Dialogic Imagination*, Austin: University of Texas Press.

———— (1983) *Bakhtin School Papers*, ed. A. Shukman, Russian Poetics in Translation 10, Somerton: RPT Publications in association with Department of Literature, University of Essex.

—— (1986) *Speech Genres, and Other Late Essays*, ed. C. Emerson and M. Holquist, Austin: University of Texas Press.

Baldwin, S. (1928) *Our Inheritance*, London: Hodder and Stoughton.

Barker, E. (1927) *National Character and the Factors in its Formation*, London: Methuen.

Barnes, W. (1869) *Poems of Rural Life in the Dorset Dialect*, 3rd collection, 2nd edn, London.

—— (1885) *A Glossary of the Dorset Dialect with a Grammar of its WordShapening and Wording*, Dorchester.

Barrell, J. (1983) *English Literature in History 1730–80: An Equal Wide Survey*, London: Hutchinson.

Barron, P. (1835) *Ancient Ireland*, nos 1–5, Dublin.

Bayly, A. (1758) *An Introduction to Languages, Literary and Philosophical*, London.

—— (1772) *A Plan and Complete Grammar of the English Language*, London.

Begly, C., and Mac Curtin, H. (1732) *The English–Irish Dictionary (An Focloir Bearla Gaoidheilge)*, Paris.

Benjamin, W. (1970) *Illuminations*, London: Cape.

Benzie, W. (1983) *Dr F. J. Furnivall: Victorian Scholar Adventurer*, Norman: Pilgrim Books.

Besant, W. (1894) *Children of Gibeon*, London: Chatto and Windus.

Blount, T. (1656) *Glossographia*, London.

Bourdieu, P. (1977) *Outline of a Theory of Practice*, Cambridge: Cambridge University Press.

—— (1982) *Ce que parler veut dire: L'économie des échanges linguistiques*, Paris: Fayard.

—— (1990) *The Logic of Practice*, trans. R. Nice, Cambridge: Polity Press.

—— (1991) *Language and Symbolic Power*, ed. John B. Thompson, trans. G. Raymond and M. Anderson, Cambridge: Polity Press.

Bourke, U. (1856) *The College Irish Grammar*, Dublin.

—— (1862) *Easy Lessons: or, Self-Instruction in Irish*, 3rd edn, Dublin.

Bradley, H. (1928) *The Collected Papers of Henry Bradley: With a Memoir by Robert Bridges*, Oxford: Clarendon Press.

Brightland, J. (1711) *A Grammar of the English Tongue with Notes*, London.

Brontë, C. (1979) *Shirley* [1849], ed. H. Rosengarten and M. Smith, Oxford: Clarendon Press.

Brooke, C. (1789) *Reliques of Irish Poetry*, Dublin.

—— (1795) *Bolg An Tsaolair: or, Gaelic Magazine*, Belfast.

Buchanan, J. (1753) *The Complete English Scholar*, London.

—— (1757a) *Linguae Britannicae vera pronunciatio*, London.

—— (1757b) *A New Pocket Book for Young Gentlemen and Ladies or:, A Spelling Dictionary of the English Language*, London.

—— (1762) *The British Grammar*, London.

—— (1769) *A Regular English Syntax*, London.

Bullokar, J. (1616) *An English Expositor*, London.

Bunreacht Na hÉireann (Constitution of Ireland) (1937), Dublin: Government Publications.

Burnett, Lord James: *see* Monboddo.

Burrow, J. (1967) 'The Uses of Philology in Victorian Britain', in *Ideas and Institutions of Victorian Britain: Essays In Honour of George Kitson Clarke*, ed. R. Robson, New York: Barnes and Noble.

Butler, M. E. L. (undated) *Irishwomen and the Home Language*, Dublin: Gaelic League.

Cahill, E. (1935) 'The Irish National Tradition', *The Irish Ecclesiastical Record*, 46, pp. 2–10.

—— (1939) 'The Irish Language and Tradition, 1540–1691', *The Irish Ecclesiastical Record*, 54, pp. 123–42.

—— (1940) 'The Irish Language in the Penal Era', *The Irish Ecclesiastical Record*, 55: 591–617.

Calvet, L. J. (1975) *Pour et contre Saussure: Vers une linguistique sociale*, Paris: Payot.

—— (1990) *La Guerre des langues*, Paris: Payot.

Campbell, G. (1776) *The Philosophy of Rhetoric*, 2 vols, London.

Cawdry, R. (1604) *A Table Alphabeticall, Conteyning and Teaching the True Writing, and Understanding of Hard Usual Words*, London.

Cockeram, H. (1623) *The English Dictionarie: or, An Interpreter of Hard English Words*, London.

Colley, L. (1992) *Britons. Forging the Nation 1707–1837*, London: Yale University Press.

Connellan, T. (1814) *An English–Irish Dictionary Intended for the Use of Schools*, Dublin.

—— (1815) *An Irish–English Primer Intended for the Use of Schools*, Dublin: Graisberry.

—— (1824) *The Irish–English Guide to the English Language, Intended to Assist the Native Irish through the Medium of the Irish Language. By His Majesty's Special Command*, London: Watts.

Coulter, P. (1862) *The West of Ireland: Its Existing Condition, and Prospects*, Dublin: Hodges and Smith.

Craik, G. (1861) *A Compendious History of English Literature and of the English Language from the Norman Conquest; with Numerous Specimens*, London.

Croce, B. (1953) *Aesthetic as Science of Expression and General linguistic* [1909], London: Peter Owen.

Crowley, T. (1989a) *The Politics of Discourse; the Standard Language Question in British Cultural Debates*, Basingstoke: Macmillan.

—— (1989b) 'Language in History: That Full Field', *News From Nowhere*, Oxford, 6, pp. 23–37.

—— (1989c) 'Bakhtin and the History of the Language', in *Bakhtin and Cultural Theory*, ed. K. Hirschkop and D. Shepherd, Manchester: Manchester University Press.

—— (1991) *Proper English? Readings in Language, History and Cultural Identity*, London: Routledge.

—— (1992) 'The Return of the Repressed: Swift and Saussure on Language and History', in *New Departures in Linguistics*, ed. G. Woolf, New York: Garland.

Daniel, W. [Uilliam O Domhnuill] (1602) *Tiomna Nuadh (New Testament)*, Dublin.

Daunt, W. (1848) *Personal Recollections of the Life of Daniel O'Connell*, London: Chapman and Hall.

Davis, T. (1914) *Essays Literary and Historical*, Dundalk: Dundalga Press.

Defoe, D. (1972) *The Life and Surprising Adventures of Robinson Crusoe, Of York, Mariner* [1719], ed. J. D. Crowley, London: Oxford University Press.

De Fréine, S. (1965) *The Great Silence*, Dublin: Foilseacháin Náisiúnta Teoranta.

De Mauro, T. (1972) *Edition critique du 'Cours de linguistique générale' de F. de Saussure*, Paris: Payot.

De Quincey, T. (1890) 'The English Language' [1839], in *Collected Writings New and Enlarged*, vol. XIV, Edinburgh.

Descartes, R. (1968) 'The Principles of Philosophy', in *The Philosophical Works of Descartes*, trans. E. S. Haldane and G. R. T. Ross, Cambridge: Cambridge University Press.

Dewar, D. (1812) *Observations on the Character, Customs and Superstitions of the Irish*, London.

Dinneen, P. (1904) *Lectures on the Irish Language Movement*, Dublin: Gill.

Donaldson, J. W. (1839) *The New Cratylus*, London.

Donlevy, A. (1742) *The Catechism: or, Christian Doctrine by Way of Question and Answer*, Paris: Guerin.

Dowling, L. (1986) *Language and Decadence in the Victorian Fin de Siècle*, Princeton: Princeton University Press.

Duffy, C. G. (1896) *Young Ireland: A Fragment of Irish History 1840–50*, London.

Durham, W. H., ed. (1915) *English Essays of the Eighteenth Century*, London: Oxford University Press.

Dyche, Y. and Pardon, W. (1735) *A New General English Dictionary*, London.

Eagleton, T. (1984) *The Function of Criticism From 'The Spectator' to Post-Structuralism*, London: Verso.

Edgeworth, M. (1833) *Forgive and Forget, and Rosanna*, trans. T. Feenachty, Belfast: Ulster Gaelic Society.

Eliot, G. (1877) Letter to Skeat, in *A Bibliographical List of the Various Dialects of English*, ed. W. W. Skeat and J. H. Nodal, London.

Ellis, A. (1869–89) *On Early English Pronunciation*, 5 pts, London.

Elworthy, F. T. (1875–6) *The Dialect of West Somerset*, 2 vols, London.

Fáinne An Lae (1898–1900), vols 1–5, Dublin.

Fanon, F. (1986) *Black Skin, White Masks*, London: Pluto.

Farquharson, L. (undated) *Ireland's Ideal*, Dublin: Gaelic League.

Farro, D. (1754) *The Royal Universal British Grammar and Vocabulary*, London.

Fenning, D. (1767) *The New and Complete Spelling Dictionary*, London.

Fichte, J. G. (1968) *Addresses to the German Nation* [1808], ed. George Armstrong Kelly, New York: Harper.

Fielding, H. (1977) *Joseph Andrews* [1742], Harmondsworth: Penguin.

Fisher, G. (1740) *The Instructor: or, Young Man's Best Companion*, 5th edn, London.

Foley, D. (1849) *A Missionary Tour through the South and West of Ireland*, Dublin: The Irish Society.

—— (1855) *An English–Irish Dictionary*, Dublin: Curry.

Forde, P. (undated) *The Irish Language Movement: Its Philosophy*, Dublin: Gaelic League.

Foucault, M. (1974) *The Order of Things: An Archaeology of The Human Sciences*, London: Tavistock.

Fowler, H. W. (1926) *A Dictionary of Modern English Usage*, Oxford: Clarendon Press.

Free, J. (1749) *Essay Towards an History of the English Tongue*, London.

Friel, B. (1981) *Translations*, London: Faber.

Gaelic League (undated) Pamphlets 1–33: see under individual authors

—— (undated) *The Gaelic League Catechism*, Dublin: Gaelic League.

—— (1910) *Programme of the Irish Language Procession, Language Sunday*, Dublin: Gaelic League.

Gaelic Society of Dublin (1808) *Transactions*, ed. E. O'Reilly, Dublin: Barlow.

Galsworthy, J. (1924) *On Expression*, Oxford: English Association.

Garnett, R. (1859) *Philological Essays*, London.

Gil, A. (1619) *Logonomia Anglica*, London.
Gissing, G. (1892) *Demos: A Story of English Socialism*, new edn, London: Smith, Elder.
————— (1978) *Born in Exile* [1892], ed. P. Coustillas, Hassocks: Harvester.
Graham, G. F. (1869) *A Book about Words*, London.
Gramsci, A. (1985) *Selections from Cultural Writings*, London: Lawrence and Wishart.
Greenbaum, S., ed. (1985) *The English Language Today*, Oxford: Pergamon.
Greenwood, J. (1711) *An Essay towards a Practical English Grammar*, London.
Gregory, Lady (1901) *Ideals in Ireland*, London: Unicorn.
Guest, E. (1882) *A History of English Rhythms* [1838], 2nd edn rev., ed. W. W. Skeat, London.
Gwynn, S. (1903) *Today and Tomorrow in Ireland: Essays on Irish Subjects*, Dublin: Hodges Figgis.
Habermas, J. (1989) *The Structural Transformation of the Public Sphere: An Inquiry into a Category of Bourgeois Society*, trans. Thomas Burger and Frederick Lawrence, Cambridge: Polity Press.
Haliday, W (1808) *Úrmicecht Na Gaedilge (Grammar of the Gaelic Language)*, Dublin: Barlow.
Harris, G. (1752) *Observations upon the English Language in a Letter to a Friend*, London.
Harris, J. (1751) *Hermes: or, A Philosophical Inquiry Concerning LANGUAGE and UNIVERSAL GRAMMAR*, London.
Harris, R. (1987) *Reading Saussure: A Critical Commentary on the 'Cours de linguistique générale'*, London: Duckworth.
Heaney, S. (1978) 'The Interesting Case of John Alphonsus Mulrennan', *Planet*, 41, pp. 34–40.
Herder, J. G. (1966) *On the Origin of Language* [1772]: see Rousseau 1966.
Higginson, E. (1864) *An English Grammar Intended for Classical Schools and Private Students*, London.
Hirschkop, K. (1986) 'Bakhtin, Discourse and Democracy', *New Left Review*, 160, pp. 92–113.
Hirschkop, K. and Shepherd, D., eds (1989) *Bakhtin and Cultural Theory*, Manchester: Manchester University Press.
History Workshop Journal (1989), special feature 27: *Language and History*, London: Redwood.
Humboldt, W. von (1988) *On Language: The Diversity of Human Language Structure and its Influence on the Mental Development of Mankind* [1836], trans. P. Heath, Cambridge: Cambridge University Press.
Hyde, D. (1986) *Language, Lore and Lyrics* [1892], ed. B. O'Conaire, Dublin: Irish Academic Press.
Ingram, J. (1807) *The Utility of Anglo-Saxon: An Inaugural Lecture*, Oxford.
Irish Archaeological Society (1842) *Tracts Relating to Ireland*, vols I–II, Dublin.
Jackson, D. (1973) 'The Irish Language and Tudor Government', *Eire–Ireland*, 8:1, pp. 21–8.
Jameson, F. (1972) *The Prison House of Language*, Princeton: Princeton University Press.
Johnson, S. (1806) *The Works of Samuel Johnson*, vol. II, London.
————— (1952) *The Letters of Samuel Johnson*, vol. I, ed. R. W. Chapman, Oxford: Clarendon Press.
Jones, D. (1907) *Phonetic Transcriptions of English Prose*, Oxford: Clarendon Press.

———— (1908) *A Chart of English Speech Sounds*, Oxford: Clarendon Press.
———— (1912) *Phonetic Readings in English*, Heidelberg: Carl Winter.
———— (1972) *An Outline of English Phonetics* [1919], Cambridge: Heffer's.
Jones, G. S. (1983) *Languages of Class: Studies in English Working Class History 1832–1932*, Cambridge: Cambridge University Press.
Jones, J. (1701) *Practical Phonography: or, The New Art of Rightly Spelling and Writing Words by the Sound Thereof and of Rightly Sounding and Reading Words by the Sight Thereof*, London.
Jones, R. F. (1953) *The Triumph of the English Language*, Stanford: Stanford University Press.
Jones, Sir W. (1807) *The Works of Sir William Jones*, London.
Joyce, J. (1960) *A Portrait of the Artist as a Young Man* [1916], Harmondsworth: Penguin.
Kant, I. (1957) *Perpetual Peace* [1795], New York: Liberal Arts Press.
Kavanagh, P. F. (undated) *Ireland's Defence – Her Language*, Dublin: Gaelic League.
Kelly, A. Cline (1984) *Swift and the English Language*, Philadelphia: University of Pennsylvania Press.
Kemble, J. M. (1846) 'On the North Anglian Dialect', *Proceedings of the Philological Society*, 2, pp. 131–42.
Kington-Oliphant, T. L. (1873) *The Sources of Standard English*, London.
Ladies Gaelic Society (1838) *An Irish Primer*, Belfast.
Lane, A. (1700) *A Key to the Art of Letters*, London.
Lehmann, W. (1967) *A Reader in Nineteenth Century Historical Indo-European Linguistics*, London: Indiana University Press.
Lemon, W. (1783) *English Etymology: or, A Derivative Dictionary of the English Language*, London.
Lhuyd, E. (1707) *Archaeologica Britannica*, Oxford.
Lo Piparo, F. (1979) *Lingua intellettuali egemonia in Gramsci*, Bari: Laterza.
Locke, J. (1975) *An Essay Concerning Human Understanding* [1690], ed. P. Nidditch, Oxford: Clarendon Press.
———— (1823) 'Some Thoughts Concerning Education' [1690], in *The Works of John Locke*, vol. IX, London.
Loughton, W. (1739) *A Practical Grammar of the English Language*, London.
Lounsbury, T. (1894) *A History of the English Language*, 2nd edn, rev., New York.
Lowth, R. (1762) *A Short Introduction to English Grammar*, London.
Lukács, G. (1971) *History and Class Consciousness: Studies in Marxist Dialectics*, trans. R. Livingstone, Cambridge, Mass.: MIT Press.
Mac Curtin, H. (1728) *The Elements of the Irish Language*, Louvain: Overbeke.
McQuige, J. (1818) *The Importance of Schools for Teaching the Native Irish Language*, London.
MacHale, J. (1844) *An tIliad*, Dublin: Cumming.
McKerrow, R. B. (1921) *A Note on the Teaching of English Language and Literature*, London: English Association.
Marsh, G. P. (1860) *Lectures on the English Language*, New York.
———— (1862) *The Students' Manual of the English Language*, London: Murray.
Martin, B. (1749) *Lingua Britannica Reformata: or, A New English Dictionary*, London.
———— (1754) *An Introduction to the English Tongue and Learning*, London.
Martyn, E. (undated) *Ireland's Battle for her Language*, Dublin: Gaelic League.
Mason, H. J. M. (1829) *History of the Irish Society*, Dublin: Goodwin.
———— (1830) *Grammar of the Irish Language*, Dublin.
Mason, J. (1748) *An Essay on Elocution*, London.

Masterman, C. F. G. (1901) 'Realities at Home', in *The Heart of the Empire: Discussions of the Problems of Modern City Life in England, with an Essay on Imperialism*, London: Fisher Unwin.

—— (1902) *From the Abyss: Of Its Inhabitants by One of Them*, London: Johnson.

—— (1904) 'The English City', in *England: A Nation. Being the Papers of the Patriots' Club*, ed. L. Oldshaw, London: Johnson.

Mathews, W. (1882) *Words: Their Use and Abuse*, Toronto.

Mazrui, A., ed. (1975) *The Political Sociology of the English Language: An African Perspective*, The Hague: Mouton.

Meiklejohn, J. (1891) *The Book of the English Language*, London.

Molloy, F. (1908) *De prosodia Hibernica* [1677], trans. O Flannghaile, Dublin: Gill.

Monboddo, Lord James Burnett (1774–1792) *Of the Origin and Progress of Language*, 6 vols, London.

Moran, D. P. (1905) *The Philosophy of Irish Ireland*, Dublin: Duffy.

Müller, M. (1862) *Lectures on the Science of Language delivered at the Royal Institute of Great Britain in 1861*, 2nd edn, London.

Murray, J. A. H. (1888–1928) *A New English Dictionary on Historical Principles*, 20 vols (10 pts), Oxford: Clarendon Press.

Nation, The (1842–5), 3 vols, Dublin.

Neilson, W. (1808) *An Introduction to the Irish Language*, Dublin.

Newbolt, Sir H. (1921) *The Teaching of English in England: Being the Report of the Departmental Committee Appointed by the President of the Board of Education to Enquire into the Position of English in the Educational System of England*, London: HMSO.

Ngũgĩ Wa Thiong'o (1986) *Decolonising the Mind. The Politics of Language in African Literature*, London: Currey.

Nichols, G. (1990) *I Is a Long Memoried Woman*, London: Karnak Press.

Nolan, J. (1877) *Irish Grammar in Prose and Verse*, Dublin: Gill.

O'Brien, (1768) *Focaloir Gaoidhilge-Sax-Bhéarla: or, an Irish–English Dictionary*, Paris.

O'Conor, C. (1753) *Dissertations on the Antient History of Ireland*, Dublin: Hoey.

O'Donovan, J. O. (undated) *An O'Growney Memorial Lecture*, Dublin: Gaelic League.

O'Farrell, A. (1904) *Leabar An Atar Eozan: The O'Growney Memorial Volume*, Dublin: Gill.

—— (undated) *The Reign of Humbug*, Dublin: Gaelic League.

O'Growney, E. (1910) *Simple Lessons in Irish*, 8th edn, Dublin: Gaelic League.

O'Hickey, M. P. (undated) *The True National Idea*, Dublin: Gaelic League.

Oldmixon, J. (1712) *Reflections on Dr. Swift's Letter to the Earl of Oxford about the English Tongue*, London.

O'Maolchraoibhe, P. (1984) *The Role of Language in Ireland's Cultural Revival*, Belfast: Sinn Féin.

O'Neill, H. C., ed. (1915) *A Guide to the English Language*, London: Jack.

O'Neill, P. (1976) 'The Reception of German Literature in Ireland 1750–1850', *Studia Hibernica*, 16, pp. 122–36.

O'Reilly, E. (1808): see Gaelic Society of Dublin.

—— (1817) *Sanas Gaoidhilge Sagsbherla (An Irish–English Dictionary)*, Dublin.

O'Reilly, J. M. (1902) *The Trusty Vehicle of the Faith of the Gael*, Dublin: Irish Book Company.

—— (undated) *The Threatening Metempsychosis of a Nation*, Dublin: Gaelic League.

Orpen, C. (1821) *The Claims of Millions of Our Fellow Countrymen or Present and Future Generations to be Taught in Their Own and Only Language, the Irish*, Dublin.

Paul, H. (1890) *Principles of the History of Language*, trans. H. A. Strong, London: Sonnenschein.

Paulin, T. (1984) 'A New Look at the Language Question', in *Ireland and the English Crisis*, Newcastle: Bloodaxe.

Peile, J. (1877) *Philology*, London.

Peyton, V. J. (1771) *The History of the English Language*, London: Hilton.

Plato (1970) 'Cratylus', in *Timaeus, and other Dialogues*, trans. B. Jowett, London: Sphere.

Proposal for the Publication of a New English Dictionary (1858), London: Philological Society.

Puttenham, G. (1936) *The Arte of English Poesie* [1589], ed. Gladys Doidge Willcock and Alice Walker, Cambridge: Cambridge University Press.

Quiller-Couch, Sir A. (1918) *Studies in Literature*, Cambridge: Cambridge University Press.

Roehrig, L. O. F. (1884) *The Irish Language*, New York.

Reynolds, S. (1909) *A Poor Man's House*, 2nd edn, London: Bodley Head.

Reynolds, S. and B. and T. Woolley (1911) *Seems So! A Working Class View of Politics*, London: Macmillan.

Rousseau, J.-J. (1966) *Essay on the Origin of Language* [1781], trans. J. H. Moran and A. Gode, London: University of Chicago Press.

Sampson, G. (1924) *The Problem of Grammar*, English Association Pamphlet 56, London: English Association.

—— (1925) *English for the English*, 2nd edn rev., London.

Saussure, F. de (1957) *Les Sources manuscrites du 'Cours de linguistique générale' de F. de Saussure*, ed. R. Godel, Geneva: Droz.

—— (1964) 'Letter to Antoine Meillet' [4 Jan. 1894], *Cahiers Ferdinand de Saussure*, vol. XXI, p. 95.

—— (1983) *Course in General Linguistics* [1916], ed. Charles Bally and Albert Sechehaye, trans. R. Harris, London: Duckworth.

Schlegel, F. von (1847) *The Philosophy of Life and Philosophy of Language in a Course of Lectures by Friedrich von Schlegel*, trans. A. J. W. Morrison, London: Bohn.

—— (1849) 'On the Language and Wisdom of the Indians' [1808], in *The Aesthetic and Miscellaneous Works of Friedrich von Schlegel*, trans. E. J. Millington, London: Bohn.

Schleicher, A. (1863) *Die Darwinische Theorie und die Sprachwissenschaft*, trans. as *Darwinism Tested By the Science of Language* (1869), London: Hotten.

Scurry, J. (1827) *Remarks on the Irish Language*, Dublin: Graisberry.

Semiotica (1991), special issue 83: *History and Semiotics*, Berlin: De Gruyter.

Shaw, G. B. (1941) *Pygmalion*, with a preface, Harmondsworth: Penguin.

Shaw, W. (1778) *An Analysis of the Galic Language*, 2nd edn, Edinburgh: Ruddiman.

—— (1780) *A Galic and English Dictionary*, London: Strahan.

Sheridan, R. B. (1975) *Sheridan's Plays*, ed. Cecil Price, Oxford: Oxford University Press.

Sheridan, T. (1756) *British Education: or, The Source of the Disorders of Great Britain*, London.

—— (1759) *A Discourse being Introductory to His Course of Lectures on Elocution and the English Language*, London.

—— (1761) *A Dissertation on the Causes of the Difficulties which Occur in the Learning of the English Tongue*, London.

——— (1762) *A Course of Lectures on Elocution*, London.
——— (1780) *A General Dictionary of the English Language, One Object of Which is to Establish a Plain and Permanent Standard of Pronunciation*, London.
Skeat, W. W. (1873) *Questions for Examination in English Literature: With An Introduction on the Study of English*, Cambridge.
——— (1895) 'The Proverbs of Alfred', in *Transactions of the Philological Society* (1895-8), pp. 399–418.
Smart, B. H. (1836) *Walker Remodelled: A New Critical Pronouncing Dictionary of the English Language. Adapted to the Present State of Literature and Science*, London.
Smith, A. (1760) *Theory of Moral Sentiments*, 2nd edn (1761), London: A. Millar.
Smith, O. (1984) *The Politics of Language 1791–1819*, Oxford: Clarendon Press.
SPIL (Society for the Preservation of the Irish Language) (1877) *An Cheud Leabar Gaedilge (The First Irish Book)*, Dublin: Gill.
——— (1877–1914) *Transactions*, Dublin: SPIL.
Spenser, E. (1949) *The Works of Edmund Spenser: The Prose Works*, ed. E. Greenlaw et al., Baltimore: Johns Hopkins University Press.
Stalker, J. (1985) 'Attitudes towards Language in the Eighteenth and Nineteenth Centuries', in *The English Language Today*, ed. S. Greenbaum, Oxford: Pergamon.
Stokes, W. (1799) *Projects for Re-establishing the Internal Peace and Tranquillity of Ireland*, Dublin: Moore.
Swayne, G. C. (1862) 'Characteristics of Language', *Blackwood's Edinburgh Magazine*, pp. 360–72.
Sweet, H. (1877) *A Handbook of Phonetics*, Oxford.
——— (1890) *A Primer of Spoken English*, Oxford.
——— (1891–8) *A New English Grammar Logical and Historical*, 2 pts, Oxford.
——— (1908) *The Sounds of English*, Oxford: Clarendon Press.
Swift, J. (1955) *Irish Tracts 1728–1733*, ed. H. Davis, Oxford: Blackwell.
——— (1957) *A Proposal for Correcting the ENGLISH TONGUE Polite Conversation, etc*, [1712], ed. H. Davis with L. Landa, Oxford: Blackwell.
——— (1966) *The Poems of Jonathan Swift*, ed. H. Williams, 2nd edn, 3 vols, Oxford: Clarendon Press.
Taylor, J. S. (1817) *Reasons for Giving Moral Instruction to the Native Irish, Through the Medium of their Vernacular Language*, London.
Thomas, D. (1787) *Observations on the Pamphlets Published by the Bishop of Cloyne, Mr Trant, and Theophilus, on One Side. And on Those by Mr O'Leary, Mr Barber, and Dr Campbell, on the Other*, Dublin.
Thomson, J. (1981) *The Seasons* [1746], ed. J. Sambrook, Oxford: Clarendon Press.
Timpanaro, S. (1975) *On Materialism*, London: New Left Books.
Trench, D. C. (1912) *What is the Use of Reviving Irish?*, Dublin: Maunsel.
Trench, R. C. (1851) *On the Study of Words*, London.
——— (1855) *English Past and Present*, London.
Ussher, G. N. (1785) *The Elements of English Grammar*, London.
Vallancey, C. (1772) *An Essay on the Antiquity of the Irish Language*, Dublin.
——— (1782) *A Grammar of the Iberno-Celtic or Irish Language*, 2nd edn, Dublin.
——— (1786) *A Vindication of the Ancient History of Ireland*, Dublin: White.
——— (1797) *Proof of the Ancient History of Ireland*, Dublin.
——— (1802) *Prospectus of a Dictionary of the Language of the AIRE COTI or Ancient Irish*, Dublin.
——— (1804) *Collecteana de rebus Hibernicus*, vol. VI, Dublin.

——— (1812) *An Account of the Ancient Stone Amphitheatre Lately Discovered in the County of Kerry*, Dublin: Graisberry.

Vološinov, V.N. (1973) *Marxism and the Philosophy of Language* [1930], London: Seminar Press.

Walker, J. (1774) *A General Idea of a Pronouncing Dictionary of the English Language*, London.

——— (1781) *Elements of Elocution*, London.

——— (1783) *Hints for Improvement in the Art of Reading*, London.

Wallis, J. (1653) *Grammatica linguae Anglicanae*, London.

Watts, T. (1850) 'On the Probable Future Position of the English Language', *Proceedings of the Philological Society*, 4, pp. 207–14.

Webster, N. (1789) *Dissertations on the English Language*, Boston: Thomas.

Wedgwood, H. (1844) 'Notices of English Etymology', *Proceedings of the Philological Society*, 2, pp. 1–14, 177–87.

Welsted, L. (1724) 'Dissertation concerning the Perfection of the English Language and the State of English Poetry', in *English Essays of the Eighteenth Century*, ed. W. H. Durham, London: Oxford University Press, 1915.

White, R. G. (1880) *Everyday English*, Boston.

Whiteing, R. (undated) *No. 5 John Street*, London: Nelson.

Whorf, B. L. (1956) *Language, Thought, and Reality*, Cambridge, Mass.: MIT Press.

Williams, R. (1977) *Marxism and Literature*, London: Oxford University Press.

——— (1983) *Keywords: A Vocabulary of Culture and Society*, London: Fontana.

——— (1984) *Writing in Society*, London: Verso.

——— (1986) 'The Uses of Cultural Theory', *New Left Review*, 158, pp. 19–31.

Wills, C. (1993) *Improprieties, Politics and Sexuality in Northern Irish Poetry*, Oxford: Clarendon Press.

Wilson, J. Dover, ed. (1928) *The Schools of England: A Study in Renaissance*, Cambridge: Cambridge University Press.

Wilson, T. (1724) *The Many Advantages of a Good Language to a Nation*, London.

Withers, P. (1789) *Aristarchus: or, The Principles of Composition*, London.

Wright, E. M. and J. Wright (1913) *Rustic Speech and Folk Lore*, Oxford: Clarendon Press.

——— (1924) *An Elementary Historical New English Grammar*, Oxford: Clarendon Press.

Wyld, H. (1907) *The Growth of English*, London: Murray.

——— (1909) *Elementary Lessons in English Grammar*, Oxford: Clarendon Press.

——— (1927) *A Short History of English, with a Bibliography of Recent Books on the Subject*, 3rd edn rev., London: Murray.

——— (1934) *The Best English: A Claim for the Superiority of Received Standard English*, Society for Pure English 4, *Tract* no. xxi, Oxford: Clarendon Press.

Yeats, W. B. (1975) *Uncollected Prose*, vol. II, ed. J. P. Frayne and C. Johnson, Basingstoke: Macmillan.

Young, A. (1780) *A Tour in Ireland*, 2 vols, Dublin: Bonham.

Young, G. M. (1936) *Victorian England: Portrait of an Age*, Oxford: Clarendon Press.

Index

Lightning Source UK Ltd.
Milton Keynes UK
UKOW04f0424140314

228110UK00001B/65/A